Cooking Light
way to
cook
grilling

Flexi ISBN-13: 978-0-8487-3593-7
Flexi ISBN-10: 0-8487-3593-5
Hardcover ISBN-13: 978-0-8487-3594-4
Hardcover ISBN-10: 0-8487-3594-3

Library of Congress Control Number: 2011941430
Printed in the United States of America
First printing 2012

Be sure to check with your health-care provider before making any changes in your diet.

Oxmoor House

VP, Publishing Director: Jim Childs
Editorial Director: Susan Payne Dobbs
Creative Director: Felicity Keane
Brand Manager: Michelle Turner Aycock
Senior Editor: Heather Averett

Cooking Light® Way to Cook: Grilling

Editor: Rachel Quinlivan West, RD
Project Editor: Emily Chappell
Senior Designer: Emily Albright Parrish
Assistant Designer: Allison Sperando Potter
Director, Test Kitchen: Elizabeth Tyler Austin
Assistant Directors,
Test Kitchen: Julie Christopher, Julie Gunter
Test Kitchen Professionals: Wendy Ball, RD;
Allison E. Cox; Victoria E. Cox;
Margaret Monroe Dickey;
Alyson Moreland Haynes;
Stefanie Maloney; Callie Nash;
Catherine Crowell Steele;
Leah Van Deren
Photography Director: Jim Bathie
Senior Photo Stylist: Kay E. Clarke
Associate Photo Stylist: Katherine Eckert Coyne
Assistant Photo Stylist: Mary Louise Menendez
Senior Production Manager: Greg Amason

Contributors

Designer: Teresa Cole
Copy Editors: Jacqueline Giovanelli, Tara Trenary
Proofreader: Adrienne Davis
Indexer: Mary Ann Laurens
Interns: Erin Bishop, Laura Hoxworth,
Alison Loughman, Lindsay A. Rozier
Test Kitchen Professionals: Martha Condra, Erica Hopper,
Kathleen Royal Phillips
Photographers: Brian Francis, Beau Gustafson,
Lee Harrelson, Mary Britton
Senseney, Jason Wallis
Photo Stylist: Mindi Shapiro Levine, Anna Pollock

Time Home Entertainment Inc.

Publisher: Richard Fraiman
Vice President, Strategy &
Business Development: Steven Sandonato
Executive Director,
Marketing Services: Carol Pittard
Executive Director,
Retail & Special Sales: Tom Mifsud
Director, New Product
Development: Peter Harper
Director, Bookazine
Development & Marketing: Laura Adam
Assistant Director,
Publishing Director: Joy Butts
Finance Director: Glenn Buonocore
Associate General Counsel: Helen Wan

Cooking Light®

Editor: Scott Mowbray
Creative Director: Carla Frank
Deputy Editor: Phillip Rhodes
Executive Editor, Food: Ann Taylor Pittman
Special Publications Editor: Mary Simpson Creel, MS, RD
Senior Food Editor: Julianna Grimes
Senior Editor: Cindy Hatcher
Associate Food Editor: Timothy Q. Cebula
Assistant Editor, Nutrition: Sidney Fry, MS, RD
Assistant Editors: Kimberly Holland, Phoebe Wu
Test Kitchen Director: Vanessa T. Pruett
Assistant Test Kitchen Director: Tiffany Vickers Davis
Recipe Testers and Developers: Robin Bashinsky,
Adam Hickman, Deb Wise
Art Directors: Fernande Bondarenko, Shawna Kalish
Junior Deputy Art Director: Alexander Spacher
Associate Art Director: Rachel Lasserre
Junior Designer: Hagen Stegall
Photo Director: Kristen Schaefer
Assistant Photo Editor: Amy Delaune
Senior Photographer: Randy Mayor
Senior Photo Stylist: Cindy Barr
Photo Stylist: Leigh Ann Ross
Food Styling Assistant: Blakeslee Wright
Chief Food Stylist: Charlotte Autry
Senior Food Stylist: Kellie Gerber Kelley
Copy Chief: Maria Parker Hopkins
Assistant Copy Chief: Susan Roberts
Research Editor: Michelle Gibson Daniels
Editorial Production Director: Liz Rhoades
Production Editor: Hazel R. Eddins
Assistant Production Editor: Josh Rutledge
Administrative Coordinator: Carol D. Johnson
Cookinglight.com Editor: Allison Long Lowery
Nutrition Editor: Holley Johnson Grainger, MS, RD
Production Assistant: Mallory Brasseale

To order additional publications, call 1-800-765-6400
or 1-800-491-0551.

For more books to enrich your life, visit **oxmoorhouse.com**

To search, savor, and share thousands of recipes,
visit **myrecipes.com**

Cooking Light
way to
cook
grilling

Oxmoor
House®

Contents

way to grill 8

burgers 18

meats 78

poultry 136

fish & shellfish 194

vegetables & fruits 252

ingredient substitution guide 306

nutritional analysis 307

seasonal produce guide 308

metric equivalents 309

indexes 310

Welcome

Grilling is easy, social, and happens outdoors—no wonder it's America's favorite way to cook, woven deeply into the fabric of our backyard lives and town-square celebrations.

It can also be healthy: the tang and aroma of smoke and char mean you can use less fat to flavor food than you might in a frying pan or baking dish. But grilling is not an automatic passport to a healthy diet. An 8-ounce high-fat burger patty topped with cheese and bacon on a mayo-slathered bun with a side of old-fashioned potato salad...well, you get the idea.

At *Cooking Light* we grill all the time, but tend to favor leaner cuts of meat, which need a bit of care. We like to grill fish and seafood, which require their own methods. And we love to load the grill with vegetables and even fruit, so they can soak up the same benefits that coals or gas convey to proteins. We also like flavorful marinades, healthy-fat oils, global-pantry spices and sauces, and other ways to boost flavor without layering on a lot of saturated fat and salt.

Healthy grilling can be as happy a way of life as any other kind of grilling. It's not work, it's fun. This book is your passport to a healthy-grilling state of mind. Enjoy!

Scott Mowbray
Cooking Light *Editor*

Cooking Light
way to grill

way to grill

Grilling is a casual, versatile cooking technique that works wonders on all types of meats, poultry, and seafood, as well as fruits and vegetables. The heat of the fire creates charred edges, gorgeous grill marks, and smoky, robust flavors that no other cooking technique can mimic. All these delicious qualities come with little or no added fat, ranking it as one of the most healthful cooking methods.

direct

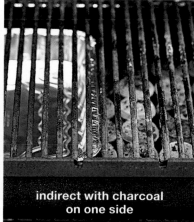

indirect with charcoal
on one side

indirect with charcoal
on two sides

Direct vs. Indirect Heat

Direct grilling involves cooking food directly above the fire. Similar to broiling, this method cooks food quickly and works best with thin cuts of meat, such as burgers, fish fillets, several kinds of steak, chops, and vegetables. It's not ideal for larger cuts of meat because the high heat will burn the outside before the inside is done.

For foods that need to cook longer, such as whole chickens, whole fish, and pork shoulder, indirect grilling is the best choice. The fire is built on one or both sides of the food (but not directly under it), and the grill is covered, which allows the hot air to circulate around the food. It's a gentler cooking method. Delicate fish fillets also benefit from this method. Although fish fillets are thin and generally cook quickly, direct heat can some-times cook them too quickly, drying them out and burning the oils in the skin.

Sometimes, both direct and indirect heat is used, particularly for larger cuts of meat. The meat might be placed over direct heat to sear it, and then transferred to indirect heat to cook more slowly. Let the recipes help guide you in choosing the best method.

Equipment

Here are the tools you need to create big grilled flavors:
• **Grill:** Choosing between a gas or charcoal grill is really a lifestyle choice since they perform equally well. Gas grills are convenient because they're easy to operate and maintain a consistent heat. Charcoal grills are more hands-on, requiring a bit more time and prep to get the fire going. Unlike gas grills, charcoal grills provide the characteristic smoky flavor that is a hallmark of many grilled foods.
• **Grill pan:** For indoor grilling, a grill pan is a must. With ridges that elevate food so air can circulate underneath and fat can drip away, a grill pan adds more than just pretty grill marks.
• **Chimney starter:** For charcoal grills, this is a helpful piece of equipment to get your fire going. We show you how to use it on page 12.
• **Drip pans:** Inexpensive disposable aluminum foil pans are necessary if you plan to smoke. They hold wood chips and chunks, and catch meat drippings.
• **Grill basket or tray:** When grilling thin or bite-sized pieces of food, a grill basket is an ideal tool since it prevents small pieces from falling through the grates.

• **Wire brush:** You'll need this tool each time you grill to clean the grates. A brass-bristle brush is best since steel bristles can damage the enamel finish of some grates.

• **Tongs:** Long-handled tongs are useful for turning meats, poultry, and seafood. Forks and utensils with sharp edges can pierce the exterior, causing the juices to seep out.

• **Thermometer:** A thermometer is an essential tool for gauging the temperature and doneness of cooked meats. Instant-read thermometers are inexpensive options. Another option is a remote digital thermometer. The probe stays in the meats as they cook, and an alarm sounds when the meats reach the correct temperature.

kitchen how-to: get the fire going

For gas grills, simply ignite the burners and preheat them to the correct temperature specified in the recipe. If you're using indirect heat, turn off one side of the grill once it's preheated. **For charcoal grills,** follow these steps:

1. A chimney starter is indispensable for charcoal grilling. Stuff newspaper in the bottom, place charcoal in the top, and light the paper. Now wait until the coals catch fire. Avoid using lighter fluid because it can give food a bitter flavor. If you don't see smoke pouring out of the top and eventually flames, you need to relight.

2. Wait, and then wait a bit more. Yes, it can take its sweet time. But don't rush: Allow the flames to die down and the coals to take on a bright-red glow with a gray, ashy look. These cues signal that it's time to put down your beverage and dump the coals into the bottom of the grill.

3. Spread the bed of coals. Arrange the coals in a pattern for indirect or direct heat suited to what you're cooking. For veggies that take longer than 20 minutes to cook (like dense potatoes), pile coals to one side of the grill for indirect heat. For quicker-cooking ingredients, pile coals in the center of the grill for direct heat.

Keep It Clean

Each time you grill, preheat the rack with all burners on high for 10 to 15 minutes (whether you're using direct or indirect heat) to incinerate any remaining residue from the last cookout, making it easy to clean off. Then brush the grate with a grill brush. Clean the grates vigorously so they're smooth and free from food that may have stuck from your previous grilling session.

Oil the Food

Whenever possible, coat the food and the grill rack with oil or cooking spray to promote caramelization and grill marks, and also to prevent sticking. If you don't coat the food, its natural juices may evaporate as it grills, leaving the food dry—this is especially disastrous when grilling sliced vegetables.

Keep Food Safe

When handling meats, poultry, or seafood, food safety is crucial. Follow these tips to keep grilling safe and delicious.

• Store raw meats, poultry, or seafood in the refrigerator until you're ready to grill—remove it 20 minutes before to allow it to come to room temperature.

• Trim excess fat to prevent flare-ups. When cooking a fatty piece of meat, the fat drips down onto the flames, which can lead to burned food.

• Never use cooking spray around a lit grill. Coat the grate before you put it on the grill or before you've lit your burners.

• Don't place cooked meats back on the plates or bowls that contained the raw meats. To keep cleanup easy, cover the plate with aluminum foil before placing the raw meats on it. Once the meats are on the grill, remove and discard the foil.

• Use a thermometer to be certain burgers, meats, poultry, and seafood have reached a safe temperature, and make sure the thermometer isn't touching bone. The color of the food and how it feels aren't accurate ways to check doneness.

• When marinating, refrigerate the food; don't leave it out on the counter. If you plan to use any leftover marinade for basting or as a sauce, you'll need to boil it to ensure it's safe. See page 108 and 163 for more information about marinating.

Feeling the Heat?

When determining if your grill is preheated to the right temperature, place your hand, palm side down, 5 inches above the grate, and count how long you can comfortably hold it there.

7 to 8 seconds = medium-low
(250° to 300°)
5 to 6 seconds = medium
(300° to 350°)
3 to 4 seconds = medium-high
(350° to 400°)
2 seconds or less = high
(400° to 450°)

way to

smoke

Smoking food over smoldering wood is an easy cooking method that adds depth and complexity in taste to food without added fat or salt. Meats are the foods typically associated with smoking, but vegetables can also benefit from the technique.

Getting Started

Unlike traditional grilling in which direct or indirect heat cooks food, smoking occurs at a lower temperature for a longer period of time—it can take less than an hour to more than 8 hours depending on the food. The heat stays sufficiently high to cook the food thoroughly, but the longer cook time gives food a chance to absorb the woodsy aroma and flavor of the wood chips or chunks.

You don't need specialty equipment to get started. Your backyard grill—gas or charcoal—will work just fine (see how to set them up on page 12) along with a few other pieces of equipment mentioned on pages 11–12 and wood chips or chunks.

Chips vs. Chunks

You can use wood chips or chunks when smoking, but here's the difference: Wood chips work best for meats that smoke for a relatively short time (2 hours or less), such as chicken or steak. For heftier cuts of meat that cook for several hours, such as pork shoulder or brisket, the larger dimensions of wood chunks work best. As a rule of thumb, use hardwoods for smoking. Avoid soft woods (pine, spruce, and other evergreens), as they produce sooty, unpleasant smoke. Never use scraps of pressure-treated wood since they can potentially contain hazardous chemicals and other toxins.

Mesquite: Gives food a strong, distinctive, slightly bitter flavor. Ideal for beef and other robust meats.

Apple and cherry: Their mild, sweet smoke works well with pork, poultry, game, and seafood.

Oak: A versatile wood, full-flavored enough to stand up to beef and pork, yet refined enough not to overpower poultry or seafood.

Hickory and pecan: Very popular smoking woods that both have a rich flavor and earthy sweetness. This smoke enhances pork.

Alder: This wood has a medium-level smoke intensity and pairs well with seafood.

Maple: Generates a mild, delicately sweet smoke that nicely flavors poultry, pork, and vegetables.

Keep the Heat Even

For those cuts of meat that need to smoke for hours, maintaining an even cooking temperature is crucial to prevent the meat from overcooking and drying out. On a gas grill you can regulate the temperature easily with the burners and monitor it from the built-in thermometer in the lid, but charcoal grills require a little more finesse. Here's how:

• **Work the vents.** Charcoal grills have vents at the top and bottom. To raise the heat, open the vents wide. To decrease the heat, partially close the vents. Remember, more oxygen means a hotter fire; less oxygen means a cooler one.

• **Adjust the charcoal.** When smoke-roasting at temps of 300° to 350° in a charcoal grill, use the normal amount (one chimney-full) of charcoal. When low-heat smoking (200° to 275°), use a half-chimney's worth. Replenish as needed.

• **Keep it moist.** For a longer-cooking dish, keep a small pan of water in the grill. This humidifies the air and helps prevent the meat from drying out. This is good practice in gas grills, too.

kitchen how-to: smoke on a charcoal grill

Smoking foods requires a covered grill and indirect heat. Here's the setup:

1. Soak the wood chips for 30 minutes, and drain. Wood chunks need to soak longer—at least one hour. Fire up your charcoal or briquettes using a chimney starter, and then pour the coals on one side of the lower grate. The charcoal is ready when it's coated with thick, gray ash.

2. Place an aluminum foil pan filled with water on the other side of the lower grate, and toss a handful of soaked wood chips on the charcoal. Place the upper grate, or grill rack, coated with cooking spray on the grill. Arrange the food on the grill rack above the aluminum foil pan on the unheated side.

3. The ideal smoking temperature is 200° to 225°. Close or open the grill's vents as needed to maintain this temperature range.

kitchen how-to: smoke on a gas grill

On some gas grills, it's impossible to hold the heat down to the desirable smoking temperature range of 200° to 225°. In that case, smoke on the lowest heat level your grill can maintain, and reduce the cooking time. You won't get as much smokiness, but you'll still get some of the aroma and flavor.

1. Soak the wood chips for 30 minutes, and drain. If your gas grill has a smoker box, add the soaked wood chips; they'll smolder from the heat of the nearest burner. If your gas grill doesn't have a built-in box, place the soaked chips on a piece of heavy-duty aluminum foil, fold it up, and close loosely; pierce the foil about six times with a fork to allow smoke to escape. You can also use an aluminum foil pan. Just pierce the pan several times, and add the soaked wood chips.

2. Turn on the burner at the end of the grill nearest the smoker box. If you're using a foil pouch, turn on the burner at one end of the grill, and arrange the pouch close to that burner. If your grill is longer than 36 inches, you may need to turn on two burners to get the proper heat.

3. Place an aluminum foil pan filled with water on the unheated side of the grill. Place the grill rack coated with cooking spray on the grill. Arrange the food on the grill rack directly above the aluminum foil pan. Adjust the grill knobs as needed to maintain the proper temperature.

burgers

burgers

Burgers are truly an American classic. The problem is, in recent years this culinary icon has gained a hefty amount of weight. In this chapter, we reclaim the favorite for those who want a juicy, delicious, and satisfying burger that fits into a healthy diet.

The Secrets to Making Juicy, Healthy Burgers

Healthier burgers using leaner meats require a few tricks in the kitchen to keep them juicy and delicious. Those tricks are here.

• For the best charred flavor, cook on a grill. A grill pan works, too, but the quality of the char is more subtle.

• Use your hands. They're seriously the best tools for shaping a burger. We give you more details on page 21.

• Once the burgers are on the grill, avoid moving them before they're ready to be turned so the outside develops a good char.

• Use a spatula that's wide enough to accommodate the size of your burger.

• Do not press the patties with the spatula as they cook. Doing so squeezes out the flavorful juices.

• Like other meats, burgers should rest for 5 minutes after they come off the grill to allow the juices to redistribute.

How Do Burgers Stack Up?

A ¼-pound patty of each:

Lamb
241 calories, 6.9g sat fat

Chuck (20% fat)
209 calories, 5.2g sat fat

Round (15% fat)
185 calories, 4.2g sat fat

Sirloin (10% fat)
177 calories, 3.8g sat fat

Extra-Lean Ground Beef (5% fat)
141 calories, 2.3g sat fat

Bison (grass-fed)
124 calories, 2.5g sat fat

Veal
146 calories, 2.6g sat fat

Pork
182 calories, 4.1g sat fat

Chicken
150 calories, 2.5g sat fat

Chicken Breast
101 calories, 0g sat fat

Turkey
193 calories, 2.8g sat fat

Turkey Breast
91 calories, 0.5g sat fat

Soy Crumbles
90 calories, 0g sat fat

kitchen how-to: shape burgers

There's nothing better to use than your hands to shape the perfect patty. You'll notice that some recipes in this book call for you to shape ground meat into patties without any additional seasonings. This is done to keep the flavor of the patties simple and meaty. For these simply seasoned burgers, sprinkle the patties with salt and pepper before they go on the grill so you'll get a hit of those flavors as you bite in. Pair them with strongly flavored condiments and cheeses. Both simply seasoned burgers and the method described below produce excellent results, and you'll find options in this chapter to suit your tastes.

1. Combine the ground meat and any burger ingredients—such as blue or feta cheese, minced shallots or onions, herbs, and spices—in a large bowl. As you work with the meat, be careful not to compact it. Just work the ingredients evenly and lightly into the meat—overworking will produce tough burgers.
2. Divide the mixture into equal portions, shaping each into a patty.
3. To ensure that the meat cooks evenly, make a thumbprint indentation into each patty before it goes on the grill. The indentation helps the patty hold its shape—rather than swelling—as it shrinks during cooking.

Why Grinding's Good

There's no question: Freshly ground beef, lamb, or poultry yields a superior, juicier burger. That includes meat you've had ground to order in a butcher shop at a supermarket and loosely wrapped (tight wraps compress the meat). It also includes meat you've ground yourself using a meat grinder or grinding attachment on a stand mixer. See a step-by-step technique on page 45 for more information.

Testing Doneness

Use a meat thermometer to test for doneness—and make sure you wash it between tests. For the burgers to be safe to eat, their internal temperature should reach the USDA's recommendation of 160° for ground beef, veal, lamb, and pork, and 165° for ground poultry.

The Best Bun for Your Burger

Great buns can greatly enhance your burger. Try focaccia, baguette, Hawaiian bread rolls, sourdough bread, Texas toast, English muffins, or garlic toast. Opt for whole-grain options as often as possible. It really does make a difference—more nutrients, more fiber, and a more satisfying taste.

Good Burger-to-Bun Ratio

It's best to shape the burgers into ¼- to ½-inch-thick patties to ensure that the size of the burger matches the bun, thus avoiding an off-kilter burger-to-bun ratio.

no bun overhang   **the burger is even**

Bad Burger-to-Bun Ratio

bun overhangs patties, leaving bready bite around the exterior   **center is too thick, which can leave a wet bottom bun**

Cheese Glossary

Cheese is one of those glorious toppings that can add so much richness and texture that it utterly transforms the burger. The calcium is a great bonus, but portions are key. Picture four dice lying end-to-end; that's about 1 ounce of cheese (i.e. one serving). If you're going to melt a firm cheese, grate it—less will go further. Here is how a few cheese options stack up.

1. Cheddar: 200mg calcium per ounce is a fifth of your daily need, but 6g saturated fat is more than 25% of your daily allowance.

2. Brie: With luscious, spread-able creaminess, it has a gram less sat fat than cheddar and less calcium, too.

3. Goat Cheese: It's not a great calcium source, but this tangy, pungent cheese is lower in calories and sat fat than many other varieties.

4. Swiss: One of the calcium kings (272mg per ounce), this nutty cheese also has less sat fat than cheddar and the lowest sodium content at 74mg.

5. Part-Skim Mozzarella: It has 3g of sat fat, a milky flavor, and is a good cheese for melting. You can also use fresh, which has 4.5g sat fat.

1   2   3   4   5

Pile on the Good Stuff!

Fresh vegetables and fruits, with their flavors, crunch, fiber, and nutrients, can bolster a burger. Get creative with:

- Arugula
- Spinach
- Bibb lettuce
- Tomato slices
- Sprouts
- Radish slices
- Cucumber
- Mango chutney
- Fruit salsas
- Tomato-based salsas
- Avocado slices
- Sweet peppers
- Grilled onions and mixed vegetables

Condiments are another way to add extra layers of flavor. Experiment with store-bought options, or make your own at home.

kitchen how-to: make mayonnaise

The key to creamy homemade mayo is to add just a few drops of oil at a time to the egg mixture, and then pour in a slow, thin drizzle—whisking constantly—to ensure the mayonnaise emulsifies (blends smoothly).

1. Combine 2 teaspoons fresh lemon juice, 1 teaspoon Dijon mustard, and 1 large pasteurized egg yolk in a medium bowl; stir well with a whisk.

2. Combine ½ cup canola oil and ¼ cup olive oil. Add oil mixture to egg yolk mixture drop by drop at first, and then in a thin, slow drizzle, stirring constantly with a whisk until the mixture is thick and smooth. Stir in ¼ teaspoon salt and ⅛ teaspoon freshly ground black pepper. **Yield: 12 tablespoons (serving size: 1 tablespoon).**

CALORIES 127; FAT 14.4g (sat 1.5g, mono 9g, poly 3.5g), PROTEIN 0.2g; CARB 0.2g; FIBER 0g; CHOL 17mg; IRON 0mg; SODIUM 53mg; CALC 2mg

kitchen how-to: make tomato ketchup

Both store-bought and home-made ketchup contain lycopene, an antioxidant associated with decreased risk of chronic diseases. We found this rendition well worth making because it captures the vibrant flavor of summer tomatoes and has about half the sodium of commercial ketchup. Serve with hamburgers, oven-baked fries, or with meat loaf.

1. Place ½ teaspoon yellow mustard seeds, ½ teaspoon celery seeds, ¼ teaspoon whole allspice, and ¼ teaspoon black peppercorns on a double layer of cheesecloth.

2. Gather edges of cheesecloth together; tie securely.

3. Combine cheesecloth bag; 2 chopped garlic cloves; 3 pounds heirloom tomatoes (about 4½ cups), cut into chunks; 2 cups chopped onion (1 medium); 1 cup chopped red bell pepper (1 small); and ⅓ cup cider vinegar in a large Dutch oven; bring to a boil. Cover, reduce heat, and simmer 20 minutes.

4. Remove cheesecloth bag, and set aside.

5. Place half of tomato mixture in a blender. Remove center piece of blender lid (to allow steam to escape); secure blender lid on blender. Place a clean towel over opening in blender lid (to avoid splatters). Blend until smooth.

6. Strain smooth mixture through a fine sieve back into pan; discard solids. Repeat procedure with remaining cooked tomato mixture.

7. Add cheesecloth bag, 1 tablespoon sugar, and ½ teaspoon salt to pan, and bring to a boil.

8. Reduce heat, and simmer, uncovered, until reduced to 1 cup (about 45 minutes). **Yield: 1 cup (serving size: 1 tablespoon).**

CALORIES 23; FAT 0.2g (sat 0g, mono 0g, poly 0.1g); PROTEIN 0.9g; CARB 5g; FIBER 1.2g; CHOL 0mg; IRON 0.3mg; SODIUM 79mg; CALC 11mg

Pesto Mayonnaise:

You'll find this quick-to-make mayo paired with Pancetta and Swiss Cheese–Stuffed Burgers with Pesto Mayonnaise on page 30, but feel free to use it to dress up any burger.

Easy Tzatziki Sauce:

Serve this tangy, creamy Greek sauce with lamb or beef, or any burger with Mediterranean or Middle Eastern spices. It's also a good dip for vegetable sticks or soft pita wedges. Combine ¾ cup plain low-fat yogurt, 2 tablespoons grated peeled seeded cucumber, 1½ teaspoons minced onion, ⅛ teaspoon salt, and ⅛ teaspoon freshly ground black pepper. Refrigerate in an airtight container up to 2 days. **Yield: about ¾ cup (serving size: 1 tablespoon).**

CALORIES 10; FAT 0.2g (sat 0.1g, mono 0.1g, poly 0g); PROTEIN 0.8g; CARB 1.2g; FIBER 0g; CHOL 1mg; IRON 0mg; SODIUM 35mg; CALC 28mg

Chipotle-Poblano Ketchup:

Two types of chiles provide smoky heat to this sauce, which goes with any type of meat or poultry burger. It's also great with oven fries or chicken fingers. Preheat broiler. Pierce 1 poblano chile (about 5 ounces) 2 times with the tip of a knife. Place on a foil-lined baking sheet; broil 10 minutes or until blackened, turning occasionally. Place in a zip-top plastic bag; seal. Let stand 15 minutes. Peel and discard skins. Cut a lengthwise slit in poblano; discard seeds and stem. Finely chop poblano. Combine poblano, 1 cup ketchup, 2 tablespoons minced seeded chipotle chiles canned in adobo sauce (about 2 chiles), and ½ teaspoon ground cumin. Refrigerate in an airtight container up to 2 weeks. **Yield: 1¼ cups (serving size: 1 tablespoon).**

CALORIES 15; FAT 0.2g (sat 0g, mono 0g, poly 0.1g); PROTEIN 0.3g; CARB 3.6g; FIBER 0.4g; CHOL 0mg; IRON 0.2mg; SODIUM 150mg; CALC 3mg

Blue Cheese Mayo:

Look for the recipe for this sharp mayo flavored with herbs and hot sauce on page 33.

Ginger-Honey Mustard:

This sweet and pungent condiment enlivens poultry or fish burgers. To make it, simply stir together 1 cup Dijon mustard, ¼ cup honey, 1½ tablespoons dry mustard, 1½ tablespoons minced peeled fresh ginger, and ⅛ teaspoon hot pepper sauce. Refrigerate in an airtight container up to 2 weeks. **Yield: 1¼ cups (serving size: 1 tablespoon).**

CALORIES 16; FAT 0.2g (sat 0.1g, mono 0g, poly 0g); PROTEIN 0.2g; CARB 3.7g; FIBER 0.1g; CHOL 0mg; IRON 0.1mg; SODIUM 156mg; CALC 2mg

Canola mayonnaise:

This option has fewer calories than regular mayo and provides healthy unsaturated fats.

Spicy Poblano Burgers with Pickled Red Onions and Chipotle Cream

2 poblano chiles
1 tablespoon 1% low-fat milk
1 (1-ounce) slice white bread, crusts removed, and torn into ½-inch pieces
3 tablespoons minced fresh cilantro, divided
1 teaspoon ground cumin
½ teaspoon ground coriander
½ teaspoon paprika
½ teaspoon kosher salt, divided
½ teaspoon freshly ground black pepper, divided
1 pound ground sirloin
½ cup light sour cream
1 tablespoon minced shallots
1 teaspoon fresh lime juice
1 (7-ounce) can chipotle chiles in adobo sauce
Cooking spray
4 (1½-ounce) hamburger buns, toasted
¼ cup Pickled Red Onions (recipe on page 27)

1. Preheat broiler.
2. Place poblano chiles on a foil-lined baking sheet, and broil 8 minutes or until blackened, turning after 6 minutes. Place in a zip-top plastic bag; seal. Let stand 15 minutes. Peel chiles, and discard seeds and membranes. Finely chop.
3. Combine milk and bread in a large bowl; mash bread mixture with a fork until smooth. Add poblano chile, 1½ tablespoons cilantro, cumin, coriander, paprika, ¼ teaspoon salt, ¼ teaspoon black pepper, and beef to milk mixture, tossing gently to combine. Divide mixture into 4 equal portions, gently shaping each into a ½-inch-thick patty. Press a nickel-sized indentation in the center of each patty. Cover and chill until ready to grill.
4. Preheat grill to medium-high heat.
5. Combine remaining 1½ tablespoons cilantro, remaining ¼ teaspoon salt, and remaining ¼ teaspoon black pepper in a medium bowl. Stir in sour cream,

shallots, and juice. Remove 1 chipotle pepper and 2 teaspoons adobo sauce from can; reserve remaining chipotle peppers and adobo sauce for another use. Chop chile. Stir chopped chipotle and 2 teaspoons adobo sauce into sour cream mixture. Set aside.

6. Place patties on grill rack coated with cooking spray; grill 3 minutes or until grill marks appear. Carefully turn patties; grill an additional 3 minutes or until desired degree of doneness. Place 1 patty on bottom half of each bun; top each serving with 3 tablespoons chipotle cream and 1 tablespoon Pickled Red Onions. **Yield: 4 servings (serving size: 1 burger).**

CALORIES 325; FAT 9.8g (sat 4.5g, mono 2.5g, poly 1.4g); PROTEIN 29.5g; CARB 30.2g; FIBER 2.1g; CHOL 70mg; IRON 3.9mg; SODIUM 621mg; CALC 81mg

Pickled Red Onions

The tangy zip of these pickled onions cuts through the rich chipotle cream. Use leftovers in bean burritos, on a beef sandwich, or mixed with fresh cilantro and orange sections as a quick relish for grilled Alaskan salmon.

  ½ **cup sugar**
  ½ **cup rice vinegar**
  ½ **cup water**
  1 **jalapeño pepper, halved lengthwise**
2½ **cups thinly vertically sliced red onion**

1. Combine first 4 ingredients in a medium saucepan; bring to a boil, stirring until sugar dissolves. Add onion to pan, and cover. Remove from heat, and cool to room temperature. Store in an airtight container in the refrigerator up to 1 month. **Yield: 2 cups (serving size: 1 tablespoon drained pickled onions).**

CALORIES 3; FAT 0g (sat 0g, mono 0g, poly 0g); PROTEIN 0.1g; CARB 0.8g; FIBER 0.1g; CHOL 0mg; IRON 0mg; SODIUM 0mg; CALC 1mg

kitchen how-to:
use a panade to keep lean burgers juicy

A panade, a pastelike mixture that's often used to bind meatballs, is used here to add moisture and keep this lean ground sirloin burger juicy.

1. Combine milk and torn sliced bread in a large bowl.
2. Mash with a fork until smooth. This milk mixture acts much like fat, keeping the meat moist and tender.
3. Combine the panade with the other burger ingredients, tossing to combine, and then shape the mixture into patties.

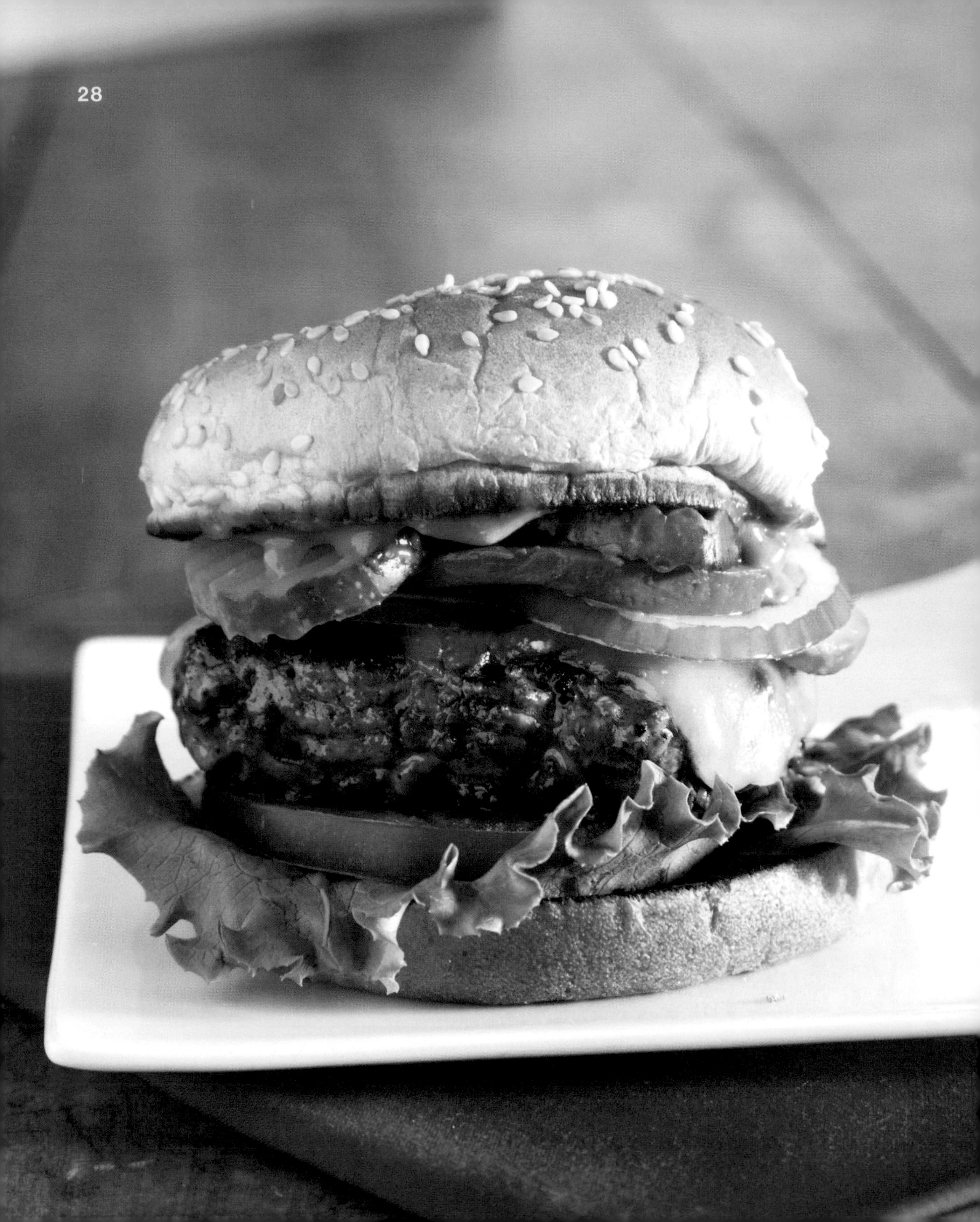

Out-N-In California Burger

- 3 tablespoons ketchup
- 2 tablespoons canola mayonnaise
- 2 teaspoons sweet pickle relish
- 1 teaspoon Dijon mustard
- 1 pound ground sirloin
- ⅛ teaspoon salt
- ⅛ teaspoon freshly ground black pepper

Cooking spray

- 4 (1-ounce) slices reduced-fat, reduced-sodium Swiss cheese
- 4 green leaf lettuce leaves
- 4 (1½-ounce) hamburger buns with sesame seeds, toasted
- 8 (¼-inch-thick) slices tomato
- 4 (¼-inch-thick) slices red onion
- ½ ripe peeled avocado, cut into ⅛-inch-thick slices
- 8 bread-and-butter pickle chips

1. Combine first 4 ingredients in a small bowl.

2. Divide beef into 4 equal portions, gently shaping each into a ½-inch-thick patty. Press a nickel-sized indentation in the center of each patty; sprinkle patties evenly with salt and pepper. Heat a grill pan or large skillet over medium-high heat. Coat pan with cooking spray. Add patties to pan; cook 3 minutes on each side. Top each patty with 1 cheese slice; cook 2 minutes or until cheese melts and patties are desired degree of doneness.

3. Place 1 lettuce leaf on bottom half of each hamburger bun; top with 2 tomato slices, 1 patty, 1 onion slice, about 2 avocado slices, 2 pickle chips, about 1½ tablespoons sauce, and top half of bun. **Yield: 4 servings (serving size: 1 burger).**

CALORIES 417; FAT 19.5g (sat 5.6g, mono 5.3g, poly 4.3g); PROTEIN 38g; CARB 34.6g; FIBER 2.8g; CHOL 73mg; IRON 3.2mg; SODIUM 802mg; CALC 272mg

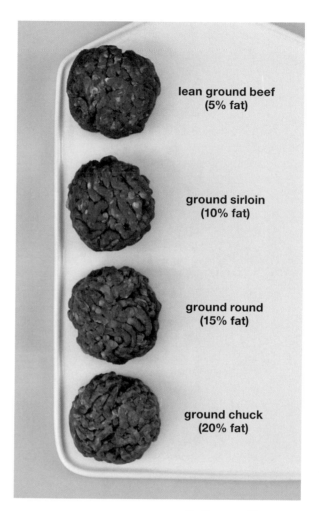

lean ground beef
(5% fat)

ground sirloin
(10% fat)

ground round
(15% fat)

ground chuck
(20% fat)

all about ground beef

When it comes to ground beef, there are a number of options in the meat section. Let the percentages of fat guide you. If the package is labeled 80% lean, that means it contains 20% fat. In addition to the standard options of ground chuck (20% fat), ground round (15% fat), and ground sirloin (10% fat), you'll also find lean ground beef with either 5% or 7% fat, the two leanest options available. If the package simply says "ground beef," that's an indication that it contains more than 20% fat.

Pancetta and Swiss Cheese–Stuffed Burgers with Pesto Mayonnaise

Cooking spray
- 1 ounce pancetta (about 2 slices), chopped into ¼-inch pieces
- ⅓ cup diced onion
- 2 garlic cloves, minced
- ½ teaspoon freshly ground black pepper
- ¼ teaspoon salt
- ¼ teaspoon dried Italian seasoning
- 1 pound ground sirloin
- ½ cup (2 ounces) shredded reduced-fat Swiss cheese
- 3 tablespoons light canola mayonnaise
- 1 tablespoon commercial pesto
- 4 Boston lettuce leaves (optional)
- 4 (2-ounce) white-wheat hamburger buns

1. Preheat grill to medium-high heat.
2. Heat a large nonstick skillet over medium heat. Coat pan with cooking spray. Add pancetta to pan; cook 4 minutes or until crisp. Remove pancetta from pan, reserving drippings in pan; set pancetta aside. Add onion and garlic to pan; cook 5 minutes or until softened, stirring frequently. Combine onion mixture, pepper, salt, seasoning, and beef in a bowl. Shape beef mixture into 8 (¼-inch-thick) patties. Top each of 4 patties with pancetta and 2 tablespoons Swiss cheese, leaving a ¼-inch border around edge. Top with remaining 4 patties; pinch edges to seal. Press a nickel-sized indentation in the center of each patty.
3. Place patties on grill rack coated with cooking spray; grill 5 minutes. Turn and grill 5 minutes or until a meat thermometer inserted in center measures 160°. Combine mayonnaise and pesto. Place 1 lettuce leaf on bottom half of each hamburger bun, if desired; top with 1 patty, about 1 tablespoon mayonnaise mixture, and top half of bun. **Yield: 4 servings (serving size: 1 burger).**

CALORIES 417; FAT 14.8g (sat 5.4g, mono 6.2g, poly 2.7g); PROTEIN 41.2g; CARB 30g; FIBER 3.4g; CHOL 78mg; IRON 4.6mg; SODIUM 676mg; CALC 226mg

kitchen how-to: make stuffed burgers

Stuffed burgers are open to many interpretations. They're a way to use high-fat ingredients in smaller amounts that still makes a big impact.

1. You'll need to cook the filling ingredients before stuffing the burgers since they won't see enough heat or time on the grill to cook them.
2. Combine the ground meat with seasonings.
3. Shape the beef mixture into 8 (¼-inch-thick) patties.
4. Top 4 patties with the filling ingredients, leaving a border around the edge.
5. Top with the remaining 4 patties, and pinch the edges to seal.

Grilled Vidalia Onions

What they add: Grown in the rich soil of Georgia, Vidalia onions are a sweet, juicy variety. Grilling enhances their flavor by caramelizing the onions' sugars, and tossing them with sherry vinegar lends a tangy sweetness.

Blue Cheese Mayo

What it adds: The sharpness of the blue cheese combined with thyme and hot sauce give this burger an anything-but-ordinary flavor. Feel free to add more hot sauce for more kick.

Burgers with Blue Cheese Mayo and Sherry Vidalia Onions

½ cup (2 ounces) crumbled blue cheese
¼ cup canola mayonnaise
2 teaspoons chopped fresh thyme, divided
¼ teaspoon hot pepper sauce
1 pound ground sirloin
1 teaspoon black pepper, divided
⅛ teaspoon kosher salt
½ teaspoon extra-virgin olive oil
4 (¼-inch-thick) slices Vidalia or other sweet onion
Cooking spray
2 teaspoons sherry vinegar
4 (1½-ounce) whole-wheat hamburger buns with sesame seeds, toasted
4 (¼-inch-thick) slices tomato
2 cups loosely packed arugula

1. Preheat grill to medium-high heat.
2. Combine blue cheese, mayonnaise, 1 teaspoon thyme, and hot pepper sauce in a small bowl; stir well.
3. Divide beef into 4 equal portions, shaping each portion into a ½-inch-thick patty. Press a nickel-sized indentation in the center of each patty. Sprinkle beef evenly with ½ teaspoon black pepper and salt.
4. Brush oil evenly over both sides of onion slices; sprinkle with remaining ½ teaspoon pepper. Place patties and onions on grill rack coated with cooking spray; cover and grill 3 minutes on each side. Set patties aside; keep warm. Place onion slices in a zip-top plastic bag; seal. Let stand 5 minutes; toss with remaining 1 teaspoon thyme and vinegar.
5. Spread cut sides of buns evenly with mayonnaise mixture. Place 1 tomato slice on bottom half of bun; top with ½ cup arugula, 1 patty, 1 onion slice, and top half of bun. **Yield: 4 servings (serving size: 1 burger).**

CALORIES 424; FAT 21.8g (sat 5.1g, mono 10.6g, poly 5.2g); PROTEIN 31.7g; CARB 27.5g; FIBER 4.4g; CHOL 76mg; IRON 3.3mg; SODIUM 624mg; CALC 151mg

Southwest Salsa Burgers

Chipotle chiles and fresh salsa give these burgers a southwestern kick that will heat up the dinner table in less than 20 minutes.

¼ **cup finely chopped shallots**
⅜ **teaspoon salt**
¼ **teaspoon ground chipotle chile pepper**
⅛ **teaspoon black pepper**
1 **pound ground sirloin**
¼ **cup refrigerated fresh salsa, divided**
Cooking spray
4 **(1-ounce) slices Monterey Jack cheese (optional)**
4 **Boston lettuce leaves**
4 **(1½-ounce) hamburger buns, toasted**
8 **(⅛-inch-thick) slices tomato**

1. Combine first 5 ingredients in a large bowl; add 2 tablespoons salsa. Divide mixture into 4 equal portions, shaping each into a ½-inch-thick patty. Press a nickel-sized indentation in the center of each patty.
2. Heat a grill pan over medium-high heat. Coat pan with cooking spray. Add patties to pan; cook 5 minutes on each side or until desired degree of doneness. Top each patty with 1 cheese slice, if desired; cook 1 minute or until cheese melts.
3. Place 1 lettuce leaf on bottom half of each bun; top with 2 tomato slices, 1 patty, 1½ teaspoons salsa, and 1 bun top. **Yield: 4 servings (serving size: 1 burger).**

CALORIES 310; FAT 11.1g (sat 4g, mono 4.3g, poly 1.2g); PROTEIN 26g; CARB 24.2g; FIBER 1.2g; CHOL 69mg; IRON 4mg; SODIUM 516mg; CALC 78mg

kitchen how-to:
grill burgers indoors

There's no need to heat up the grill every time you have a hankering for a burger. A grill pan can produce delicious results (including great grill marks) inside.

1. Heat a grill pan over medium-high heat, and then coat with cooking spray to prevent sticking.
2. Add the patties to the pan, and cook 5 minutes on each side or until desired degree of doneness.
3. Add a slice of cheese, if you like, and let it cook for 1 minute or until it's melted.

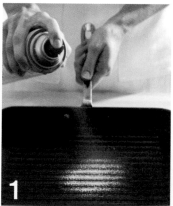

Sautéed Mushrooms
What they add: The chopped mushrooms in the burger mixture add low-fat moisture to the lean beef as it cooks.

Truffle Oil
What it adds: This ingredient is a less expensive way to impart the flavor and aroma of truffles to a dish.

Mushroom Burgers with Fried Eggs and Truffle Oil

Cooking spray
  3 cups finely chopped cremini
     mushrooms (about 8 ounces)
  ⅓ cup minced shallots
  1 tablespoon chopped fresh
     thyme
  5 garlic cloves, minced
  ⅓ cup cabernet sauvignon or
     other dry red wine
  ½ teaspoon kosher salt
  ¾ teaspoon freshly ground
     black pepper, divided
  1 pound extra-lean ground beef
  4 large eggs
  2 cups baby arugula leaves
  ¼ cup (1 ounce) grated
     Parmigiano-Reggiano cheese
  1 tablespoon white truffle oil
  1 tablespoon minced fresh
     chives
  1 tablespoon light canola
     mayonnaise
  1 tablespoon no-salt-added
     ketchup
  2 teaspoons Dijon mustard
  4 (1½-ounce) hamburger buns,
     toasted

1. Preheat grill to medium-high heat.
2. Heat a large nonstick skillet over medium-high heat. Coat pan with cooking spray. Add mushrooms and next 3 ingredients to pan; sauté 5 minutes or until mushrooms are browned. Add wine; cook 3 minutes or until liquid evaporates. Remove from heat; cool completely.
3. Combine mushroom mixture, salt, ½ teaspoon pepper, and beef in a large bowl. Divide mixture into 4 equal portions, gently shaping each into a ½-inch-thick patty. Press a nickel-sized indentation in the center of each patty. Place patties on grill rack coated with cooking spray; grill 4 minutes or until grill marks appear. Carefully turn patties; grill 4 minutes or until desired degree of doneness.
4. Return pan to medium heat; coat with cooking spray. Crack eggs into pan; cook 4 minutes or until whites are set. Remove from heat.
5. Combine remaining ¼ teaspoon pepper, arugula, cheese, and oil in a medium bowl; toss gently to coat. Combine chives and next 3 ingredients in a small bowl. Spread 2 teaspoons mayonnaise mixture on bottom half of each bun; top with 1 patty. Top each serving with 1 egg, ½ cup arugula mixture, and top half of bun. **Yield: 4 servings (serving size: 1 burger).**

CALORIES 429; FAT 17.5g (sat 5.5g, mono 7.4g, poly 2g); PROTEIN 37.5g; CARB 31.2g; FIBER 1.8 g; CHOL 244mg; IRON 4.7mg; SODIUM 767mg; CALC 185mg

Chipotle Barbecue Burgers with Slaw

The cool sour cream dressing in the slaw balances the spiciness of chiles in the burger. Toast the buns while the patties cook. Serve with baked sweet potato chips.

- ½ cup dry breadcrumbs
- 2 tablespoons barbecue sauce
- 1 tablespoon chopped chipotle chile, canned in adobo sauce
- 1 teaspoon bottled minced garlic
- 1 pound lean ground beef
- 1 large egg, lightly beaten

Cooking spray

- 2 cups cabbage-and-carrot coleslaw
- 1 tablespoon reduced-fat mayonnaise
- 1 tablespoon reduced-fat sour cream
- 1 teaspoon sugar
- 1 teaspoon cider vinegar
- ⅛ teaspoon salt
- ⅛ teaspoon freshly ground black pepper
- 4 (1.5-ounce) hamburger buns

1. Combine first 6 ingredients. Divide mixture into 4 equal portions, shaping each into a ½-inch-thick patty. Press a nickel-sized indentation in the center of each patty.
2. Heat a grill pan over medium-high heat. Coat pan with cooking spray. Add patties to pan; cook 4 minutes on each side or until a meat thermometer registers 160°.
3. Combine coleslaw and next 6 ingredients in a large bowl; toss well. Place 1 patty on bottom half of each bun; top each serving with ½ cup coleslaw mixture and top half of bun. **Yield: 4 servings (serving size: 1 burger).**

CALORIES 358; FAT 9.1g (sat 3g, mono 2.7g, poly 1.9g); PROTEIN 32.1g; CARB 36.3g; FIBER 2.6g; CHOL 115mg; IRON 4.3mg; SODIUM 609mg; CALC 112mg

kitchen how-to:
amp up burgers with homemade slaw

A homemade slaw can add extra flavor and moisture to lean burgers and provide a cool contrast to hot-off-the-grill burgers, particularly those made with fiery seasoning. A packaged cabbage-and-carrot coleslaw mix makes easy work of it. You can add some tang by using a mix of mayonnaise and sour cream, if you like, and then toss together for an easy topping.

Korean Barbecue Burgers

Top these burgers with a splash of rice vinegar and kimchi, a spicy-hot pickled vegetable condiment available at Asian markets. Serve with rice crackers.

½ cup chopped green onions
1½ tablespoons brown sugar
1½ tablespoons minced peeled fresh ginger
3 tablespoons lower-sodium soy sauce
1 tablespoon dark sesame oil
½ teaspoon freshly ground black pepper
2 garlic cloves, minced
1½ pounds ground sirloin
Cooking spray
6 (1½-ounce) whole-wheat hamburger buns, split
6 red leaf lettuce leaves
6 tablespoons thinly sliced radishes

1. Preheat grill to medium-high heat.
2. Combine first 8 ingredients. Divide mixture into 6 equal portions, shaping each into a ½-inch-thick patty. Press a nickel-sized indentation in the center of each patty.
3. Place patties on grill rack coated with cooking spray; grill 6 minutes on each side or until desired degree of doneness. Remove from grill; let patties stand 5 minutes.
4. Place buns, cut sides down, on grill rack; grill 1 minute or until toasted. Place 1 patty on bottom half of each bun; top each serving with 1 lettuce leaf, 1 tablespoon radishes, and top half of bun. **Yield: 6 servings (serving size: 1 burger).**

CALORIES 343; FAT 14.4g (sat 4.7g, mono 5.7g, poly 2.3g); PROTEIN 26.7g; CARB 27.4g; FIBER 3.7g; CHOL 72mg; IRON 3.8mg; SODIUM 534mg; CALC 72mg

Burger Seasonings
What they add: Soy sauce, brown sugar, sesame oil, and garlic are typical marinade ingredients for *bulgogi,* a traditional Korean barbecue sirloin specialty. They create a sweet and savory burger version reminiscent of the original dish.

Radishes
What they add: Thinly sliced fresh radishes provide a cool crunch.

Pesto Sliders

Mixing salt and pepper into the beef seasons it more thoroughly than sprinkling the surface of the patties. Serve with baked chips.

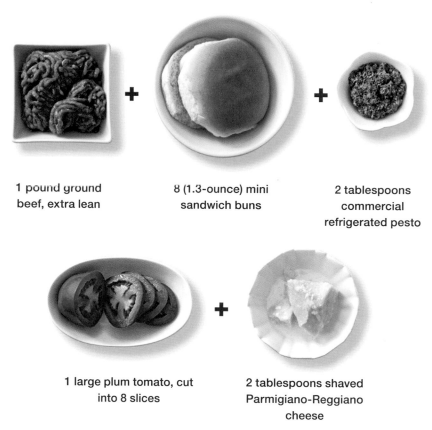

1 pound ground beef, extra lean

+

8 (1.3-ounce) mini sandwich buns

+

2 tablespoons commercial refrigerated pesto

1 large plum tomato, cut into 8 slices

+

2 tablespoons shaved Parmigiano-Reggiano cheese

Gently combine ground beef, ¼ teaspoon salt, and ¼ teaspoon freshly ground black pepper in a bowl. Divide beef mixture into 8 equal portions, shaping each into a ¼-inch-thick patty. Press a nickel-sized indentation in the center of each patty. Heat a grill pan over medium-high heat. Coat pan with cooking spray. Add patties to pan; cook 3 minutes on each side or until desired degree of doneness. Spread bottom half of each bun with ¾ teaspoon pesto, and top each with 1 tomato slice and 1 patty. Top each patty with ¾ teaspoon shaved Parmigiano-Reggiano cheese and top half of bun. **Yield: 4 servings (serving size: 2 sliders).**

CALORIES 416; FAT 16.5g (sat 6.2 g, mono 6.9g, poly 2.3g); PROTEIN 29.7g; CARB 38.8g; FIBER 2.3g; CHOL 65mg; IRON 4.4mg; SODIUM 754mg; CALC 149mg

Brisket Burgers

Grinding the meat for this burger produces fresh flavor from inexpensive beef brisket. (See page 45 for grinding tips). Ask for the flat cut of brisket for the leanest and the lowest in saturated fat.

- 1 (1-pound) beef brisket, trimmed and cut into 1-inch pieces
- 2 tablespoons olive oil
- ¼ teaspoon kosher salt
- ⅛ teaspoon freshly ground black pepper
- Cooking spray
- 4 (½-ounce) slices cheddar cheese
- 4 (1½-ounce) hamburger buns, toasted
- 4 green leaf lettuce leaves
- 4 (¼-inch-thick) slices tomato

1. To prepare grinder, place feed shaft, blade, and ¼-inch die plate in freezer 30 minutes or until well chilled. Assemble grinder just before grinding.

2. Arrange meat in a single layer on jelly-roll pan, leaving space between each piece. Freeze 15 minutes or until meat is firm but not frozen. Combine meat and oil in large bowl, and toss to combine. Pass meat through meat grinder completely. Immediately pass meat through grinder a second time. Divide mixture into 4 equal portions, gently shaping each into a ½-inch-thick patty. Press a nickel-sized indentation in the center of each patty. Cover and chill until ready to grill.

3. Preheat grill to medium-high heat.

4. Sprinkle patties with salt and pepper. Place on grill rack coated with cooking spray; grill 2 minutes or until grill marks appear. Carefully turn patties; grill 3 minutes. Top each patty with 1 cheese slice; grill 1 minute or until cheese melts and beef reaches desired degree of doneness. Place 1 patty on bottom half of each bun; top each serving with 1 lettuce leaf, 1 tomato slice, and top half of bun. **Yield: 4 servings (serving size: 1 burger).**

CALORIES 386; FAT 17.9g (sat 6.1g, mono 8.7g, poly 1.9g); PROTEIN 32.4g; CARB 22.1g; FIBER 1.2g; CHOL 64mg; IRON 4mg; SODIUM 496mg; CALC 181mg

kitchen how-to: grind meat for burgers

1

2

3

4

When grinding meat at home, a grinder attachment for your stand mixer is ideal, but an old-fashioned hand grinder works, too. You can also use your food processor; in that case, be sure to work in small batches, pulsing the meat 8 to 10 times or until the meat is finely chopped but not pureed.

1. No matter what grinding tool you use, it's important to keep the meat and the grinding equipment as cold as possible. If the meat gets too warm, it will begin to smear rather than grind cleanly, giving the finished product an unappetizing mashed texture. Putting the meat and grinding equipment in the freezer for 15 minutes beforehand helps guarantee optimum results. Arrange the meat in a single layer on a jelly-roll pan, leaving a space between each piece, and then freeze for 15 minutes or until the meat is firm but not frozen.

2. Combine meat and oil in a large bowl, and toss to combine. Oil is added to ensure juiciness and rich, meaty flavor.
3. Pass the meat through the meat grinder completely.

4. Immediately pass the meat through the grinder a second time to ensure meat is well ground, and then use as you would ground meat.

Vadouvan

What it adds: *Vadouvan* is an Indian condiment made by cooking onions, shallots, and garlic until deeply caramelized, and then flavoring them with a combination of toasted dried spices. For a shortcut, you can substitute 2 teaspoons of garam masala or Madras curry powder for all the ground spices here.

Roasted Peppers

What they add: Roasted peppers have a silky texture and sweet flavor that rounds out this burger. For tips on roasting peppers, see page 269.

Yogurt-Mint Sauce
What it adds: Yogurt and mint provide a cool counterpoint to the spice mix.

Lamb Burgers with Indian Spices and Yogurt-Mint Sauce

- 1   tablespoon olive oil
- ¾   cup finely chopped onion
- ¼   cup finely chopped shallots
- 2   tablespoons minced garlic, divided
- ¾   teaspoon ground cumin
- ¾   teaspoon ground coriander
- ¼   teaspoon ground cardamom
- ¼   teaspoon ground mustard
- ¼   teaspoon ground turmeric
- ⅛   teaspoon ground red pepper

Dash of grated whole nutmeg

- ½   pound ground lamb
- ½   pound ground turkey breast
- 2   tablespoons finely chopped fresh mint, divided
- ¾   teaspoon kosher salt, divided
- 2   red bell peppers
- ½   cup plain 2% reduced-fat Greek yogurt
- 1   tablespoon fresh lemon juice
- ¼   teaspoon freshly ground black pepper, divided

Cooking spray

- 4   (1½-ounce) hamburger buns, toasted
- 2   cups torn radicchio

1. Heat oil in a medium nonstick skillet over medium heat. Add onion and shallots; cook 15 minutes or until onions are golden, stirring frequently. Stir in 1½ tablespoons garlic, cumin, and next 6 ingredients; cook 1 minute. Remove from heat; cool to room temperature.

2. Combine onion mixture, lamb, turkey, 1 tablespoon mint, and ¼ teaspoon salt. Divide mixture into 4 equal portions, gently shaping each into a ½-inch-thick patty. Press a nickel-sized indentation in the center of each patty. Cover and chill until ready to grill.

3. Preheat broiler.

4. Cut bell peppers in half lengthwise; discard seeds and membranes. Place pepper halves, skin sides up, on a foil-lined baking sheet; flatten with hand. Broil 9 minutes or until blackened. Place in a zip-top plastic bag; seal. Let stand 10 minutes. Peel and cut each pepper portion in half.

5. Preheat grill to medium-high heat.

6. Combine remaining 1½ teaspoons garlic, remaining 1 tablespoon mint, yogurt, juice, ¼ teaspoon salt, and ⅛ teaspoon black pepper in a medium bowl. Set aside.

7. Sprinkle patties evenly with remaining ¼ teaspoon salt and remaining ⅛ teaspoon black pepper. Place patties on grill rack coated with cooking spray; grill 4 minutes or until grill marks appear. Carefully turn patties; grill 3 minutes or until a thermometer registers 165°. Place 1 patty on bottom half of each bun; top each serving with 2 tablespoons yogurt mixture, ½ cup radicchio, 2 bell pepper strips, and top half of bun. **Yield: 4 servings (serving size: 1 burger).**

CALORIES 420; FAT 18.2g (sat 6g, mono 6.5g, poly 1.9g); PROTEIN 30.3g; CARB 33.7g; FIBER 3.2g; CHOL 75mg; IRON 4.1mg; SODIUM 660mg; CALC 132mg

Greek Lamb Burgers

Fresh rosemary, oregano, and lemon rind harmonize with the richness of lamb and feta cheese. Tuck chopped tomato and lettuce into the pita pockets, if desired. Serve with fresh fruit and lemonade.

½ cup (2 ounces) crumbled reduced-fat
    feta cheese
1 tablespoon chopped fresh rosemary
2 teaspoons grated lemon rind
2 teaspoons chopped fresh oregano
½ teaspoon salt
3 garlic cloves, minced
¾ pound lean ground lamb
¾ pound ground turkey breast
Cooking spray
3 (6-inch) pitas, cut in half
6 tablespoons Easy Tzatziki Sauce (page 25)

1. Preheat grill to medium-high heat.
2. Combine first 8 ingredients. Divide mixture into 6 equal portions, shaping each into a ½-inch-thick patty. Press a nickel-sized indentation in the center of each patty.
3. Place patties on grill rack coated with cooking spray; grill 6 minutes on each side or until a thermometer registers 165°. Remove from grill; let stand 5 minutes.
4. Place 1 patty in each pita half; drizzle each serving with 1 tablespoon Easy Tzatziki Sauce. **Yield: 6 servings (serving size: 1 stuffed pita half).**

CALORIES 275; FAT 10.3g (sat 4.4g, mono 3.6g, poly 0.8g); PROTEIN 25.9g; CARB 19.1g; FIBER 0.8g; CHOL 62mg; IRON 1.9mg; SODIUM 576mg; CALC 78mg

Easy Tzatziki Sauce
What it adds: This creamy, cool sauce lends authentic Greek flavor to this burger. If you don't want to make the sauce, serve with a drizzle of plain, fat-free yogurt.

Pita Bread
What it adds: Pita bread is a staple in Middle Eastern and Mediterranean cuisine. Opt for a whole-wheat version, if you like.

Two Ground Meats
What they add: Ground lamb contains about 20% fat, which can carry a hefty load of calories and saturated fat. Pairing it with lean ground turkey breast keeps those numbers in check.

Mini Lamb Burgers with Blue Cheese

1¼ teaspoons olive oil
1⅔ cups thinly sliced onion (about 1 large)
¾ teaspoon brown sugar
⅜ teaspoon salt, divided
¼ teaspoon freshly ground black pepper
13 ounces lean ground lamb
Cooking spray
1 cup arugula leaves
8 (1.3-ounce) mini sandwich buns, toasted
2 tablespoons crumbled blue cheese

1. Heat oil in a large nonstick skillet over medium heat. Add onion and sugar to pan; cook 10 minutes, stirring frequently. Stir in ⅛ teaspoon salt. Reduce heat; cook 8 minutes or until tender and browned, stirring occasionally. Keep warm.
2. Preheat grill to high heat.
3. Combine remaining ¼ teaspoon salt, pepper, and lamb in a large bowl. Divide lamb mixture into 8 equal portions, shaping each into a ½-inch-thick patty. Press a nickel-sized indentation in the center of each patty. Place patties on grill rack coated with cooking spray. Grill 3 minutes on each side.
4. Place arugula evenly on bottom halves of buns; top with 1 patty, 1½ tablespoons caramelized onion, and about ¾ teaspoon blue cheese. Cover with top halves of buns. **Yield: 8 servings (serving size: 1 slider).**

CALORIES 226; FAT 10.4g (sat 3.8g, mono 4.8g, poly 1g); PROTEIN 11.8g; CARB 21.2g; FIBER 1.6g; CHOL 33mg; IRON 1.8mg; SODIUM 347mg; CALC 68mg

kitchen how-to:
shape mini burgers

Mini burgers take on various forms, but the method for making them is standard. You can prepare them outdoors on your grill or indoors on a grill pan.

1. Divide the meat mixture into equal portions about the size of large meatballs.
2. Shape each into a ¼- to ½-inch-thick patty. Place patties on grill rack coated with cooking spray (to help prevent these mini burgers from sticking). Grill 3 minutes on each side or until desired degree of doneness. You may need to adjust your cooking time based on the thickness of your patties.

Swedish Meatball Burgers

Although we suggest serving these on potato or Kaiser rolls, you can also perch the patties atop egg noodles.

⅓ cup finely chopped onion
2 tablespoons chopped fresh parsley
1 tablespoon paprika
1 tablespoon brown sugar
1½ tablespoons white wine vinegar
1 teaspoon salt
⅛ teaspoon ground allspice
⅛ teaspoon ground nutmeg
1½ pounds ground veal
Cooking spray
6 (2-ounce) potato sandwich rolls or Kaiser rolls, split
6 Bibb lettuce leaves (optional)
6 (¼-inch-thick) slices tomato (optional)
6 tablespoons fat-free sour cream

1. Preheat grill to medium-high heat.
2. Combine first 9 ingredients. Divide mixture into 6 equal portions, shaping each into a ½-inch-thick patty. Press a nickel-sized indentation in the center of each patty.
3. Place patties on grill rack coated with cooking spray; grill 5 minutes on each side or until a thermometer registers 160°. Remove from grill; let stand 5 minutes.
4. Place rolls, cut sides down, on grill rack; grill 1 minute or until toasted. Place 1 lettuce leaf and 1 tomato slice, if desired, on bottom half of each roll; top each serving with 1 patty, 1 tablespoon sour cream, and top half of roll. **Yield: 6 servings (serving size: 1 burger).**

CALORIES 326; FAT 10.6g (sat 3.2g, mono 4.3g, poly 1.9g); PROTEIN 25.5g; CARB 31.9g; FIBER 1.5g; CHOL 89mg; IRON 2.1mg; SODIUM 718mg; CALC 45mg

all about ground veal

Nutritionally, ground veal has a lot going for it. It's a lean option (just 8% fat)—a ¼-pound patty contains 2.6 grams saturated fat and 146 calories—and an alternative to standard burger fare. When buying ground veal, it's best to use it within 1 to 2 days. You can also freeze it, if you like; but for best quality, use it within 3 to 4 months.

Saté Burgers

Serve these patties on a bed of brown rice with spinach and lime wedges for an alternative to the classic burger.

½ cup chopped fresh cilantro
¼ cup finely chopped unsalted, dry-roasted peanuts
1½ tablespoons brown sugar
2 tablespoons fresh lime juice
1½ tablespoons fish sauce
1½ teaspoons ground cumin
½ teaspoon salt
¼ teaspoon hot pepper sauce
3 garlic cloves, minced
¾ pound ground pork
¾ pound ground turkey breast
Cooking spray

1. Preheat grill to medium-high heat.
2. Combine first 11 ingredients. Divide mixture into 6 equal portions, shaping each into a ½-inch-thick patty. Press a nickel-sized indentation in the center of each patty.
3. Place patties on grill rack coated with cooking spray; grill 7 minutes on each side or until a thermometer registers 165°. Remove from grill; let stand 5 minutes.
Yield: 6 servings (serving size: 1 patty).

CALORIES 166; FAT 7.5g (sat 2.1g, mono 3.1g, poly 1.3g); PROTEIN 20.1g; CARB 4.9g; FIBER 0.8g; CHOL 49mg; IRON 0.7mg; SODIUM 599mg; CALC 16mg

Saté Flavors
What they add: Peanuts, cilantro, brown sugar, lime juice, and fish sauce create the flavors of the Indonesian meat skewers called saté.

Mix of Meats
What they add: Using equal amounts of ground turkey breast and pork keeps these burgers lean. Since the mix includes poultry, you'll need to be sure to cook the burgers to 165°.

Turkey Burgers with Roasted Eggplant

Marmite is a concentrated yeast paste that helps give this burger meaty flavor—find it in supermarket baking aisles and health-food stores.

1 (8-ounce) eggplant
Cooking spray
2 tablespoons finely chopped fresh parsley, divided
4 teaspoons olive oil, divided
1 teaspoon fresh lemon juice
1 garlic clove, minced
¾ teaspoon kosher salt, divided
½ teaspoon freshly ground black pepper, divided
1 pound turkey tenderloins, cut into 1-inch pieces

1 teaspoon lower-sodium soy sauce
¼ teaspoon Marmite
4 (1½-ounce) hamburger buns with sesame seeds, toasted
4 Bibb lettuce leaves
4 (¼-inch-thick) slices tomato

1. Preheat oven to 400°.
2. Lightly coat eggplant with cooking spray; wrap eggplant in foil. Place eggplant on a jelly-roll pan; bake at 400° for 45 minutes or until very tender, turning once. Remove from foil; cool slightly. Cut eggplant in half. Carefully scoop out pulp to measure 1¼ cups; discard skin. Place pulp in a food processor; process until smooth. Reserve ¼ cup pureed pulp. Combine remaining pulp, 1 tablespoon parsley, 2 teaspoons oil,

juice, and garlic. Stir in ½ teaspoon salt and ¼ teaspoon pepper; set aside.

3. To prepare grinder, place feed shaft, blade, and ¼-inch die plate in freezer 30 minutes or until well chilled. Assemble the grinder just before grinding.

4. Arrange turkey pieces in a single layer on a jelly-roll pan, leaving space between each piece. Freeze 15 minutes or until meat is firm but not frozen. Combine meat and remaining 2 teaspoons oil in a large bowl; toss to combine. Pass meat through meat grinder completely. Immediately pass meat through grinder a second time. Combine reserved ¼ cup eggplant puree, turkey, remaining 1 tablespoon parsley, soy sauce, and Marmite in a large bowl. Divide mixture into 4 equal portions, gently shaping each

into a ½-inch-thick patty. Press a nickel-sized indentation in the center of each patty. Cover and chill until ready to grill.

5. Preheat grill to medium-high heat.

6. Lightly coat patties with cooking spray; sprinkle with remaining ¼ teaspoon salt and remaining ¼ teaspoon pepper. Place patties on grill rack; grill 4 minutes until well marked. Carefully turn patties over; grill 3 minutes or until done. Place 1 patty on bottom half of each bun; top each with 1 tablespoon eggplant mixture, 1 lettuce leaf, 1 tomato slice, and top half of bun. Reserve remaining eggplant mixture for another use. **Yield: 4 servings (serving size: 1 burger).**

CALORIES 311; FAT 12.5g (sat 3g, mono 2.8g, poly 1.5g); PROTEIN 26.9g; CARB 23.3g; FIBER 1.9g; CHOL 65mg; IRON 3.6mg; SODIUM 522mg; CALC 70mg

kitchen how-to: make perfect poultry burgers

How do you get a burger made from mild, low-fat turkey to have some of the juiciness and meaty richness of beef? You add ingredients to lend moisture and mimic those flavors. It's also a matter of getting the burger off the grill before it dries out (or sticks and falls apart)—a job made trickier by needing to cook poultry to 165°.

1. Turkey isn't the juiciest meat, but the addition of mildly flavored eggplant solves that problem in these burgers. Simply roast the eggplant, and then puree it. Next, blend it with the ground meat. You can also mix in olive oil to avoid the sawdust syndrome. Stirring in

2 tablespoons olive oil per pound of ground poultry keeps burgers moist and juicy, and also helps them form a nicely browned crust on the outside that won't stick to the grill.

2. Another way to add savory flavor is with Marmite. Here's the kitchen science: Beef and other red meats contain compounds called glutamates. So do soy sauce and Marmite, which is a powerfully strong yeast extract found in a lot of supermarkets (the Aussies love a version called Vegemite). We add both the eggplant and the Marmite to the turkey mixture, lending this burger the umami flavors of red meat.

Apricot Turkey Burgers

For a more unusual offering, fold these burgers into flatbread, Indian naan, or Middle Eastern lavash.

¾ cup drained canned chickpeas (garbanzo beans)
½ cup dried apricots, chopped
⅓ cup minced shallots
½ teaspoon salt
½ teaspoon ground ginger
½ teaspoon ground cumin
½ teaspoon ground cinnamon
⅛ teaspoon ground red pepper
1½ pounds ground turkey
Cooking spray
6 (1½-ounce) multigrain hamburger buns, split
6 romaine lettuce leaves (optional)
6 tablespoons Easy Tzatziki Sauce (page 25)

1. Preheat grill to medium-high heat.
2. Place chickpeas in a food processor; pulse 3 times or until chopped. Combine chickpeas, apricots, and next 7 ingredients. Divide mixture into 6 equal portions, shaping each into a ½-inch-thick patty. Press a nickel-sized indentation in the center of each patty.
3. Place patties on grill rack coated with cooking spray; grill 6 minutes on each side or until a meat thermometer registers 165°. Remove from grill; let stand 5 minutes.
4. Place buns, cut sides down, on grill rack; grill 1 minute or until toasted. Place 1 lettuce leaf on bottom half of each bun, if desired; top with 1 patty, 1 table-spoon Easy Tzatziki Sauce, and top half of bun. **Yield: 6 servings (serving size: 1 burger).**

CALORIES 320; FAT 9.2g (sat 2.3 g, mono 3.6g, poly 2.3g); PROTEIN 24.9g; CARB 35.4g; FIBER 4.6g; CHOL 53mg; IRON 3.5mg; SODIUM 541mg; CALC 89mg

Multigrain Buns
What they add: Multigrain buns amp up the fiber in these burgers, but you could substitute flatbread, Indian naan, or Middle Eastern *lavash* for something a bit different.

Dried Apricots
What they add: Along with the chickpeas, tangy dried apricots keep these Moroccan-spiced burgers moist.

Southwest Turkey Burgers

2 poblano chiles, halved and seeded
1 ounce French bread baguette
¼ cup 1% low-fat milk
½ teaspoon chili powder, divided
1 teaspoon ground cumin
½ teaspoon salt
¼ teaspoon black pepper
¼ teaspoon ground red pepper
1 pound ground turkey breast
Cooking spray
2 tablespoons canola mayonnaise
4 (1½-ounce) hamburger buns, toasted
4 (½-inch-thick) slices tomato
4 green leaf lettuce leaves

1. Preheat grill to medium-high heat.
2. Place poblanos, skin sides down, on grill rack; grill 10 minutes or until blackened. Place poblanos in a small zip-top plastic bag; seal. Let stand 15 minutes. Peel and dice.
3. Place bread in a food processor; pulse 5 times or until coarse crumbs measure ½ cup. Combine breadcrumbs and milk in a bowl; let stand 5 minutes. Add poblanos, ¼ teaspoon chili powder, cumin, and next 4 ingredients; gently mix just until combined. Divide mixture into 4 equal portions, shaping each portion into a ½-inch-thick patty. Press a nickel-sized indentation in the center of each patty. Place patties on grill rack coated with cooking spray; grill 3 minutes on each side or until done.
4. Combine remaining ¼ teaspoon chili powder and mayonnaise. Top bottom half of each bun with 1 tomato slice, 1 lettuce leaf, 1 patty, about 1½ teaspoons mayonnaise mixture, and 1 bun top. **Yield: 4 servings (serving size: 1 burger).**

CALORIES 321; FAT 8.5g (sat 1.1g, mono 4.2g, poly 2.9g); PROTEIN 27.8g; CARB 32.5g; FIBER 2.6g; CHOL 56mg; IRON 3.5mg; SODIUM 658mg; CALC 108mg

kitchen how-to: grill poblanos

Dark-green poblano chiles have mild to moderate heat. In general, the darker the chile, the more fiery it will be.

1. Cut poblanos in half lengthwise; discard seeds and membranes.
2. Place poblanos, skin sides down, on a grill rack coated with cooking spray; grill until blackened.
3. Place the poblanos in a zip-top plastic bag, and seal. Let peppers stand in bag 15 minutes. The heat from the poblanos creates steam in the sealed bag, which helps the charred skins separate from the flesh of the pepper.
4. The charred skins should easily separate from the peppers. Then just chop or dice.

Turkey Burger Pitas with Tahini Sauce

You can divide the mixture into 8 smaller patties, if you like.

- ½ cup plain 2% reduced-fat Greek yogurt
- 1 tablespoon tahini (sesame seed paste)
- 1 teaspoon fresh lemon juice
- 1 garlic clove, minced
- Dash of salt
- ¼ cup chopped green onions
- 3 tablespoons finely chopped fresh parsley
- ½ teaspoon salt
- ¼ teaspoon onion powder
- 1 pound ground turkey
- Cooking spray
- 2 (6-inch) whole-wheat pitas, cut in half
- 4 green leaf lettuce leaves
- 4 (¼-inch) slices tomato

1. Combine first 5 ingredients in a small bowl.
2. Combine onions and next 4 ingredients in a large bowl. Divide mixture into 4 equal portions, shaping each into a ½-inch-thick patty. Press a nickel-sized indentation in the center of each patty.
3. Heat a grill pan over medium-high heat. Coat pan with cooking spray. Add patties to pan, and cook 4 minutes on each side or until done.
4. Line each pita half with 1 lettuce leaf; add 1 patty, 1 tomato slice, and 2 tablespoons tahini sauce to each pita half. **Yield: 4 servings (serving size: 1 filled pita half).**

CALORIES 302; FAT 11.9g (sat 3.5g, mono 3.9g, poly 3.3g); PROTEIN 30.6g; CARB 21.1g; FIBER 2.8g; CHOL 73mg; IRON 2.7mg; SODIUM 599mg; CALC 93mg

Tahini
What it adds: Made from ground sesame seeds that have been lightly roasted, this paste has a texture similar to nut butter.

2% Reduced-Fat Greek Yogurt
What it adds: This yogurt is an ideal base for the tahini sauce, adding rich flavor and a creamy texture.

Chicken Parmesan Burgers

These burgers will remind you of chicken Parmesan—the patties are drenched in marinara and topped with cheese.

2 (3-ounce) square ciabatta rolls
1 garlic clove, halved
½ pound ground chicken
⅓ cup plus 2 tablespoons lower-sodium marinara sauce, divided
½ teaspoon chopped fresh rosemary
½ teaspoon chopped fresh thyme
¼ teaspoon crushed red pepper
⅛ teaspoon kosher salt
⅛ teaspoon black pepper
Cooking spray
¼ cup shredded part-skim mozzarella cheese
8 fresh basil leaves

1. Preheat broiler.
2. Cut rolls in half. Place rolls, cut sides up, on a baking sheet. Broil 3 minutes or until lightly browned. Remove rolls from pan. Rub each slice with cut side of garlic. Set aside.
3. Preheat oven to 375°.
4. Combine chicken, ⅓ cup marinara, rosemary, thyme, red pepper, salt, and black pepper. Divide into 2 equal portions, shaping each into a ¼-inch-thick patty. Press a nickel-sized indentation in the center of each patty. Heat an ovenproof skillet over medium-high heat. Coat pan with cooking spray. Add patties to pan; cook 3 minutes. Turn patties, and place pan in oven. Bake at 375° for 8 minutes. Top each patty with 2 tablespoons cheese; bake 1 minute.
5. Layer bottom half of each roll with 2 basil leaves, 1 patty, 1 tablespoon marinara, 2 basil leaves, and roll top. **Yield: 2 servings (serving size: 1 burger).**

CALORIES 427; FAT 14.4g (sat 4.5g, mono 5.3g, poly 2.3g); PROTEIN 28.9g; CARB 55.4g; FIBER 1.2g; CHOL 83mg; IRON 2.9mg; SODIUM 742mg; CALC 112mg

all about
ground chicken vs. ground chicken breast

When it comes to ground chicken (or any ground poultry for that matter), pay attention to the labels. Regular "ground chicken" is a mix of white and dark meat, which means it contains anywhere from 10% to 15% fat. Ground chicken *breast* contains just the white meat.

ground chicken breast

ground chicken

Jamaican Chicken Burgers

Pickapeppa sauce—a tangy, sweet Jamaican condiment found near the steak sauces in most supermarkets—would be a fitting accompaniment. Or try our Chipotle-Poblano Ketchup on page 25.

1 cup thinly sliced soft black plantains (about 1 medium)
¼ cup chopped green onions
1 tablespoon cider vinegar
1 tablespoon Worcestershire sauce
1 teaspoon dried thyme
½ teaspoon ground allspice
½ teaspoon salt
¼ teaspoon ground red pepper
1½ pounds ground chicken breast
Cooking spray
6 (2-ounce) onion sandwich buns, split
6 Bibb lettuce leaves
6 (¼-inch-thick) slices tomato
6 (⅛-inch-thick) slices red onion

1. Preheat grill to medium-high heat.
2. Cook plantain in boiling water 15 minutes or until very tender. Drain; place in a large bowl. Mash plantain with a fork until smooth; cool 5 minutes. Add green onions and next 7 ingredients. Divide mixture into 6 equal portions, shaping each into a ½-inch-thick patty. Press a nickel-sized indentation in the center of each patty.
3. Place patties on grill rack coated with cooking spray; grill 4 minutes on each side or until a thermometer registers 165°. Remove from grill, and let stand 5 minutes.
4. Place buns, cut sides down, on grill rack; grill 1 minute or until toasted. Place 1 lettuce leaf on bottom half of each bun; top with 1 tomato slice, 1 patty, 1 red onion slice, and top half of bun. **Yield: 6 servings (serving size: 1 burger).**

CALORIES 309; FAT 5.5g (sat 1.3g, mono 2.4g, poly 1g); CARB 24.5g; PROTEIN 40.7g; FIBER 3.1g; CHOL 50mg; IRON 3mg; SODIUM 577mg; CALC 91mg

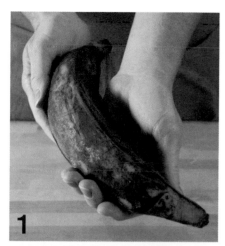

1

kitchen how-to:
make island-inspired burgers

Sweet flavors with a hit of heat rev up these lean burgers.

1. Mashed plantains bind and moisten these island-inspired burgers. Be sure to choose ripe plantains with black skins; they're tender and slightly sweet.
2. Cook plantains in boiling water 15 minutes or until very tender.

3. Drain plantains; place in a large bowl. Using a fork or potato masher, mash the plantain until smooth, and then cool for 5 minutes.
4. Add green onions, cider vinegar, Worcestershire sauce, dried thyme, ground allspice, salt, ground red pepper, and ground chicken breast; shape into patties.

2

3

4

Salmon Burgers

1 pound skinless center-cut salmon fillets, cut into 1-inch pieces and divided
2 tablespoons Dijon mustard, divided
2 teaspoons grated lemon rind
2 tablespoons minced fresh tarragon
1 tablespoon finely chopped shallots (about 1 small)
½ teaspoon kosher salt
¼ teaspoon freshly ground black pepper
1 tablespoon honey
1 cup arugula leaves
½ cup thinly sliced red onion
1 teaspoon fresh lemon juice
1 teaspoon extra-virgin olive oil
Cooking spray
4 (1½-ounce) hamburger buns with sesame seeds, toasted

1. Place ¼ pound salmon, 1 tablespoon mustard, and rind in a food processor; process until smooth. Spoon puree into a large bowl. Place remaining ¾ pound salmon in food processor; pulse 6 times or until coarsely chopped. Fold chopped salmon, tarragon, shallots, salt, and pepper into puree. Divide mixture into 4 equal portions, gently shaping each into a ½-inch-thick patty. Press a nickel-sized indentation in the center of each patty. Cover and chill until ready to grill.
2. Preheat grill to medium heat.
3. Combine remaining 1 tablespoon mustard and honey in a small bowl, and set aside.
4. Combine arugula, onion, juice, and oil in a medium bowl. Set aside.
5. Lightly coat both sides of burgers with cooking spray. Place patties on grill rack; grill 2 minutes. Carefully turn patties, and grill an additional 1 minute or until desired degree of doneness. Place 1 patty on bottom half of each bun; top each serving with ¼ cup arugula mixture, 1½ teaspoons honey mixture, and top half of bun. **Yield: 4 servings (serving size: 1 burger).**

CALORIES 372; FAT 16g (sat 3.2g, mono 5.9g, poly 5.8g); PROTEIN 27.3g; CARB 28.2g; FIBER 1.5g; CHOL 67mg; IRON 2.1mg; SODIUM 569mg; CALC 92mg

kitchen how-to:
make delicious salmon burgers

For best results, choose salmon from the meaty center of the fish, and avoid portions cut from the tail section (where the body starts to taper). Tail-end flesh contains more connective tissue than center-cut fillets.

1. The trick when working with salmon for burgers is to get the texture right. Ground beef will stick together firmly to form a patty, but ground salmon alone can be soft and difficult to work with, and a binder like breadcrumbs or eggs can blur the salmon flavor. For perfect texture, puree one-quarter of the salmon into a fine puree, and use it to bind the rest of the roughly chopped salmon.
2. To make quick work of roughly chopping the salmon, use your food processor. Be sure to watch how much you pulse—6 pulses should be a good estimate. You just need a rough chop.
3. Combine the salmon puree, chopped salmon, and other seasonings in a large bowl, and divide mixture into equal portions. Gently shape each portion into a patty.

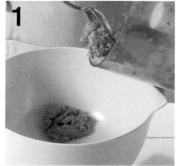

Black Bean Burgers with Mango Salsa

2 (15-ounce) cans black beans, rinsed and drained
¾ cup finely chopped fresh cilantro, divided
¾ cup (3 ounces) shredded Monterey Jack cheese
¼ cup panko (Japanese breadcrumbs)
2 teaspoons ground cumin
1 teaspoon dried oregano
½ teaspoon sea salt
½ medium jalapeño pepper, finely chopped
2 large egg whites, lightly beaten
Cooking spray
1¼ cups chopped peeled mango (about 1 medium)
3 tablespoons chopped shallots
1½ tablespoons fresh lime juice
1 avocado, peeled and chopped
1 garlic clove, minced
6 (2-ounce) whole-wheat hamburger buns, lightly toasted
6 green leaf lettuce leaves

1. Place black beans in a medium bowl; mash with a fork. Stir in ½ cup finely chopped cilantro and next 7 ingredients. Shape bean mixture into 6 (½-inch-thick) patties.
2. Heat a grill pan over medium-high heat. Coat pan with cooking spray. Add patties to pan; cook 3 to 4 minutes on each side.
3. Combine remaining ¼ cup cilantro, mango, and next 4 ingredients in a medium bowl. Place 1 patty on bottom half of each hamburger bun; top each with 1 lettuce leaf, ⅓ cup mango salsa, and top half of bun.
Yield: 6 servings (serving size: 1 burger).

CALORIES 320; FAT 11.9g (sat 3.9g, mono 5g, poly 1.7g); PROTEIN 13.4g; CARB 46.2g; FIBER 10.1g; CHOL 13mg; IRON 3.3mg; SODIUM 777mg; CALC 201mg

kitchen how-to:
make veggie burgers

Veggie burgers are not a substitute for the classic beef burger—nothing is. But done right, they're full of unexpected, delicious flavors and packed with nutrition, courtesy of lean vegetable protein and fiber.

1. Veggie burgers can be made with chickpeas, black beans, white beans, potatoes, lentils, and pretty much any other vegetable that can be mashed and formed into a patty.
2. Even with binders like breadcrumbs, oats, or egg whites, some veggie burgers can be delicate and may be better suited to a grill pan rather than a grill.
3. Cook the burgers 3 to 4 minutes on each side. When flipping them, be gentle, and use a spatula to help you.

Amchur Powder
What it adds: *Amchur* (or amchoor) powder is a tart, green mango-based seasoning. If you can't find it, feel free to omit it.

Garam Masala
What it adds: This fragrant Indian spice blend offers pungent, smoky flavor.

Vegetable Burgers

These tender vegetable patties are meant to be soft. Prepare through Step 2 the day before and refrigerate overnight. The mixture is easier to work with when it's cold. Plus, the flavors have had more time to marry.

- 1 **(16-ounce) can chickpeas (garbanzo beans), rinsed and drained**
- 1 **cup chopped fresh cilantro**
- ½ **cup coarsely chopped carrot**
- 1 **teaspoon garam masala**
- 1 **teaspoon amchur powder**
- 1¼ **teaspoons kosher salt**
- ½ **teaspoon freshly ground black pepper**
- ¼ **teaspoon ground red pepper**
- 1 **jalapeño pepper, seeded and quartered**
- 2 **pounds peeled red potatoes, cut into 2-inch pieces**
- ¼ **cup coarsely chopped red onion**
- 1 **cup dry breadcrumbs**
- 2 **tablespoons extra-virgin olive oil**
- 2⅔ **cups fresh spinach leaves**
- 4 **(6-inch) whole-grain pitas, cut in half**
- 8 **red onion slices**

1. Place first 9 ingredients in a food processor; process until finely chopped.

2. Place potatoes in a large saucepan; cover with water. Bring to a boil; cook 13 minutes. Add onion, and cook 2 minutes or until potatoes are tender. Drain; cool 10 minutes. Place potato mixture in a large bowl; mash with a potato masher or fork. Stir in chickpea mixture and breadcrumbs; cover and chill 8 hours or overnight.

3. Divide potato mixture into 8 equal portions, shaping each portion into a ½-inch-thick patty (about ⅔ cup mixture). Heat 1 tablespoon oil in a large skillet over medium heat. Add 4 patties to pan; cook 5 minutes on each side or until browned and heated through. Remove from pan, and set aside. Repeat procedure with remaining 1 tablespoon oil and 4 patties. Place ⅓ cup spinach and 1 patty in each pita half. Top each serving with 1 onion slice. **Yield: 8 servings (serving size: 1 stuffed pita half).**

CALORIES 304; FAT 5.8g (sat 0.8g, mono 2.9g, poly 1.4g); PROTEIN 10.6g; CARB 54.1g; FIBER 7.5g; CHOL 0mg; IRON 3.2mg; SODIUM 693mg; CALC 61mg

Lentil-Barley Burgers with Fiery Fruit Salsa

Combine leftover cooked pearl barley with lentils, veggies, and seasonings for a hearty main-dish burger without the bun. Fruit salsa adds bright flavors. Serve with lime wedges for added zest.

Salsa:
- ¼ cup finely chopped pineapple
- ¼ cup finely chopped mango
- ¼ cup finely chopped tomatillo
- ¼ cup halved grape tomatoes
- 1 tablespoon fresh lime juice
- 1 serrano chile, minced

Burgers:
- 1½ cups water
- ½ cup dried lentils
- Cooking spray
- 1 cup chopped onion
- ¼ cup grated carrot
- 2 teaspoons minced garlic
- 2 tablespoons tomato paste
- 1½ teaspoons ground cumin
- ¾ teaspoon dried oregano
- ½ teaspoon chili powder
- ¾ teaspoon salt, divided
- ¾ cup cooked pearl barley
- ½ cup panko (Japanese breadcrumbs)
- ¼ cup finely chopped fresh parsley
- ½ teaspoon coarsely ground black pepper
- 2 large egg whites, lightly beaten
- 1 large egg, lightly beaten
- 3 tablespoons canola oil

1. To prepare salsa, combine first 6 ingredients; cover and refrigerate.

2. To prepare burgers, combine 1½ cups water and lentils in a saucepan; bring to a boil. Cover, reduce heat, and simmer 25 minutes or until lentils are tender. Drain. Place half of lentils in a large bowl. Place remaining lentils in a food processor; process until smooth. Add processed lentils to whole lentils in bowl.

3. Heat a large nonstick skillet over medium-high heat. Coat pan with cooking spray. Add onion and carrot; sauté 6 minutes or until tender, stirring occasionally. Add garlic; cook 1 minute, stirring constantly. Add tomato paste, cumin, oregano, chili powder, and ¼ teaspoon salt; cook 1 minute, stirring constantly. Add onion mixture to lentils. Add remaining ½ teaspoon salt, barley, and next 5 ingredients; stir well. Cover and refrigerate 1 hour or until firm.

4. Divide mixture into 8 equal portions, shaping each into a ½-inch-thick patty. Heat 1½ table-spoons oil in a large nonstick skillet over medium-high heat. Add 4 patties; cook 3 minutes on each side or until browned. Remove from pan, and set aside. Repeat procedure with remaining 1½ tablespoons oil and 4 patties. Serve with salsa.

Yield: 4 servings (serving size: 2 patties and ¼ cup salsa).

CALORIES 315; FAT 12.8g (sat 1.2g, mono 6.8g, poly 3.5g); PROTEIN 12.8g; CARB 39.2g; FIBER 9.5g; CHOL 53mg; IRON 3.9mg; SODIUM 539mg; CALC 60mg

kitchen how-to: cook dried lentils

Lentils cook quickly, and don't require soaking like other dried legumes do. They lend mild, nutty flavor to these burgers.

1. Combine the water and lentils in a large saucepan— 3 cups of water for 1 cup of dried lentils is a good standard ratio to use.

2. Bring to a boil.

3. Cover, reduce the heat, and simmer 25 to 30 minutes or until the lentils are tender.

Sweet Potato–Pecan Burgers with Caramelized Onions

Onions:
- 1 teaspoon canola oil
- 3 cups sliced onion
- 2 tablespoons balsamic vinegar
- 1 teaspoon sugar
- ⅛ teaspoon salt

Burgers:
- 2½ cups (½-inch) cubed peeled sweet potato
- Cooking spray
- 2½ cups chopped onion
- 3 garlic cloves
- 1 cup regular oats
- 1½ teaspoons ground cumin
- ¾ teaspoon salt
- ¼ teaspoon pepper
- ½ cup chopped pecans, toasted
- 6 Boston lettuce leaves
- 6 (1½-ounce) 100% whole-wheat or whole-grain buns
- 6 tablespoons chili sauce

1. To prepare onions, heat 1 teaspoon oil in a large nonstick skillet over medium-high heat. Add sliced onion to pan; sauté 12 minutes or until browned, stirring occasionally. Stir in vinegar, sugar, and ⅛ teaspoon salt; cook 30 seconds or until vinegar is absorbed. Remove onion mixture from pan; keep warm. Wipe pan dry with a paper towel.

2. To prepare burgers, place potato in a large saucepan; cover with water. Bring to a boil. Reduce heat, and simmer 15 minutes or until tender; drain.

3. Heat large nonstick skillet over medium-high heat. Coat pan with cooking spray. Add chopped onion and garlic to pan; sauté 5 minutes or until tender.

4. Place potato, chopped onion mixture, oats, cumin, ¾ teaspoon salt, and pepper in a food processor; process until smooth. Place potato mixture in a bowl; stir in nuts. Divide potato mixture into 6 equal portions, shaping each portion into a ½-inch-thick patty.

5. Heat a grill pan over medium-high heat. Coat pan with cooking spray. Add patties to pan; cook 4 minutes or until browned. Carefully turn patties over; cook 3 minutes or until browned. Place 1 lettuce leaf on bottom half of each bun; top each with 1 patty, 1 tablespoon chili sauce, about 3 tablespoons onion mixture, and top halves of buns. **Yield: 6 servings (serving size: 1 burger).**

CALORIES 376; FAT 12.3g (sat 0.9g, mono 5.8g, poly 3.2g); PROTEIN 11.3g; CARB 59g; FIBER 7.9g; CHOL 0mg; IRON 3.4mg; SODIUM 785mg; CALC 89mg

kitchen how-to: make sweet potato–pecan burgers

Nuts add healthful unsaturated fats and filling protein to this tasty vegetarian sandwich.

1. Place sweet potatoes in a large saucepan; cover with water. Bring to a boil. Reduce heat, and simmer 15 minutes or until tender to make them more mashable.

2. Browning onions and garlic will caramelize some of the natural sugars found in these vegetables and give greater depth of flavor to the burger mixture.

3. Place patty ingredients in a food processor, and process until the mixture is smooth.

4. Add nuts for texture and crunch; divide the mixture, and shape into patties.

5. These patties are a bit delicate, so cooking them in a grill pan is best. When you're flipping them, turn them carefully with a spatula.

meats

meats

Because lean meat doesn't have a lot of extra fat to insulate it and keep it moist, there's less room for error on the part of the cook. It can easily go from perfectly cooked to dry and overdone in about a minute. This chapter shows you how to grill lean meat to perfection.

Marinating Safely

Any contamination in raw meat can be transferred from the meat to the marinade. If you plan to use the marinade as a sauce to baste with or serve with the grilled meat, you must boil it to kill any bacteria that might have been transferred from the raw meat. Just place the marinade in a saucepan, bring it to a boil, and boil for 1 minute. You can find more information about marinades on page 108.

Let It Stand

Meat will taste better and be juicier if given a chance to rest (5 to 10 minutes) after you take it off the grill. During cooking, the meat's juices collect in the center. By letting it rest, the juices have time to redistribute throughout the meat. If you cut into it too early, all those juices will run out, and you'll be left with a dry piece of grilled meat.

Know When to Baste

Great food can be ruined if basted too early with sugar-based sauces, which results in charring. To prevent burning, add sugar-based sauces toward the end of the cook time. You can baste with yogurt-, citrus-, and oil and vinegar–based sauces throughout cooking.

Testing for Doneness

A food thermometer is a key piece of equipment when testing the doneness of meat on the grill. It's also a way to prevent food-borne illness. You can use it for all sizes and cuts of meat. Place the food thermometer in the thickest part of the meat, and make sure you're not touching bone, fat, gristle, or the filling in stuffed meat. It's best to check the meat in several places to make sure all parts of the meat were cooked evenly. The U.S. Department of Agriculture (USDA) recommends that all beef, pork, lamb, veal chops, roasts, and steaks be cooked to at least 145°.

beef

Lean beef is very well suited for high-heat cooking methods like grilling, but you'll need a quick hand.

Rosemary Grilled Steak with Tomato Jam

Fresh rosemary brings pleasant pine notes to grilled beef. If you don't have time to make the jam, use bottled tomato chutney instead.

1 teaspoon canola oil
1 tablespoon finely chopped shallots
1 teaspoon minced garlic, divided
¾ cup finely chopped tomato
2 tablespoons water
1 tablespoon white balsamic vinegar
⅛ teaspoon salt
¼ teaspoon freshly ground pepper, divided

1 teaspoon minced fresh rosemary
¼ teaspoon salt
2 (4-ounce) beef tenderloin steaks (1 inch thick), trimmed
Cooking spray

1. Preheat grill to medium-high heat.
2. Heat a small nonstick skillet over medium heat. Add oil to pan; swirl to coat. Add shallots to pan; cook 3 minutes, stirring occasionally. Stir in ½ teaspoon garlic; cook 1 minute, stirring frequently. Add tomato, 2 tablespoons water, vinegar, and ⅛ teaspoon salt; bring to a boil. Reduce heat, and simmer 12 minutes or until liquid almost

evaporates. Stir in ⅛ teaspoon pepper; keep warm.
3. Combine remaining ½ teaspoon garlic, remaining ⅛ teaspoon pepper, rosemary, and ¼ teaspoon salt in a small bowl.
4. Place steaks on grill rack coated with cooking spray; grill 3 minutes. Turn steaks over. Sprinkle evenly with rosemary mixture; grill 3 minutes or until desired degree of doneness. Serve with tomato jam. **Yield: 2 servings (serving size: 1 steak and 2 tablespoons tomato jam).**

CALORIES 168; FAT 6.5g (sat 1.7g, mono 2.9g, poly 0.8g); PROTEIN 22.9g; CARB 5.7g; FIBER 0.9g; CHOL 60mg; IRON 3.1mg; SODIUM 504mg; CALC 19mg

kitchen how-to: determine doneness

Because lean beef turns bone-dry when well done, cooking it to medium-rare (or an internal temperature of 145°) is the ticket. It's also the temperature recommended by the USDA as safe. You'll need a thermometer (preferably an instant-read) to be sure. Remember, it's better to err on the side of undercooking. You can always cook the meat longer, but once it's overcooked, there's no fixing it.

Rare (130°)

Medium-rare (145°)

Medium (160°)

Medium-well (165°)

Well-done (170°)

Grilled Miso-Marinated Filet Mignon

3 tablespoons finely chopped green onions
2 tablespoons miso (soybean paste)
1 tablespoon rice vinegar
1 tablespoon honey
1 tablespoon lower-sodium soy sauce
2 teaspoons Dijon mustard
1 teaspoon dark sesame oil
4 (4-ounce) beef tenderloin steaks, trimmed
Cooking spray

1. Combine first 7 ingredients in a large zip-top plastic bag. Add steaks to bag; turn to coat. Let stand at room temperature 20 minutes, turning occasionally.
2. Preheat grill to medium-high heat.
3. Remove steaks from bag; discard marinade. Place steaks on grill rack coated with cooking spray; grill 5 minutes on each side or until desired degree of doneness. **Yield: 4 servings (serving size: 1 steak).**

CALORIES 207; FAT 10.2g (sat 3.7g, mono 4.1g, poly 0.7g); PROTEIN 23.9g; CARB 3.5g; FIBER 0.2g; CHOL 71mg; IRON 1.6mg; SODIUM 330mg; CALC 19mg

kitchen how-to: create great grill marks

Grill marks are a sign of a well-grilled steak. When grilling steaks, use tongs to turn the meat. Forks and other sharp utensils can puncture the meat causing the delicious juices that keep steaks moist to leach out.

1. Preheat the grill to medium-high or high heat. Once hot, place the steaks on the grill.
2. Halfway through the cooking time for the first side of the steak, rotate the meat a quarter-turn (45° for diamond-shaped crosshatches and 90° for square-shaped marks).
3. Flip the steak over, and complete cooking. You can create grill marks on this side of the steak if you like, but you don't have to since only one side will show when you serve the steaks. Be sure not to flip the steak back onto the marked side while grilling.

New York Strip
What it adds: Based on the classic *bistecca Fiorentina*—grilled porterhouse—this dish uses sirloin strip steaks, which are leaner (and, because they're boneless, a little easier to grill) than porterhouse.

Lemon Juice
What it adds: Lemon juice is a traditional accent, meant to cut the richness of the meat.

Tuscan-Style New York Strip with Arugula-Artichoke Salad

Use a mandoline to slice the artichokes thinly and evenly.

    4 tablespoons extra-virgin olive oil, divided
   10 garlic cloves, crushed
   10 thyme sprigs
    6 (2-inch) strips lemon rind
    2 (12-ounce) New York strip steaks, trimmed
    1 teaspoon kosher salt, divided
    1 teaspoon freshly ground black pepper,
       divided
    6 medium red potatoes
    1 bay leaf
    2 cups water
   ½ cup fresh lemon juice, divided
    3 medium artichokes (about 1¾ pounds)
    5 cups baby arugula (about 5 ounces)
    1 cup thinly vertically sliced red onion
    3 lemons, quartered
       Cooking spray
    2 teaspoons fresh thyme leaves
   ½ cup (2 ounces) shaved Parmigiano-Reggiano
       cheese

1. Combine 1 tablespoon oil, garlic, thyme sprigs, and lemon rind in a large zip-top plastic bag. Add steaks to bag; seal and marinate in refrigerator 3½ hours, turning occasionally. Remove bag from refrigerator, and let stand 30 minutes. Remove steaks from marinade, and discard marinade. Sprinkle with ½ teaspoon salt and ½ teaspoon black pepper.

2. Place potatoes and bay leaf in a saucepan; cover with water. Bring to a boil; reduce heat, and simmer 15 minutes or until crisp-tender. Drain; discard bay leaf. Cool completely; cut potatoes into 24 (⅓-inch-thick) slices.

3. Preheat grill to medium-high heat.

4. Combine 2 cups water and ¼ cup juice in a large bowl. Trim about 2 inches from top of each artichoke. Cut each in half vertically. Remove fuzzy thistle from bottom with a spoon. Trim any remaining leaves and dark green layer from base. Place artichoke halves in lemon water. Combine 2 tablespoons oil, 2 tablespoons juice, ¼ teaspoon salt, and ¼ teaspoon pepper in a large bowl; stir with a whisk. Thinly vertically slice artichokes. Add sliced artichokes, arugula, and thinly vertically sliced onion to bowl; toss gently to combine.

5. Place steaks, potato slices, and lemons on grill rack coated with cooking spray. Grill steaks 4 minutes on each side or until desired degree of doneness. Grill potatoes 3 minutes on each side or until tender. Grill lemons 2 minutes on each cut side. Let steak stand 5 minutes. Cut steak diagonally across grain into thin slices.

6. Place 4 potato slices on each of 6 plates. Sprinkle evenly with remaining ¼ teaspoon salt, remaining ¼ teaspoon black pepper, and thyme leaves. Place 1 cup arugula mixture on each plate, and top each serving with 4 teaspoons cheese. Arrange 3 ounces steak on each serving, and drizzle evenly with remaining 1 tablespoon olive oil and remaining 2 tablespoons lemon juice. Serve with grilled lemon. **Yield: 6 servings.**

CALORIES 429; FAT 17.5g (sat 5.5g, mono 7.4g, poly 2g); PROTEIN 37.5g; CARB 31.2g; FIBER 1.8 g; CHOL 244mg; IRON 4.7mg; SODIUM 767mg; CALC 185mg

Fresh & Dried Herbs

What they add: Five different herbs lend the steaks bright, fresh flavor. Experiment with your own blends. For lighter flavor, refrigerate the herb-rubbed steaks for only 2 hours before cooking.

Grilled Herb Steak

2 tablespoons fresh thyme leaves, minced
1 tablespoon fresh oregano leaves, minced
1 teaspoon fresh rosemary leaves, minced
1 teaspoon dried marjoram
1 teaspoon dried lavender buds
1 large garlic clove, minced
4 (8-ounce) rib-eye steaks
½ teaspoon salt
½ teaspoon freshly ground black pepper
Cooking spray

1. Combine first 6 ingredients in a small bowl. Rub both sides of steaks with herb mixture. Place steaks in a shallow dish; cover and refrigerate 4 hours.
2. Remove steaks from refrigerator. Sprinkle both sides of steaks with salt and pepper; let stand at room temperature 20 minutes.
3. Preheat grill to medium-high heat.
4. Place steaks on grill rack coated with cooking spray; grill 2 minutes on each side or until desired degree of doneness. Remove from grill. Cover steaks loosely with foil; let stand 5 minutes. **Yield: 4 servings (serving size: 1 steak).**

CALORIES 354; FAT 15.4g (sat 6.2g, mono 6.6g, poly 0.6g); PROTEIN 49g; CARB 1g; FIBER 0.3g; CHOL 155mg; IRON 3.8mg; SODIUM 394mg; CALC 43mg

Rib-eye Steak
What it adds: This cut has excellent marbling, which adds flavor and keeps the steak tender.

Chipotle Chile Powder
What it adds: Chipotle chile powder gives the rub a smoky flavor.

Flank Steak
What it adds: Flank steak is a great all-purpose cut of beef, but it needs to be sliced very thinly across the grain to keep it from being tough.

Spice-Rubbed Flank Steak with Fresh Salsa

Salsa:
 2 cups chopped seeded tomato
 ½ cup finely chopped red onion
 ¼ cup chopped fresh cilantro
 3 tablespoons fresh lime juice
 1 tablespoon extra-virgin olive oil
 ½ teaspoon kosher salt
 ¼ teaspoon ground red pepper

Steak:
 1 teaspoon garlic powder
 2 teaspoons ground cumin
 2 teaspoons paprika
 1 teaspoon chipotle chile powder
 ¾ teaspoon freshly ground black pepper
 ½ teaspoon kosher salt
 ½ teaspoon ground cinnamon
 1 (1½-pound) flank steak, trimmed
 1 tablespoon extra-virgin olive oil
 Cooking spray

1. Preheat grill to high heat.
2. To prepare salsa, combine first 7 ingredients in a bowl.
3. To prepare steak, combine garlic powder and next 6 ingredients. Brush both sides of steak with olive oil, and sprinkle with spice mixture. Place steak on grill rack coated with cooking spray; grill 4 minutes on each side or until desired degree of doneness. Let stand 5 minutes. Cut steak diagonally across grain into thin slices. Serve with salsa. **Yield: 6 servings (serving size: about 3 ounces steak and ⅓ cup salsa).**

CALORIES 253; FAT 14.4g (sat 4.2g, mono 8.1g, poly 1g); PROTEIN 25g; CARB 5.6g; FIBER 1.7g; CHOL 65mg; IRON 3.2mg; SODIUM 415mg; CALC 30mg

kitchen how-to:
slice flank steak

When a recipe says to cut "across the grain," that means you need to cut across the fibers of the meat rather than with them. In some cuts like tenderloin and loin, the grain is fine, and those cuts will usually be tender no matter how you slice them. But for cuts like flank steak, which come from harder-working muscles and generally have a tougher, larger grain, cutting across them shortens those tough muscle fibers, which makes it easier to chew. For flank steak, this means slicing across the width of the steak rather than the length.

Grilled Flank Steak with Onions, Avocado, and Tomatoes

Use colorful in-season heirloom tomatoes for a pretty presentation.

2 medium red onions, cut into ½-inch-thick slices + **1 (1½-pound) flank steak, trimmed**

2 cups cherry tomatoes, halved + **¼ cup balsamic vinegar** + **1 ripe peeled avocado, cut into 8 wedges**

Preheat grill to high heat. Lightly coat onions with cooking spray. Place onions on grill rack; grill 10 minutes on each side or until tender. Place onions in a medium bowl; cover tightly with foil. Keep warm. Lightly coat steak with cooking spray; sprinkle steak with ¾ teaspoon kosher salt and ¾ teaspoon black pepper. Place steak on grill rack; grill 6 minutes on each side or until desired degree of doneness. Let stand 3 minutes. Cut steak diagonally across grain into thin slices. Add tomatoes, balsamic vinegar, ¼ teaspoon kosher salt, and ¼ teaspoon black pepper to onions; toss gently to combine. Divide steak evenly among 6 plates; top with ½ cup tomato mixture. Cut avocado wedges in thirds crosswise. Top each serving with 4 avocado pieces. **Yield: 6 servings.**

CALORIES 262; FAT 13.6g (sat 4g, mono 7.7g, poly 1g); PROTEIN 24.3g; CARB 10.3g; FIBER 3.6g; CHOL 50mg; IRON 2.9mg; SODIUM 393mg; CALC 31mg

Steak with Cucumber-Radish Salad

If you can't find mâche, use butter lettuce.

3 tablespoons red wine vinegar, divided
2 teaspoons extra-virgin olive oil, divided
1 teaspoon black pepper, divided
⅝ teaspoon salt, divided
1 (1-pound) flank steak, trimmed
Cooking spray
1½ cups thinly sliced radishes
1 English cucumber, halved lengthwise, peeled, and cut into ¼-inch-thick slices
1 (5-ounce) package prewashed mâche (about 8 cups)
¼ cup (1 ounce) crumbled blue cheese

1. Heat a grill pan over medium-high heat. Combine 1 tablespoon vinegar, 1 teaspoon oil, ½ teaspoon pepper, and ⅜ teaspoon salt; rub evenly over surface of steak. Coat grill pan with cooking spray. Add steak to pan, and cook 5 minutes on each side or until desired degree of doneness. Remove steak from pan, and let stand 5 minutes. Cut steak diagonally across grain into thin slices.

2. While steak cooks, combine remaining 2 tablespoons red wine vinegar, remaining 1 teaspoon oil, remaining ½ teaspoon pepper, remaining ¼ teaspoon salt, radishes, and cucumber in a large bowl, and toss well to coat. Add mâche; toss gently to combine. Serve steak with salad. Sprinkle evenly with cheese. **Yield: 4 servings (serving size: about 3 ounces steak, about 2 cups salad, and 1 tablespoon cheese).**

CALORIES 229; FAT 10.7g (sat 4g, mono 3.9g, poly 0.5g); PROTEIN 27.2g; CARB 3.9g; FIBER 0.9g; CHOL 44mg; IRON 2.1mg; SODIUM 560mg; CALC 113mg

kitchen how-to: grill steak indoors

You can cook delicious steak indoors, which is an ideal solution for those who don't have a grill or when Mother Nature doesn't cooperate. Here's how:

1. A grill pan is the must-have tool of your indoor grilling arsenal. The grooves in the pan can recreate the grill marks and crusty, seared exterior indicative of great grilled steak. Heat the pan over medium-high heat, and coat it with cooking spray to help prevent sticking.

2. Add the steak to the pan, and cook for 5 minutes on each side or until desired degree of doneness.

3. Remove the steak from the pan, and be sure to let the meat rest for 5 minutes so the flavorful juices have time to redistribute in the meat.

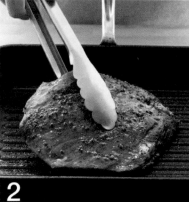
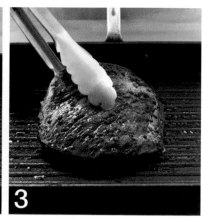

Santa Maria Smoked Tri-Tip

Flavorful tri-tip steak is a cut of beef also known as bottom sirloin or sirloin tip. Compared to other styles of barbecue, this recipe for smoked tri-tip comes together quickly, making it ideal for a weeknight dinner.

    3 cups hickory wood chips
    1 teaspoon kosher salt
    1 teaspoon freshly ground black pepper
    ½ teaspoon garlic powder
    1 (2¼-pound) tri-tip steak, trimmed
    Cooking spray
    2 cups Santa Maria Salsa
    Cilantro sprigs (optional)

1. Soak wood chips in water 1 hour; drain well.
2. Combine salt, pepper, and garlic powder; sprinkle evenly over steak. Let stand at room temperature 30 minutes.

3. Remove grill rack; set aside. Preheat grill, heating one side to high and one side to medium. Place wood chips on hot coals on medium-heat side of grill; heat wood chips 10 minutes. Coat grill rack with cooking spray; place on grill.
4. Lightly coat steak with cooking spray. Place steak on grill rack over high-heat side of grill; grill 6 minutes, turning 3 times. Place steak on grill rack over medium-heat side of grill; grill 40 minutes or until a thermometer registers 145° (medium-rare) or until desired degree of doneness. Remove steak from grill; let stand 10 minutes. Cut steak diagonally across grain into thin slices. Serve with Santa Maria Salsa; garnish with cilantro sprigs, if desired. **Yield: 8 servings (serving size: 3 ounces steak and ¼ cup salsa).**

CALORIES 259; FAT 13.1g (sat 4.8g, mono 6.9g, poly 0.5g); PROTEIN 30.9g; CARB 2.6g; FIBER 0.7g; CHOL 66mg; IRON 3.9mg; SODIUM 514mg; CALC 26mg

Santa Maria Salsa

This sprightly, crunchy relish is a California original that's served alongside or over smoked steak.

    2 (14.5-ounce) cans fire-roasted diced tomatoes
       with green chiles, undrained
    1 cup finely chopped celery
    ½ cup finely chopped onion
    1½ teaspoons white vinegar
    ½ teaspoon Worcestershire sauce
    ½ teaspoon freshly ground black pepper
    ¼ teaspoon kosher salt
    ¼ teaspoon garlic powder
    ¼ teaspoon hot pepper sauce

1. Drain 1 can tomatoes. Combine drained tomatoes, undrained tomatoes, and remaining ingredients; cover and chill salsa at least 30 minutes before serving. **Yield: 4 cups (serving size: ¼ cup).**

CALORIES 10; FAT 0.1g (sat 0g, mono 0g, poly 0g); PROTEIN 0.4g; CARB 2.4g; FIBER 0.6g; CHOL 0mg; IRON 0.2mg; SODIUM 206mg; CALC 13mg

kitchen how-to:
quick-smoke meats

Smoking meats can easily be an all-day event, but you can achieve a smoky flavor and tender meat in less time.

1. In many smoked-meat recipes, one side of the grill is heated to high heat while the other side is left off—it's this indirect heat, low temperature, and long cook time that tenderizes the meat. To speed up the process a bit while still providing smoked flavor, heat the other side to medium heat. Be sure to soak the wood chips in water for 1 hour, and then place the drained chips on hot coals on the medium-heat side of the grill. Heat the wood chips for 10 minutes. If you're using a gas grill, place the wood chips in a smoker box or foil pouch (see page 17 for more information about both), and place it under the grate directly over the burner heated to high. Once it starts smoking, transfer it to the side heated to medium.

2. Coat the grill rack with cooking spray, and place it on the grill. Place the meat over the high-heat side of the grill to quickly sear it and seal in the meat's juices.

3. Move the meat to the side heated to medium, and grill until desired degree of doneness.

4. Use a meat thermometer for accuracy. Remove the meat from the grill, and let it stand 5 to 10 minutes.

Coffee-Rubbed Texas-Style Brisket

6 cups oak or hickory wood chips
1 tablespoon ground coffee
1 tablespoon kosher salt
1 tablespoon dark brown sugar
2 teaspoons smoked paprika
2 teaspoons ancho chile powder
1 teaspoon garlic powder
1 teaspoon onion powder
1 teaspoon ground cumin
1 teaspoon freshly ground black pepper
1 (4½-pound) flat-cut brisket (about 3 inches thick)

1. Soak wood chips in water at least 1 hour; drain.
2. Combine coffee and next 8 ingredients in a bowl. Pat brisket dry; rub with coffee mixture.
3. Remove grill rack, and set aside. Preheat grill for indirect grilling, heating one side to high and leaving one side with no heat. Pierce bottom of a disposable aluminum foil pan several times with the tip of a knife. Place pan on heat element on heated side of grill; add 1½ cups wood chips to pan. Place another disposable aluminum foil pan (do not pierce pan) on unheated side of grill. Pour 2 cups water in pan. Let chips stand 15 minutes or until smoking; reduce heat to medium-low. Maintain temperature at 225°. Place grill rack on grill. Place brisket in a small roasting pan, and place pan on grill rack on unheated side. Close lid; cook 6 hours or until a meat thermometer registers 195°. Add 1½ cups wood chips every hour for first 4 hours; cover pan with foil for remaining 2 hours. Remove roasting pan from grill. Cover and let stand 30 minutes.
4. Unwrap brisket, reserving juices; trim and discard fat. Place a large zip-top plastic bag inside a 4-cup glass measure. Pour juices through a sieve into bag; discard solids. Let drippings stand 10 minutes (fat will rise to the top). Seal bag; carefully snip off 1 bottom corner of bag. Drain drippings into a bowl, stopping before fat reaches opening; discard fat. Cut brisket across grain into thin slices; serve with juices. **Yield: 18 servings (serving size: 3 ounces).**

CALORIES 156; FAT 4.4g (sat 1.6g, mono 1.8g, poly 0.2g); PROTEIN 24.9g; CARB 2.3g; FIBER 0.2g; CHOL 47mg; IRON 2.4mg; SODIUM 414mg; CALC 25mg

kitchen how-to: make Texas-style sauce

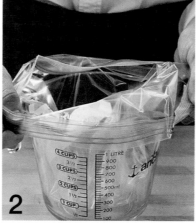

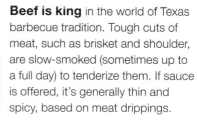

Beef is king in the world of Texas barbecue tradition. Tough cuts of meat, such as brisket and shoulder, are slow-smoked (sometimes up to a full day) to tenderize them. If sauce is offered, it's generally thin and spicy, based on meat drippings.

1. After smoking the meat, reserve the juices.
2. Place the juices in a large zip-top plastic bag inside a 4-cup glass measure.
3. Pour the juices through a sieve into the bag to remove any bits of meat; discard solids.
4. Let drippings stand for 10 minutes. The fat will rise to the top into separate layers.
5. Carefully snip off 1 corner of bag.
6. Drain drippings into a bowl, stopping before the fat reaches the opening.

bison

Bison has a deeper, richer flavor than beef. It's also lean and yields tender results on the grill.

Bison Rib-eye Kebabs

The rib-eye cut of bison is surprisingly lean, yields tender results when grilled, and stands up well to the piney rosemary.

¼ cup extra-virgin olive oil
2 tablespoons finely chopped fresh rosemary
1 tablespoon coarsely ground black pepper
2 large garlic cloves, minced
1 pound bison rib-eye, trimmed and cut into
    1¼-inch cubes
½ teaspoon salt
Cooking spray

1. Combine first 5 ingredients in a large bowl; toss well to coat. Cover and refrigerate 45 minutes.
2. Preheat grill to medium-high heat.
3. Remove bison from marinade, and discard remaining marinade. Thread bison evenly onto each of 4 (12-inch) skewers, and sprinkle with salt. Place skewers on grill rack coated with cooking spray, and grill 3 minutes on each side or until desired degree of doneness. Serve immediately. **Yield: 4 servings (serving size: 1 kebab).**

CALORIES 163; FAT 6.2g (sat 2.3g, mono 2.9g, poly 0.4g); PROTEIN 25.1g; CARB 0.2g; FIBER 0.1g; CHOL 67mg; IRON 2.5mg; SODIUM 335mg; CALC 7mg

kitchen how-to: make kebabs

Kebabs are ideal for weeknight meals or a crowd because they cook quickly and can be assembled ahead. Plus, there are endless varieties and combinations of meats, fruit, and vegetables. You'll find both reusable metal skewers and wooden skewers, which should be used only once. If you're using wooden skewers, you'll need to soak them in water for 30 minutes before assembling the kebabs so they don't burn on the grill.

1. When making kebabs, size matters. Everything— meat, poultry, seafood, fruit, vegetables—threaded onto the skewers needs to be cut to the same size. This ensures they cook evenly. In some instances, it may be best to thread fruits and vegetables on separate skewers. This is particularly useful when meats, poultry, or seafood require longer cooking times than the fruits and vegetables that accompany them.
2. Marinades can be another way to add flavor and keep meat, poultry, and seafood moist on the grill. If you're planning to baste the kebabs with the marinade, you'll need to bring the marinade to a boil to ensure it's safe.
3. Thread kebab ingredients evenly onto each skewer. Place the skewers on the preheated grill rack coated with cooking spray, and grill 3 minutes on each side or until the protein has reached the desired degree of doneness.

lamb

Lamb generally contains a good bit of marbling (the white flecks of fat distributed throughout the meat), which adds flavor and keeps the meat juicy and moist against the high heat of the grill.

Grilled Rack of Lamb with Saffron Rice

A rich, succulent cut of lamb with an earthy spice rub and a side of rice maintain a good nutrition profile. The spices add flavor to the lamb with no additional fat and negligible sodium. Serve with steamed haricots verts.

  Cooking spray
  1 cup diced onion
  2 garlic cloves, minced
  1 cup uncooked basmati rice
  2 cups fat-free, lower-sodium chicken broth
  ¼ teaspoon saffron threads, crushed
  1 bay leaf
  ½ teaspoon kosher salt
  ½ teaspoon ground cumin
  ½ teaspoon ground cinnamon
  ½ teaspoon paprika
  ⅛ teaspoon ground coriander
  ⅛ teaspoon ground cardamom
  ⅛ teaspoon ground red pepper
  1 (1½-pound) French-cut rack of lamb (8 ribs)
  1 teaspoon olive oil

1. Heat a medium saucepan over medium heat. Coat pan with cooking spray. Add onion and garlic to pan; cook 5 minutes or until golden brown, stirring frequently. Add rice and next 3 ingredients; bring to a boil. Cover, reduce heat, and simmer 20 minutes. Discard bay leaf. Keep warm.
2. Preheat grill to medium-high heat.
3. Combine salt and next 6 ingredients. Brush lamb with oil, and rub with salt mixture. Place lamb on grill rack coated with cooking spray; grill 10 minutes, turning once, or until a thermometer registers 145° (medium-rare) to 160° (medium). Let stand 5 minutes before slicing into chops. Serve lamb with rice. **Yield: 4 servings (serving size: 2 lamb chops and ¾ cup rice).**

CALORIES 294; FAT 11.3g (sat 4.5g, mono 4.7g, poly 0.5g); PROTEIN 24.1g; CARB 22.6g; FIBER 1.9g; CHOL 68mg; IRON 2.4mg; SODIUM 498mg; CALC 40mg

kitchen how-to:
French a rack of lamb

Rack of lamb is a price-cut for special occasions. It's also lean and becomes tough when overcooked, so cook with care and attention. You can ask your butcher to French the rack for you, or give it a go following our simple steps.

1. Remove the remaining fat cap from the top side of the bones. Using a sharp boning knife, keep the blade flush with the bone, and follow the contour of the bone.
2. Trim the fatty sections from between the ribs. Slice downward along one side of a rib, and then up against the side of the next rib; remove and discard fatty pieces.
3. Use the knife to scrape the bones clean. Remove any remaining flecks of fat or meat—this will give the cooked ribs an elegant appearance.

Spiced Lamb Kebabs

Yogurt works double duty as a marinade and a dipping sauce in this easy recipe.

| 1¼ cups plain fat-free Greek yogurt | 1 teaspoon ground cumin | ½ teaspoon hot paprika |

1 garlic clove, minced   **1 (1-pound) boneless leg of lamb, trimmed**

Combine yogurt, cumin, paprika, and garlic in a bowl. Cut lamb into 24 (1-inch) cubes; sprinkle with ½ teaspoon kosher salt and ¼ teaspoon black pepper. Combine lamb and ½ cup yogurt mixture in a zip-top plastic bag (refrigerate remaining yogurt mixture); seal and marinate in refrigerator at least 1 hour. Remove lamb, and discard marinade. Thread 3 lamb pieces onto each of 8 (10-inch) skewers. Heat a grill pan over medium-high heat; coat with cooking spray. Arrange 4 skewers on pan; cook 7 minutes or until desired degree of doneness, turning frequently. Remove from pan. Repeat with remaining skewers. Serve with remaining yogurt mixture. **Yield: 4 servings (serving size: 2 kebabs and 3 tablespoons sauce).**

CALORIES 187; FAT 5.2g (sat 1.8g, mono 2.1g, poly 0.5g); PROTEIN 29.6g; CARB 3.4g; FIBER 0.2g; CHOL 73mg; IRON 2.3mg; SODIUM 338mg; CALC 60mg

Grilled Lamb Chops with Roasted Summer Squash and Chimichurri

A quick blanching in boiling water mellows the garlic slightly.

2 cups water
2 garlic cloves, peeled
½ cup fresh flat-leaf parsley leaves
3 tablespoons extra-virgin olive oil, divided
1½ tablespoons coarsely chopped shallots
1 teaspoon fresh oregano leaves
1½ teaspoons sherry vinegar
1½ teaspoons fresh lemon juice
Dash of crushed red pepper
1 teaspoon salt, divided
1 teaspoon freshly ground black pepper, divided
3 medium yellow squash (about ¾ pound), cut lengthwise into ¼-inch-thick slices
3 medium zucchini (about ¾ pound), cut crosswise into ¼-inch-thick slices
6 (5-ounce) lamb loin chops (about 1 inch thick), trimmed
Cooking spray

1. Bring 2 cups water to a boil in a small saucepan. Add garlic to pan; reduce heat, and simmer 3 minutes. Remove garlic from water; cool. Coarsely chop garlic.

2. Place garlic, ½ cup parsley, 2 tablespoons oil, shallots, and next 4 ingredients in a food processor; process 1 minute or until almost smooth. Add ¼ teaspoon salt and ¼ teaspoon black pepper; pulse 2 times.

3. Preheat oven to 450°.

4. Preheat grill to medium-high heat.

5. Combine squash, zucchini, and remaining 1 tablespoon oil in a bowl; toss well. Arrange squash and zucchini in a single layer on a baking sheet. Sprinkle with ¼ teaspoon salt and ¼ teaspoon black pepper. Bake at 450° for 16 minutes or until tender, turning after 8 minutes.

6. Lightly coat lamb with cooking spray. Sprinkle with remaining ½ teaspoon salt and ½ teaspoon black pepper. Place lamb on grill rack coated with cooking spray; grill 5 minutes on each side or until desired degree of doneness. Divide squash and zucchini evenly among 6 plates. Top each serving with 1 lamb chop and 1½ teaspoons chimichurri. **Yield: 6 servings.**

CALORIES 288; FAT 15.5g (sat 4.4g, mono 8.4g, poly 1.5g); PROTEIN 30.9g; CARB 5.8g; FIBER 2.1g; CHOL 90mg; IRON 3.5mg; SODIUM 466mg; CALC 47mg

Chimichurri

What it adds: This piquant Argentinian herb sauce adds a hefty dose of flavor to the simply seasoned lamb chops. It has many variations and can be paired with a variety of meats, such as beef, chicken, or fish, or used as a marinade.

Lamb Loin Chops
What they add: These affordable, versatile chops are quick cooking, so they're great for weeknight meals. Trimming the excess fat from the chops is an important step to prevent flare-ups on the grill.

pork

Except for fattier cuts like Boston butt, spare ribs, and blade shoulder chops, pork has little or no marbling, which means it must be cooked carefully to avoid drying out. We'll show you how.

kitchen how-to: marinate meats

Marinating is an excellent way to add flavor to meats. Acidic marinades made with citrus, wine, and vinegar are very common, but be warned—they don't offer much in the way of tenderizing. Additionally, marinades that are highly acidic can actually toughen meat, particularly more delicate meats and seafood.

1. Combine the marinade ingredients. A large zip-top plastic bag is a great option and offers easy cleanup, but you can also marinate in plastic or glass containers. Avoid metal since acidic ingredients can interact with the metal and cause off flavors.
2. Remove the meat from the bag. At this point, some recipes call for discarding the marinade, while others reserve it and use it as a basting or

dipping sauce. If reserving the marinade, be sure you boil it first to prevent food-borne illness.
3. It's also good to add salt and black pepper after the meat has marinated to ensure it's well-seasoned. If those ingredients were only added to the marinade, you wouldn't get as much bang for your buck since the meat only absorbs a fraction of the marinade flavors.

Saffron-Marinated Pork Tenderloin with Grilled Pepper Relish

Pork:
- ⅓ cup sliced shallots
- ⅓ cup chopped fresh basil
- 1 tablespoon fresh lemon juice
- 2 teaspoons paprika
- 1 teaspoon ground cumin
- 2 teaspoons olive oil
- ¼ teaspoon saffron threads, crushed
- 3 garlic cloves, thinly sliced
- 1 (1-pound) pork tenderloin, trimmed
- ½ teaspoon salt
- ¼ teaspoon freshly ground black pepper
- Cooking spray

Relish:
- 2 (¼-inch-thick) slices red onion
- 1 large red bell pepper
- 1 large green bell pepper
- 1 tablespoon chopped fresh basil
- 1 teaspoon sugar
- 2 teaspoons sherry vinegar
- ¼ teaspoon salt

1. To prepare pork, combine first 9 ingredients in a large zip-top plastic bag; seal. Marinate in refrigerator 24 hours, turning occasionally.
2. Preheat grill to medium-high heat.
3. Remove pork from bag; discard marinade. Sprinkle with ½ teaspoon salt and pepper. Place pork on grill rack coated with cooking spray. Grill 18 minutes or until a thermometer registers 145°, turning occasionally. Let stand 10 minutes before slicing.

4. To prepare relish, place onion and bell peppers on grill rack coated with cooking spray. Grill onion 4 minutes on each side or until tender. Grill peppers 12 minutes or until blackened, turning occasionally. Place peppers in a large zip-top plastic bag; seal. Let stand 10 minutes. Peel peppers; cut in half lengthwise.

Discard seeds and membranes. Chop onion and peppers. Combine onion, peppers, basil, and remaining ingredients in a medium bowl. Serve relish with pork. **Yield: 4 servings (serving size: 3 ounces pork and ½ cup relish).**

CALORIES 208; FAT 6.6g (sat 1.7g, mono 3.4g, poly 0.9g); PROTEIN 25.6g; CARB 11.7g; FIBER 2.7g; CHOL 74mg; IRON 2.5mg; SODIUM 508mg; CALC 39mg

Stuffed Cuban Pork Tenderloin

While the pork is cooking, add fresh vegetables to the grill for a complete meal.

- 1 **(1-pound) pork tenderloin, trimmed**
- 2 **tablespoons whole-grain Dijon mustard**
- ⅓ **cup chopped fresh cilantro**
- 3 **thin slices Swiss cheese, halved**
- ⅓ **cup chopped bread-and-butter pickles**
- ¼ **teaspoon salt**
- ¼ **teaspoon freshly ground black pepper**
  Cooking spray

1. Preheat grill to medium-high heat.

2. Cut a lengthwise slit down the center of tenderloin two-thirds of the way through the meat. Open halves, laying tenderloin flat. Place tenderloin between 2 sheets of heavy-duty plastic wrap; pound to ½-inch thickness using a meat mallet or heavy skillet. Spread mustard evenly over pork. Sprinkle with cilantro. Arrange cheese and pickles over pork in a single layer. Roll up, jelly-roll fashion, starting with long side; secure pork at 1-inch intervals with twine. Sprinkle evenly with salt and pepper.

3. Place pork on grill rack coated with cooking spray. Grill 19 to 22 minutes or until a thermometer registers 145°, turning after 11 minutes. Remove from grill. Cover and let stand 5 minutes. Cut into 12 slices.

Yield: 4 servings (serving size: 3 slices).

CALORIES 215; FAT 8.5g (sat 4.5g, mono 2.4g, poly 0.6g); PROTEIN 30.6g; CARB 4.6g; FIBER 0g; CHOL 93mg; IRON 1.2mg; SODIUM 507mg; CALC 172mg

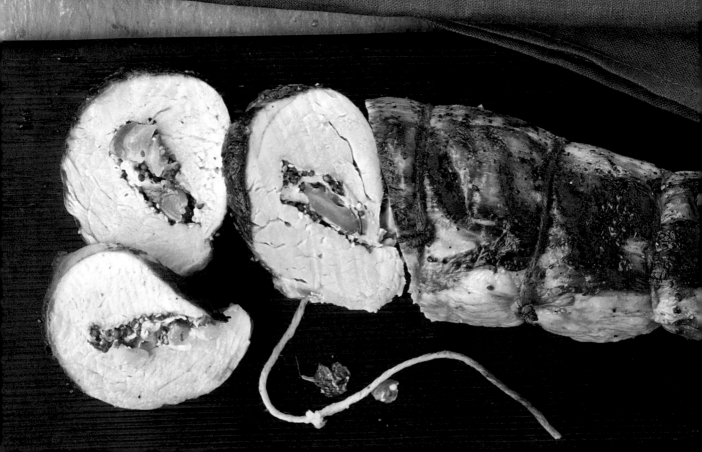

kitchen how-to:
stuff a pork tenderloin

A stuffed pork tenderloin or loin is handsome at the table, and the fillings make it versatile. If you don't have kitchen twine, you can secure the meat with wooden picks.

1. Cut the pork in half lengthwise, cutting to, but not through, the other side. Open the halves, laying the meat flat. Starting from the center, cut each half lengthwise, cutting to, but not through, the other side. Open the halves, laying the meat flat.

2. Place the meat between two sheets of heavy-duty plastic wrap, and pound with a mallet or heavy skillet to an even ½-inch thickness.

3. Remove meat from plastic wrap; discard plastic. Slide segments of kitchen twine beneath the meat in 1- to 2-inch intervals.

4. Sprinkle or spread filling evenly on the meat, leaving a ½-inch border.

5. Start at a long side of the meat, and roll up, jelly-roll fashion, tucking in the filling as you go.

6. Secure with twine, and grill until the internal temperature of the pork (not the filling) registers 145°. Let the meat stand for at least 5 minutes to allow the juices to redistribute in the meat.

Grilled Pork Tenderloin Roulade

1 (1-pound) pork
tenderloin, trimmed

¼ cup chopped shallots

¼ cup crumbled
goat cheese

3 tablespoons chopped
walnuts, toasted

2 teaspoons chopped
fresh thyme

Preheat grill to medium heat. Slice tenderloin lengthwise, cutting to, but
not through, other side. Open halves, laying tenderloin flat. Place tenderloin
between 2 sheets of heavy-duty plastic wrap; pound to ½-inch thickness
using a meat mallet or heavy skillet. Sprinkle shallots, cheese, walnuts, and
thyme on tenderloin. Roll up, starting with long side; secure pork at 1-inch
intervals with twine. Sprinkle with ¼ teaspoon salt and ¼ teaspoon black
pepper. Place pork on grill rack coated with cooking spray. Grill 24 minutes
or until a thermometer registers 145°, turning after 13 minutes. Remove from
grill; lightly cover with foil. Let stand 10 minutes; cut crosswise into 8 slices.
Yield: 4 servings (serving size: 2 slices).

CALORIES 206; FAT 9.6g (sat 3.1g, mono 2.7g, poly 3.1g); PROTEIN 26.5g; CARB 2.8g; FIBER 0.5g; CHOL 79mg; IRON 1.9mg;
SODIUM 242mg; CALC 38mg

Brined Pork Tenderloin with Plum and Jicama Relish

8 cups cold water
½ cup kosher salt
2 (1-pound) pork tenderloins, trimmed
1 tablespoon extra-virgin olive oil
½ teaspoon freshly ground black pepper, divided
1½ cups diced plums (¾ pound)
¾ cup finely chopped peeled jicama
½ cup finely chopped red onion
2 teaspoons grated lime rind
2 tablespoons fresh lime juice
1 tablespoon honey
⅛ teaspoon kosher salt
1 serrano chile, seeded and chopped
Parsley sprigs (optional)

1. Combine 8 cups cold water and ½ cup salt in a glass measuring cup, stirring until salt dissolves. Pour salt water into a 13 x 9–inch glass or ceramic baking dish. Add pork to brine; let stand at room temperature 1 hour.

2. Preheat grill to medium-high heat.

3. Drain pork; pat dry. Brush pork with oil; sprinkle with ¼ teaspoon pepper. Place pork on grill rack; grill 13 minutes or until a thermometer registers 145°, turning pork occasionally. Remove pork from grill; let stand 5 minutes. Cut across grain into ½-inch-thick slices.

4. Combine remaining ¼ teaspoon pepper, plums, and next 7 ingredients; toss gently to combine. Serve relish with pork. Garnish with parsley sprigs, if desired. **Yield: 8 servings (serving size: 3 ounces pork and about ¼ cup relish).**

CALORIES 214; FAT 8.6g (sat 2.7g, mono 4.2g, poly 0.8g); PROTEIN 25.1g; CARB 8.2g; FIBER 1.3g; CHOL 78mg; IRON 1.3mg; SODIUM 226mg; CALC 11mg

kitchen how-to: brine meats

Soaking mildly flavored lean meats and poultry like pork, chicken, and turkey in a brine—a solution of liquid (usually water) and salt—can help keep them from drying out on the grill. The meat absorbs this mixture, plumping it up and infusing it with both flavor and moisture. Brining seafood is also an option when it will be exposed to high heats that can have a drying effect. Beef and lamb aren't good candidates for brining. These meats generally contain more fat and are often cooked to a lower internal temperature than pork or poultry, so they don't lose as much of their natural moisture.

1. Combine cold water with kosher salt, stirring until salt dissolves. (Some brines also use sugar.) Kosher salt offers a cleaner flavor than table salt, which usually contains iodine and anti-caking agents that can affect the flavor. It's also less salty than table salt.

2. Add the meat to the brine, and let stand at room temperature. In general, meat should remain in the brine at least 30 minutes and can stay in it up to several days. The key: You can either soak the meat for a long time in a weak brine or for a short time in a stronger one. If you soak meat in a strong brine for too long, the result can be mushy meat.

3. Drain meat, and pat dry. Patting the meat dry is an important step. Too much moisture on the surface of the meat can prevent the exterior from browning.

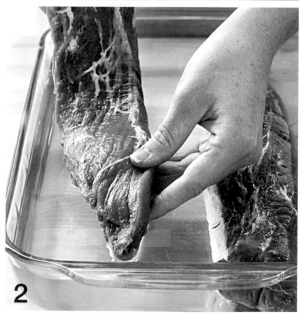

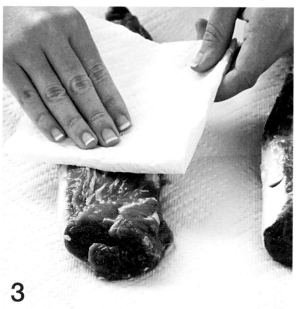

Ground Red Pepper
What it adds: Red pepper adds fiery flavor to the pork. Add more or less depending on the amount of heat you can handle.

Bacon
What it adds: Bacon's savory flavor is key to the sweet-tart sauce, which would work equally well with chicken.

Spice-Rubbed Pork Tenderloin with Mustard Barbecue Sauce

Sauce:
- 2 bacon slices, finely chopped
- 1 cup chopped onion
- ½ cup prepared yellow mustard
- 5 tablespoons honey
- 3 tablespoons ketchup
- 2 tablespoons cider vinegar
- ¼ teaspoon chili powder
- ¼ teaspoon ground cumin

Pork:
- 1 tablespoon light brown sugar
- 1 tablespoon smoked paprika
- 2 teaspoons chili powder
- 1 teaspoon garlic powder
- 1 teaspoon ground cumin
- ¾ teaspoon salt
- ½ teaspoon freshly ground black pepper
- ⅛ teaspoon ground red pepper
- 2 (1-pound) pork tenderloins, trimmed

Cooking spray

1. Preheat grill to medium-high heat.
2. To prepare sauce, cook bacon in a medium saucepan over medium-high heat 4 minutes or until almost crisp, stirring occasionally. Add chopped onion to pan; cook 4 minutes, stirring frequently. Add mustard and next 5 ingredients to pan, and bring to a boil. Reduce heat, and simmer 4 minutes or until slightly thick, stirring occasionally.
3. To prepare pork, combine brown sugar and next 7 ingredients in a small bowl, stirring well; rub mixture evenly over pork. Place pork on grill rack coated with cooking spray. Grill 20 minutes or until a thermometer registers 145°, turning once. Let pork stand 10 minutes. Cut pork crosswise into ½-inch-thick slices. Serve with sauce. **Yield: 8 servings (serving size: 3 ounces pork and about 2½ tablespoons sauce).**

CALORIES 235; FAT 6.5g (sat 2.1g, mono 2.8g, poly 0.7g); PROTEIN 26.2g; CARB 17.6g; FIBER 1.3g; CHOL 77mg; IRON 1.8mg; SODIUM 569mg; CALC 26mg

Grilled Pork Tenderloin with Salsa Verde

2 (1-pound) pork tenderloins, trimmed and
   cut into ¾-inch-thick slices
Cooking spray
½ teaspoon salt
½ teaspoon freshly ground black pepper, divided
1½ cups diced green tomato
¼ cup chopped fresh flat-leaf parsley
3 tablespoons thinly sliced fresh chives
2 tablespoons fresh lemon juice
2 tablespoons extra-virgin olive oil
1 tablespoon capers
1 teaspoon chopped fresh oregano
1 teaspoon chopped fresh thyme
1 teaspoon sugar
1 garlic clove, minced

1. Preheat grill to medium-high heat.
2. Arrange pork slices in a single layer between 2 sheets of heavy-duty plastic wrap; pound to ½-inch thickness using a meat mallet or small heavy skillet. Lightly coat pork with cooking spray; sprinkle with salt and ¼ teaspoon pepper. Place pork on grill rack; grill pork 2 minutes on each side or until done.
3. Place tomato and remaining ingredients in a food processor; pulse until minced. Stir in remaining ¼ teaspoon pepper. Serve with pork. **Yield: 6 servings (serving size: 4 ounces pork and 2 tablespoons salsa).**

CALORIES 235; FAT 9.9g (sat 2.5g, mono 5.7g, poly 1.3g); PROTEIN 32.3g; CARB 3.2g; FIBER 0.5g; CHOL 98mg; IRON 2.2mg; SODIUM 320mg; CALC 21mg

kitchen how-to: pound pork

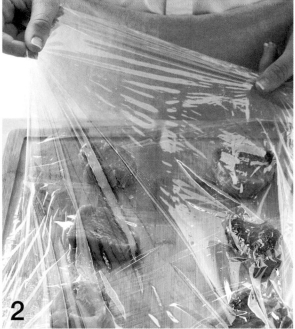

Pounding pork helps tenderize the meat by breaking down connective tissues. You can also use this technique on other meats and cuts that tend to be a bit tough.

1. Cut the pork into ¾-inch-thick slices.

2. Arrange the slices in a single layer between 2 sheets of heavy-duty plastic wrap. Placing the slices between 2 large sheets rather than smaller individual sheets is quicker because you can pound the meat all at once.

3. Pound pork to a ½-inch thickness using a meat mallet or a small heavy skillet. (A mallet is a quieter, more controlled option.) Pounding the meat to an even thickness helps the meat cook evenly on the grill—thinner parts of the meat don't overcook before a thicker section has finished cooking.

2. Combine sugar and next 4 ingredients in a bowl. Pat pork dry, and rub with sugar mixture.
3. Remove grill rack, and set aside. Preheat grill for indirect grilling, heating one side to high and leaving one side with no heat. Pierce bottom of a disposable aluminum foil pan several times with the tip of a knife. Place pan on heat element on heated side of grill; add 1½ cups wood chips to pan. Place another disposable aluminum foil pan (do not pierce pan) on unheated side of grill. Pour 2 cups water in pan. Let chips stand 15 minutes or until smoking; reduce heat to medium. Maintain temperature at 300°. Place grill rack on grill. Place pork on grill rack over unheated side. Close lid, and cook 6 hours at 300° or until a meat thermometer registers 195°, covering pork loosely with foil after 5 hours. Drain and add 1 cup additional wood chips every 45 minutes. Refill water pan, and add charcoal to fire as needed. Remove pork from grill; let stand 20 minutes. Unwrap pork; trim and discard fat. Shred pork.
4. Heat oil in a medium saucepan over medium heat; swirl to coat. Add onion; cook 2 minutes, stirring frequently. Add ⅓ cup sugar and next 5 ingredients; bring to a simmer. Cook 15 minutes or until thickened. Arrange about 3 ounces pork and 2 tablespoons sauce on each bun. **Yield: 16 servings (serving size: 1 sandwich).**

CALORIES 438; FAT 19.2g (sat 6.2g, mono 8.5g, poly 2.5g); PROTEIN 29.8g; CARB 36.1g; FIBER 3.6g; CHOL 3mg; IRON 3.3mg; SODIUM 792mg; CALC 99mg

Pulled Pork Sandwiches with Mustard Sauce

7 to 8 cups hickory wood chips	⅓ cup packed brown sugar
2 tablespoons brown sugar	⅔ cup Dijon mustard
1 tablespoon dry mustard	⅔ cup cider vinegar
1 tablespoon smoked paprika	⅓ cup molasses
1 tablespoon black pepper	1 teaspoon hot sauce
1½ teaspoons kosher salt	½ teaspoon kosher salt
1 (5-pound) boneless Boston butt pork roast	16 (1.5-ounce) whole-wheat hamburger buns
2 tablespoons olive oil	
¾ cup finely chopped onion	

1. Soak wood chips in water at least 1 hour; drain.

kitchen how-to:
make mustard sauce

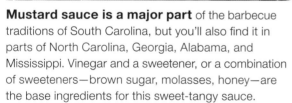

Mustard sauce is a major part of the barbecue traditions of South Carolina, but you'll also find it in parts of North Carolina, Georgia, Alabama, and Mississippi. Vinegar and a sweetener, or a combination of sweeteners—brown sugar, molasses, honey—are the base ingredients for this sweet-tangy sauce.

1. Cook finely chopped onions in a saucepan to cut their bite and bring out some of their natural sweetness.
2. Add brown sugar, Dijon mustard, cider vinegar, molasses, hot sauce, and kosher salt to the onions in the pan. Simple yellow mustard is traditional, but Dijon mustard mellows the flavor a bit. You can also vary the recipe by using different types of vinegar and sweetener combinations.
3. Bring the mixture to a simmer, and cook 15 minutes or until thickened. This sauce is thicker than a vinegar-based sauce but still pourable.

Cantonese-Style Grilled Pork

Hoisin sauce gives this dish its salty-sweet aromatic flavor. Serve these succulent slices of pork with steamed Chinese buns, or sandwich them in a hot dog bun.

 1 (1-pound) boneless pork shoulder, trimmed
 ½ teaspoon salt
 1 tablespoon sugar
 2 tablespoons hoisin sauce
 2 tablespoons ketchup
 1 tablespoon Shaoxing (Chinese cooking wine)
    or dry sherry
 2 teaspoons mirin (sweet rice wine)
 1 teaspoon grated peeled fresh ginger
 1 garlic clove, minced
    Cooking spray

1. Cover and freeze pork 45 minutes. Cut pork across grain into ⅛-inch-thick slices. Sprinkle pork evenly with salt.
2. Combine sugar and next 6 ingredients in a large zip-top plastic bag; knead to blend. Add pork to bag; seal. Marinate in refrigerator 3 hours, turning bag occasionally.
3. Preheat grill to medium-high heat.
4. Remove pork from bag, and discard marinade. Place pork on grill rack coated with cooking spray. Grill 1 minute on each side or until desired degree of doneness. **Yield: 4 servings (serving size: 3 ounces).**

CALORIES 221; FAT 8.9g (sat 2.9g, mono 3.3g, poly 0.6g); PROTEIN 23.4g; CARB 9.4g; FIBER 0.1g; CHOL 67mg; IRON 0.9mg; SODIUM 560mg; CALC 20mg

kitchen how-to: easily slice meat

Partially freezing meat can make cutting it into thin slices a lot easier.

1. Cover the meat and place it in the freezer for 45 to 60 minutes for cuts that are 1-inch-thick. Larger cuts will need to go for longer. You want the meat to be firm but not so hard that it can't be cut. This step keeps the meat rigid while slicing.
2. If you skip this step, the meat can give under the pressure of the knife, which can not only make cutting it more difficult, but may also yield slices that aren't the right thickness.

1

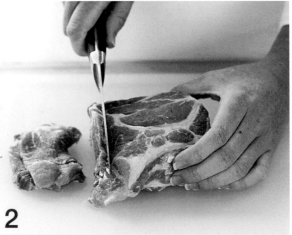

2

Memphis Pork and Coleslaw Sandwiches

Pork:
- 8 hickory wood chunks (about 4 pounds)
- 2 tablespoons paprika
- 1 tablespoon freshly ground black pepper
- 1 tablespoon turbinado sugar
- 1½ teaspoons garlic powder
- 1½ teaspoons onion powder
- 1½ teaspoons dry mustard
- 1 teaspoon kosher salt
- 1 (5-pound) bone-in pork shoulder (Boston butt)
- ⅓ cup white vinegar
- 1 tablespoon Worcestershire sauce
- 1 teaspoon canola oil
- 1 (12-ounce) can beer
- 2 cups water
- Cooking spray

Slaw:
- ¼ cup finely chopped onion
- 1½ tablespoons prepared mustard
- 1½ tablespoons white vinegar
- 1 tablespoon reduced-fat mayonnaise
- 1½ teaspoons granulated sugar
- ¼ teaspoon salt
- 6 cups chopped green cabbage

Remaining ingredients:
- 13 hamburger buns
- 1⅔ cups Memphis-style Sauce (see how-to on page 125)

1. To prepare pork, soak wood chunks in water about 16 hours; drain.

2. Combine paprika and next 6 ingredients; reserve 1 tablespoon paprika mixture. Rub half of remaining paprika mixture onto pork. Place in a large zip-top plastic bag; seal and refrigerate overnight.

3. Remove pork from refrigerator; let stand at room temperature 30 minutes. Rub remaining half of paprika mixture onto pork.

4. Combine reserved 1 tablespoon paprika mixture, ⅓ cup vinegar, Worcestershire, oil, and beer in a

small saucepan; cook over low heat 5 minutes or until warm.
5. Remove grill rack; set aside. Preheat grill for indirect grilling, heating one side to medium-low and leaving one side with no heat. Maintain temperature at 225°. Pierce bottom of a disposable aluminum foil pan several times with the tip of a knife. Place pan on heated side of grill; add half of wood chunks to pan. Place another disposable aluminum foil pan (do not pierce pan) on unheated side of grill. Pour 2 cups water in pan. Coat grill rack with cooking spray; place grill rack on grill.

6. Place pork on grill rack over foil pan on unheated side. Close lid; cook 4½ hours or until a thermometer registers 170°, gently brushing pork with beer mixture every hour (avoid brushing off sugar mixture). Add additional wood chunks halfway during cooking time. Discard any remaining beer mixture.
7. Preheat oven to 250°.
8. Remove pork from grill. Wrap pork in several layers of aluminum foil, and place in a baking pan. Bake at 250° for 2 hours or until a thermometer registers 195°. Remove from oven. Let stand, still

wrapped, 1 hour or until pork easily pulls apart. Unwrap pork; trim and discard fat. Shred pork with 2 forks.
9. While pork bakes, prepare slaw. Combine onion and next 5 ingredients in a large bowl. Add cabbage, and toss to coat. Cover and chill 3 hours before serving. Serve pork and slaw on buns with Memphis-style Sauce. **Yield: 13 servings (serving size: 1 bun, 3 ounces pork, about ⅓ cup slaw, and about 1½ tablespoons sauce).**

CALORIES 387; FAT 15.2g (sat 5.1g, mono 6.3g, poly 2.2g); PROTEIN 26.6g; CARB 33.7g; FIBER 2.3g; CHOL 74mg; IRON 3.5mg; SODIUM 769mg; CALC 120mg

kitchen how-to: make Memphis-style sauce

As the center of Southern barbecue, Memphis offers sauces that occupy the middle ground between thin-tangy sauces and thicker varieties. Memphis-style blends provide moderate amounts of sweet, heat, and tang, which add up to a lot of flavor.

1. Combine 1 cup ketchup, ¾ cup white vinegar, 2 tablespoons brown sugar, 1 tablespoon onion powder, 2 tablespoons Worcestershire sauce, 2 tablespoons

prepared mustard, ½ teaspoon freshly ground black pepper, ¼ teaspoon salt, and ⅛ teaspoon ground red pepper in a medium saucepan.
2. Bring to a simmer. Cook 5 minutes; serve warm.
3. The sauce has a consistency that's middle of the road in comparison to other sauces—not too thick and not too thin. **Yield: 2 cups (serving size: 2 tablespoons).**

CALORIES 25; FAT 0.1g (sat 0g, mono 0.1g, poly 0g); PROTEIN 0.4g; CARB 6.4g; FIBER 0.2g; CHOL 0mg; IRON 0.3mg; SODIUM 247mg; CALC 10mg

Barbecued Pork Chops

A simple 8-ingredient marinade, made with mostly pantry staples, adds vibrant flavor to these chops. Pair with kimchi-style slaw for a quick-cooking dinner solution—ready in about 40 minutes (including a 25-minute marinade).

        2   tablespoons dark brown sugar
        2   tablespoons lower-sodium soy sauce
        1   tablespoon dark sesame oil
        1   tablespoon pineapple juice
        2   teaspoons minced fresh garlic
      1½   teaspoons sake (rice wine)
        ¼   teaspoon crushed red pepper
        ¼   teaspoon freshly ground black pepper
        4   (4-ounce) bone-in pork chops (about
             ½ inch thick)
     Cooking spray
        ¼   teaspoon kosher salt
        1   teaspoon sesame seeds, toasted

1. Combine first 8 ingredients in a zip-top plastic bag; add pork to bag. Seal; marinate at room temperature 25 minutes.
2. Heat a grill pan over medium-high heat. Coat pan with cooking spray. Remove pork from bag; reserve marinade. Sprinkle pork with salt. Cook pork 3 minutes on each side or until done. Pour reserved marinade into a small saucepan; bring to a boil. Reduce heat, and simmer 2 minutes or until thickened. Brush pork with reduced marinade; sprinkle with sesame seeds. **Yield: 4 servings (serving size: 1 pork chop).**

CALORIES 195; FAT 9.4g (sat 2.5g, mono 3.9g, poly 2.4g); PROTEIN 17.7g; CARB 8.9g; FIBER 0.3g; CHOL 49mg; IRON 1mg; SODIUM 433mg; CALC 31mg

Bone-In Pork Chops
What they add: Bone-in chops are more flavorful than their boneless counterparts.

Sake

What it adds: There are many different varieties of this Japanese rice-based alcohol, and the flavor can range from dry to sweet. Opt for your favorite in this recipe.

Pork Chops with Cherry Couscous

In-season, sweet red cherries are a bountiful bargain, and they lend a wonderfully fresh, fruity element that pairs well with pork.

   3   **tablespoons olive oil, divided**
   4   **(6-ounce) bone-in center-cut pork chops**
   1   **teaspoon salt, divided**
   ¼   **teaspoon freshly ground black pepper**
Cooking spray
   1   **cup uncooked couscous**
   ¾   **cup boiling water**
   1   **cup coarsely chopped pitted cherries**
   ½   **cup sliced green onions**
   ⅓   **cup chopped dry-roasted almonds**
   2   **teaspoons grated lemon rind**
   2   **tablespoons fresh lemon juice**

1. Preheat grill to medium-high heat.
2. Brush 1 tablespoon olive oil evenly over both sides of pork, and sprinkle evenly with ½ teaspoon salt and black pepper. Place pork on grill rack coated with cooking spray, and grill 4 minutes on each side or until a thermometer inserted in the thickest portion of pork registers 145°. Let pork stand 5 minutes.
3. Place couscous in a large bowl. Add ¾ cup boiling water; cover and let stand 5 minutes. Uncover and fluff with a fork. Stir in remaining 2 tablespoons oil, remaining ½ teaspoon salt, cherries, and remaining ingredients. Serve with pork. **Yield: 4 servings (serving size: 1 pork chop and about ¾ cup couscous).**

CALORIES 495; FAT 22.3g (sat 3.6g, mono 13.4g, poly 3.3g); PROTEIN 29.7g; CARB 43.8g; FIBER 5g; CHOL 66mg; IRON 2mg; SODIUM 683mg; CALC 76mg

kitchen how-to:
test for doneness

As the USDA recommends for whole (not ground) cuts of beef, veal, and lamb, pork should be cooked to an internal temperature of 145° to ensure it's safe to eat.

1. The best way to test for doneness is by using a meat thermometer and inserting it into the thickest portion of the meat. Once it hits 145°, the meat is ready to be pulled from the grill. The internal temperature will continue to rise as the meat rests.
2. When you cut into the meat, the middle should be slightly pink.

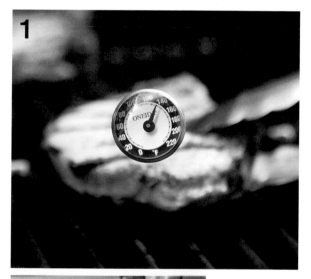

Pan-Grilled Pork Chops with Grilled Pineapple Salsa

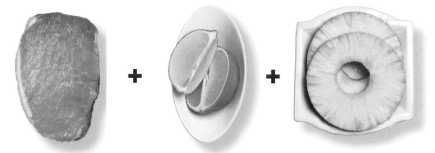

4 (4-ounce) boneless center-cut loin pork chops (about ½ inch thick)

1 tablespoon plus 2 teaspoons fresh lime juice, divided

4 (½-inch-thick) slices pineapple

1 medium red onion, cut into ½-inch-thick slices

1 tablespoon minced jalapeño pepper

Combine pork and 1 tablespoon lime juice; let stand 10 minutes. Heat a grill pan over medium-high heat. Coat pan with cooking spray. Add pineapple and onion; cook 4 minutes on each side or until onion is tender. Coarsely chop pineapple and onion; place in a medium bowl with remaining 2 teaspoons lime juice, jalapeño, and ⅛ teaspoon salt. Sprinkle pork with ½ teaspoon salt and ¼ teaspoon freshly ground black pepper. Heat grill pan over medium-high heat. Coat pan with cooking spray. Add pork; cook 4 minutes on each side or until done. **Yield: 4 servings (serving size: 1 chop and about ½ cup salsa).**

CALORIES 215; FAT 7g (sat 2.5g, mono 3.1g, poly 0.5g); PROTEIN 26.4g; CARB 10.9g; FIBER 1.4g; CHOL 70mg; IRON 1mg; SODIUM 416mg; CALC 42mg

Grilled Pork Chops with Two-Melon Salsa

Cover this quick and easy grilled pork recipe with a tasty salsa that uses summer's freshest fruits and flavors to round out the meal. Use any fruit you like in place of melons—peaches, pineapple, or mango.

Salsa:
- 1 cup chopped seedless watermelon
- 1 cup chopped honeydew melon
- 3 tablespoons finely chopped sweet onion
- 1 tablespoon finely chopped jalapeño pepper
- 1 tablespoon chopped fresh cilantro
- 1 tablespoon fresh lime juice
- ⅛ teaspoon salt

Pork chops:
- 2 teaspoons canola oil
- 1½ teaspoons chili powder
- ½ teaspoon garlic powder
- ½ teaspoon salt
- ¼ teaspoon freshly ground black pepper
- 4 (4-ounce) boneless center-cut pork chops, trimmed
- Cooking spray

1. To prepare salsa, combine first 7 ingredients; set aside.
2. To prepare pork chops, heat a grill pan over medium-high heat. Combine oil and next 4 ingredients in a small bowl. Rub oil mixture over both sides of pork chops. Coat pan with cooking spray. Add pork to pan; cook 4 minutes on each side or until desired degree of doneness. Serve with salsa. **Yield: 4 servings (serving size: 1 pork chop and ½ cup salsa).**

CALORIES 256; FAT 13.5g (sat 4.3g, mono 6.4g, poly 1.6g); PROTEIN 25g; CARB 8.7g; FIBER 0.9g; CHOL 70mg; IRON 0.9mg; SODIUM 458mg; CALC 37mg

kitchen how-to:
cut fresh watermelon
Always rinse a melon before slicing it.
Melons are grown in dirt and handled frequently. They may look clean but can harbor bacteria on the skin. Thoroughly rinse them to prevent transferring bacteria to the flesh when cutting into it.

1. Place washed melon on a cutting board, and use a sharp, heavy knife to slice about 1 inch from the stem end to make a stable cutting surface.
2. Stand the melon up, cut side down, and vertically slice the melon in half.
3. Lay halves, cut sides down, and make 1-inch cuts through the melon. All cut melon should be stored in a covered container in the refrigerator.

Grilled Pork Tacos with Summer Corn and Nectarine Salsa

Be sure to zest the lime before you slice and juice it.

2 tablespoons fresh lime juice, divided
1½ tablespoons extra-virgin olive oil, divided
4 (4-ounce) boneless center-cut loin pork chops
¾ teaspoon salt, divided
½ teaspoon ground cumin
¼ teaspoon freshly ground black pepper
1 garlic clove, minced
Cooking spray
1 ear shucked corn
¼ cup diced red bell pepper
½ cup diced ripe nectarine
½ teaspoon grated lime rind
1 minced seeded jalapeño pepper
8 (6-inch) corn tortillas
1 cup shredded cabbage

1. Preheat grill to medium-high heat.
2. Combine 2 teaspoons lime juice, 1 tablespoon oil, and pork in a zip-top plastic bag; seal. Marinate 10 minutes at room temperature. Remove pork from bag; discard marinade. Sprinkle both sides of pork with ½ teaspoon salt, cumin, pepper, and garlic. Place pork on grill rack coated with cooking spray; grill 3 minutes on each side or until desired degree of doneness. Let stand 5 minutes. Slice pork into thin strips.
3. Lightly coat corn with cooking spray. Place corn on grill rack coated with cooking spray; grill 6 minutes or until lightly charred, turning occasionally. Let corn stand 5 minutes; cut kernels from cob. Combine kernels, 2 teaspoons juice, remaining 1½ teaspoons oil, remaining ¼ teaspoon salt, bell pepper, and next 3 ingredients in a bowl; toss.
4. Place tortillas on grill rack coated with cooking spray, and grill 1 minute on each side or until lightly browned. Toss cabbage with remaining 2 teaspoons lime juice. Place 2 tortillas on each of 4 plates, and divide pork evenly among tortillas. Top each taco with about 1 tablespoon cabbage mixture and about 2 tablespoons salsa. **Yield: 4 servings (serving size: 2 tacos).**

CALORIES 131; FAT 5.4g (sat 2.4g, mono 2g, poly 0.7g); PROTEIN 1.3g; CARB 19.2g; FIBER 0.3g; CHOL 10mg; IRON 0.6mg; SODIUM 100mg; CALC 4mg

kitchen how-to: grill tortillas

Corn tortillas offer a more assertive flavor and coarser texture than their flour-based counterparts. Both corn and flour tortillas are delicious when grilled.

1. Corn tortillas can sometimes be delicate, so use tongs to place them on the grill.
2. They don't take long to grill—just 30 seconds on each side or until they're lightly browned.

poultry

poultry

Grilling brings out great flavors in poultry. Whether you're cooking over direct or indirect heat, there are tips to ensure success.

Marinating

Various pieces of poultry benefit from the added flavor that marinades provide. You'll find specific tips about marinating on pages 81 and 108. Remember, if you're using the remaining marinade as a sauce or to baste the poultry as it cooks, be sure to boil the marinade to kill any bacteria that might have been transferred from the raw meat—the bacteria will be killed once the meat is cooked.

Testing for Doneness

Always cook poultry thoroughly. Use a thermometer to test for doneness—the internal temperature of all types of poultry should reach 165°. Insert the thermometer in the middle of the thickest part of the meat, and do not touch the bone. For whole poultry, insert the thermometer into the thickest portion of the thigh.

kitchen how-to:
grill poultry

The best method for grilling poultry depends on the cut you're working with. Thin cuts can handle direct grilling since these cuts don't require much time on the grill to cook all the way through. Larger cuts, like whole birds or thick cuts of meat (some larger breast pieces can fall in this category), benefit from a mix—time over direct heat to brown the exterior, and then a move to indirect heat for the duration so that the exterior doesn't get charred while the interior is still raw.

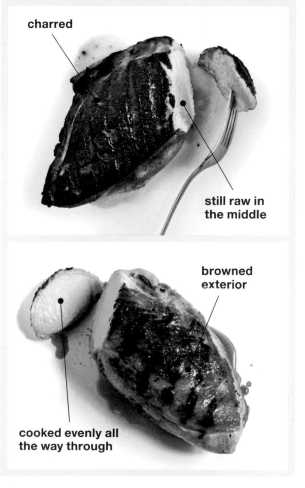

charred

still raw in the middle

browned exterior

cooked evenly all the way through

Grilled Spice-Rubbed Whole Chicken

1½ teaspoons brown sugar
1¼ teaspoons ground cumin
1   teaspoon kosher salt
½   teaspoon freshly ground black pepper
½   teaspoon paprika
½   teaspoon dried thyme
½   teaspoon chili powder
1   (4-pound) whole chicken
Cooking spray

1. Prepare grill for indirect grilling. If using a gas grill, heat one side to medium-high and leave one side with no heat. If using a charcoal grill, arrange hot coals on either side of charcoal grate, leaving an empty space in the middle.
2. Combine first 7 ingredients; set aside.
3. Remove and discard giblets and neck from chicken. Trim excess fat. Place chicken, breast side down, on a cutting surface. Cut chicken in half lengthwise along backbone, cutting to, but not through, other side. Turn chicken over. Starting at neck cavity, loosen skin from breast and drumsticks by inserting fingers, gently pushing between skin and meat. Rub spice mixture under skin. Gently press skin to secure.
4. Place chicken, breast side down, on grill rack coated with cooking spray over direct heat; cover and cook 7 minutes. Turn chicken over; cook 7 minutes. Move chicken over indirect heat; cover and cook 45 minutes or until a thermometer inserted in meaty part of thigh registers 165°. Transfer chicken to a cutting board; let rest 10 minutes. Discard skin.
Yield: 4 servings (serving size: 1 breast half or 1 thigh and 1 drumstick).

CALORIES 270; FAT 6.5g (sat 1.6g, mono 1.9g, poly 1.6g); PROTEIN 47.3g; CARB 2.6g; FIBER 0.6g; CHOL 150mg; IRON 2.8mg; SODIUM 537mg; CALC 40mg

kitchen how-to: grill a whole chicken

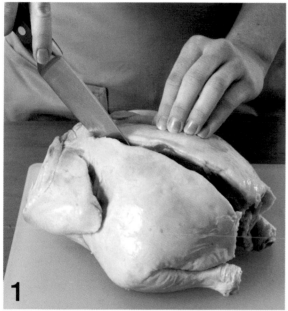

The less intense heat of indirect grilling is the best way to grill a whole chicken. The high heat of direct grilling is too intense—the exterior will overcook and burn before the interior gets done.

1. Cut the chicken in half lengthwise across the backbone, cutting to, but not through, the other side. This allows heat to more easily penetrate the interior of the bird.

2. Rub the seasonings under the skin of the bird, and press the skin so they'll stay in place. It's best to keep the skin on the bird while it grills—it helps hold in moisture. Remove and discard it after grilling.

3. Place the chicken, breast side down, over direct heat, and cook for 7 minutes on each side to quickly brown the exterior.

4. Move the chicken to indirect heat, and cover the grill. The covered grill acts like an oven allowing heat to circulate around the bird and cook it to perfection.

5. Use a thermometer to test doneness. Take a few readings in different parts of the bird to ensure the whole chicken has reached a safe temperature of 165°.

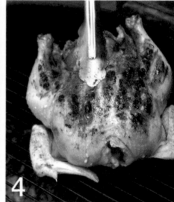

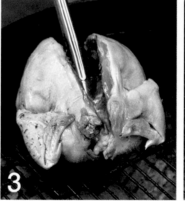

Fantastic Bourbon Smoked Chicken

- 2 **quarts water**
- 9 **tablespoons bourbon, divided**
- ¼ **cup packed dark brown sugar**
- 3 **tablespoons kosher salt**
- 2 **quarts ice water**
- 1 **tablespoon black peppercorns**
- 1 **tablespoon coriander seeds**
- 3 **bay leaves**
- 3 **garlic cloves, peeled**
- 1 **small onion, quartered**
- 1 **small Fuji apple, cored and quartered**
- 1 **lemon, quartered**
- 1 **(4-pound) whole chicken**
- 2 **cups applewood chips**
- ½ **teaspoon freshly ground black pepper**
- **Cooking spray**
- 1 **tablespoon butter, melted**

1. Combine 2 quarts water, ½ cup bourbon, sugar, and kosher salt in a large Dutch oven, and bring to a boil, stirring until salt and sugar dissolve. Add 2 quarts ice water and next 7 ingredients, and cool to room temperature. Add chicken to brine; cover and refrigerate 18 hours, turning chicken occasionally.
2. Soak wood chips in water 1 hour; drain.
3. Remove chicken from brine; pat chicken dry with paper towels. Strain brine through a sieve; discard brine, and reserve 2 apple quarters, 2 lemon quarters, 2 onion quarters, and garlic. Discard remaining solids.

Sprinkle chicken cavity with pepper; add reserved solids to chicken cavity. Lift wing tips up and over back; tuck under chicken. Tie legs.
4. Remove grill rack, and set aside. Preheat grill for indirect grilling, heating one side to high and leaving one side with no heat. Pierce the bottom of a disposable aluminum foil pan several times with the tip of a knife. Place pan on heat element on heated side of grill; add 1 cup wood chips to pan. Place another disposable aluminum foil pan (do not pierce pan) on unheated side of grill. Pour 2 cups water in pan. Let chips stand 15 minutes or until smoking; reduce heat to medium-low. Maintain temperature at 275°.
5. Coat grill rack with cooking spray; place on grill. Place chicken, breast side up, on grill rack over foil pan on unheated side. Combine remaining 1 tablespoon bourbon and butter; baste chicken with bourbon mixture. Close lid, and cook 2 hours at 275° or until thermometer inserted into meaty part of thigh registers 165°. Add remaining 1 cup wood chips halfway through cooking time. Place chicken on a platter; cover with foil. Let stand 15 minutes. Discard skin before serving. **Yield: 4 servings (serving size: 5 ounces chicken).**

CALORIES 299; FAT 12.6g (sat 4.4g, mono 4.3g, poly 2.3g); PROTEIN 35.8g; CARB 6.2g; FIBER 1g; CHOL 114mg; IRON 1.8mg; SODIUM 560mg; CALC 30mg

Bourbon Brine
What it adds: The bourbon-infused brine helps keep the bird moist and has an extra hit of bourbon flavor.

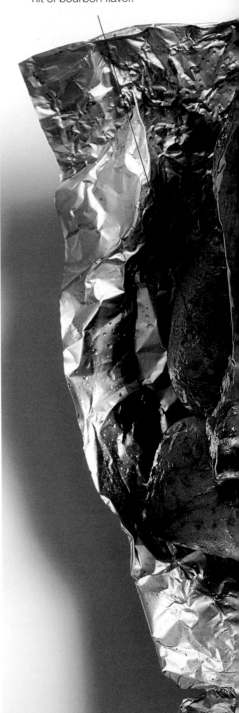

Bourbon-Butter Baste
What it adds: The bourbon-butter mixture helps create this bird's golden exterior.

Lemon and Sage Chicken

1 (4-pound) roasting chicken
1 tablespoon grated lemon rind
⅓ cup fresh lemon juice
⅓ cup Sauternes or other dessert white wine
¼ cup minced fresh sage leaves
1 tablespoon olive oil
1 teaspoon paprika
¼ teaspoon freshly ground black pepper
2 large garlic cloves, grated
½ teaspoon salt
  Cooking spray

1. Remove and discard giblets and neck from chicken. Cut chicken into drumsticks, thighs, and breasts; cut each breast in half crosswise to form 4 breast pieces total. Reserve wings and back for another use.
2. Combine rind and next 7 ingredients in a small bowl, and stir with a whisk. Place juice mixture in a large zip-top plastic bag. Add chicken to bag; seal and marinate in refrigerator 1 hour. Remove chicken from bag, and discard marinade. Sprinkle chicken evenly with salt.
3. Preheat grill to medium-high heat. After preheating, turn the left burner off (leave the right burner on), or arrange charcoal on one side of grill for indirect heat.
4. Place chicken on grill rack coated with cooking spray covering right burner; grill over direct heat 15 minutes, turning every 5 minutes. Move chicken to grill rack coated with cooking spray covering left burner; grill over indirect heat 10 minutes or until a thermometer registers 165°. Discard chicken skin. **Yield: 4 servings (serving size: 2 breast pieces or 1 leg and 1 thigh).**

CALORIES 246; FAT 13.7g (sat 3.9g, mono 5.7g, poly 3g); PROTEIN 26.3g; CARB 2.2g; FIBER 0.1g; CHOL 84mg; IRON 1.3mg; SODIUM 374mg; CALC 15mg

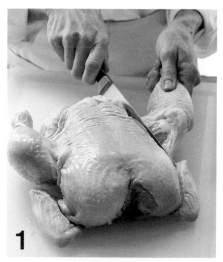

kitchen how-to:
break down a whole chicken

Purchasing a whole chicken is more economical than buying pieces separately. Here's how to break the bird down to get the cuts you want.

1. If your bird has them, remove the giblets and neck from the chicken. Many birds come with them already removed or separated in a plastic bag. Cut above the thighs to remove the whole leg.

2. Cut each piece at the joint to separate the leg and the thigh.

3. Cut the chicken in half, and carefully slice the breast meat off into two large pieces.

4. Cut each piece of breast meat in half crosswise to form 4 breast pieces. Reserve the back and wings for another use.

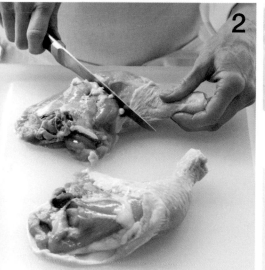

kitchen how-to: grill chicken under a brick

The weight of foil-covered bricks helps the chicken cook evenly, leaving the breast moist and tender while the legs cook fully.

1. Prepare the chicken by removing the giblets and neck, trimming the excess fat, and removing the wings. Cut the chicken in half lengthwise, and then remove the skin. Pierce the surface of each piece of chicken with a fork. Place the chicken in the marinade, turning to coat, and let it marinate.
2. Wrap two bricks with aluminum foil.
3. This technique also works best using indirect heat, so place each piece of chicken, breast side down, on the grill rack coated with cooking spray on the unheated side of the grill.
4. Place an aluminum foil–wrapped brick on each chicken half, and grill until internal temperature reaches 165° (about 1 hour). Refrigerate in an airtight container until ready to use.

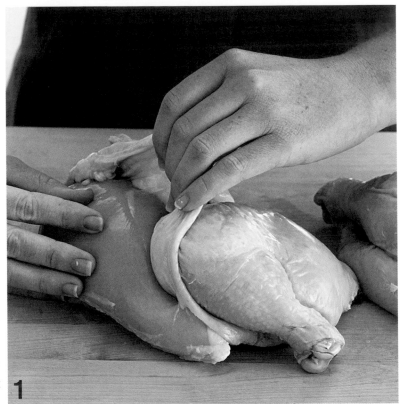

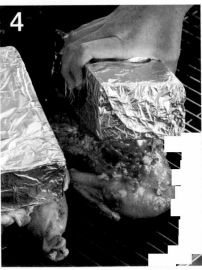

Marinated Chicken Cooked Under a Brick

¼ cup chopped shallots
1 tablespoon chopped fresh rosemary
1 teaspoon grated lemon rind
3 tablespoons fresh lemon juice
2 tablespoons balsamic vinegar
2 tablespoons honey
1 tablespoon Dijon mustard
1 tablespoon olive oil
2 teaspoons chopped fresh thyme
2 teaspoons lower-sodium soy sauce
6 garlic cloves, minced
1 (4-pound) whole chicken
Cooking spray
½ teaspoon salt
¼ teaspoon freshly ground black pepper

1. Combine first 11 ingredients in a 13 x 9–inch baking dish.
2. Remove and discard giblets and neck from chicken. Trim excess fat. With a sharp knife or kitchen shears, remove the wings at the first joint. Split chicken in half lengthwise. Remove and discard skin; pierce entire surface of chicken with a fork. Place chicken in dish, turning to coat. Cover and refrigerate 8 hours or overnight, turning occasionally.
3. Remove chicken from dish; discard marinade. Coat chicken with cooking spray; sprinkle chicken evenly with salt and pepper.
4. Prepare grill for indirect grilling, heating one side to medium-high

and leaving one side with no heat. Maintain temperature at 400°.
5. Wrap 2 bricks with aluminum foil. Place chicken halves, breast side down, on grill rack coated with cooking spray on unheated side. Place 1 prepared brick on each chicken half. Place wings on grill. Cover and grill 1 hour or until a thermometer inserted into the thickest part of thigh registers 165°. Carefully remove hot bricks; remove chicken from grill. Let chicken stand 5 minutes. Carve chicken. **Yield: 4 servings (serving size: about 4 ounces).**

CALORIES 247; FAT 9.8g (sat 2.6g, mono 3.8g, poly 2.2g); PROTEIN 35.6g; CARB 1.7g; FIBER 0.1g; CHOL 106mg; IRON 1.8mg; SODIUM 420mg; CALC 20mg

Root Beer–Can Chicken

Complete the meal with roasted red potatoes and a sweet-tart broccoli slaw. This recipe is traditional enough to appeal to any crowd, but the updated flavors add an element of fun.

1½ teaspoons Hungarian sweet paprika
1 teaspoon brown sugar
½ teaspoon garlic powder
½ teaspoon onion powder
½ teaspoon ground red pepper
½ teaspoon chili powder
¼ teaspoon ground allspice
¾ teaspoon kosher salt, divided
2 (12-ounce) cans root beer, divided
2 tablespoons chilled unsalted butter, cut into pieces
2 teaspoons cider vinegar
1 (3½-pound) whole chicken, skinned

1. Prepare grill for indirect grilling, heating one side to medium.
2. Combine first 7 ingredients and ½ teaspoon salt in a small bowl.
3. Open both root beer cans; pour 18 ounces into a small saucepan. Set remaining root beer aside (in the can). Bring 18 ounces root beer to a boil. Cook until reduced to ⅓ cup (about 20 minutes). Remove from heat. Add remaining ¼ teaspoon salt, butter, and vinegar, stirring until smooth.
4. Rub paprika mixture evenly over chicken. Holding chicken upright with the cavity facing down, insert reserved opened root beer can into cavity. Place chicken on unheated side of grill. Spread legs out to form a tripod to support the chicken. Cover and grill 1 hour and 30 minutes or until a meat thermometer inserted into meaty portion of thigh registers 165°, basting chicken every 20 minutes with sauce.
5. Lift chicken slightly using tongs; place spatula under can. Carefully remove chicken and can from grill; place on a cutting board. Let stand 10 minutes. Gently lift chicken using tongs or insulated rubber gloves; carefully twist can and remove from cavity. Discard can. Carve chicken.
Yield: 4 servings (serving size: 1 breast half or 1 leg quarter).

CALORIES 371; FAT 15.1g (sat 6.2g, mono 5g, poly 2.4g); PROTEIN 35.6g; CARB 21.4g; FIBER 0.2g; CHOL 121mg; IRON 1.9mg; SODIUM 502mg; CALC 32mg

kitchen how-to:
make root beer–can chicken

This is a family-friendly take on beer-can chicken in which we use an opened root beer can to support a whole bird on the grill.

1. Prepare the grill for indirect grilling, heating one side to medium heat. Rub seasoning over chicken.
2. Holding the chicken upright with the cavity facing down, insert the can, still halfway filled with root beer, into the cavity. The liquid inside the can adds moisture, resulting in succulent, tender meat.
3. Place the chicken on the unheated side of the grill. Spread the legs out to form a tripod to support the chicken while it cooks on the grill.
4. Cover and grill 1½ hours or until a meat thermometer registers 165°, basting the chicken every 20 minutes with sauce.

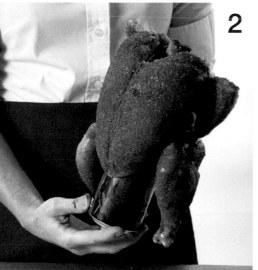

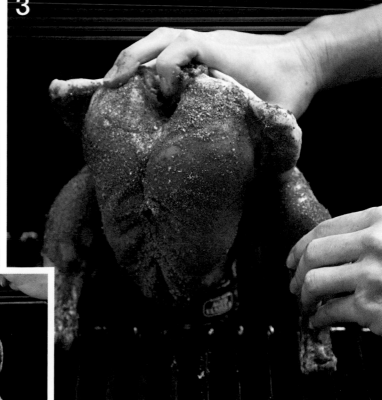

Chicken Breasts with Tomatoes and Olives

Kalamata and picholine olives add salty savor. Serve over couscous with dressed greens on the side.

| 4 (6-ounce) skinless, boneless chicken breast halves | 1 cup multicolored cherry or grape tomatoes, halved | 3 tablespoons oil and vinegar dressing, divided |

| 20 olives, halved | ½ cup (2 ounces) crumbled feta cheese |

Preheat grill to medium-high heat. Sprinkle chicken evenly with ¼ teaspoon salt and ¼ teaspoon freshly ground black pepper. Place chicken on grill rack coated with cooking spray, and grill 6 minutes on each side or until chicken is done. Keep warm. Combine tomatoes, 1½ tablespoons dressing, and olives in a medium skillet over medium heat, and cook 2 minutes or until tomatoes soften slightly and mixture is thoroughly heated, stirring occasionally. Brush chicken with remaining 1½ tablespoons dressing. Cut each chicken breast half into ¾-inch slices. Top each chicken breast half with ¼ cup tomato mixture. Sprinkle each serving with 2 tablespoons cheese and torn basil leaves, if desired. **Yield: 4 servings.**

CALORIES 348; FAT 17.3g (sat 4.4g, mono 5g, poly 1.2g); PROTEIN 41.9g; CARB 3.9g; FIBER 0.6g; CHOL 111mg; IRON 1.6mg; SODIUM 810mg; CALC 100mg

Quick Barbecue Chicken

1 teaspoon sugar
1 teaspoon chili powder
2 teaspoons olive oil
½ teaspoon salt
¼ teaspoon garlic powder
¼ teaspoon ground cumin
⅛ teaspoon ground ginger
⅛ teaspoon ground cinnamon
⅛ teaspoon freshly ground black pepper
2 (8-ounce) bone-in chicken breast halves
Cooking spray

1. Preheat grill to medium-high heat.
2. Combine first 9 ingredients in a bowl, stirring well. Loosen skin from chicken by inserting fingers, gently pushing between skin and meat; rub spice mixture evenly under skin over meat. Lightly coat skin with cooking spray. Place chicken, breast side down, on grill rack coated with cooking spray; grill 30 minutes or until a thermometer inserted in the thickest part registers 165°, turning twice. Let chicken stand 10 minutes. Remove skin; discard. **Yield: 2 servings (serving size: 1 chicken breast half).**

CALORIES 308; FAT 9.7g (sat 2.1g, mono 5g, poly 1.6g); PROTEIN 49.4g; CARB 2.7g; FIBER 0.3g; CHOL 131mg; IRON 1.7mg; SODIUM 738mg; CALC 27mg

kitchen how-to:
keep lean poultry moist on the grill

Chicken, particularly the lean white meat that's lower in fat, can dry out over the high heat of the grill. One way to help keep it moist is to leave the skin on the chicken as it cooks so the breasts will remain juicy. To season the breast halves, loosen the skin by inserting your fingers and rubbing the seasonings under the skin. Discard the skin just before serving.

Marinade
What it adds: This marinade combines sweet and salty ingredients to give you a taste of the cuisine of the Big Island.

Long-Grain White Rice
What it adds: The grains of this long, slender rice stay separate and fluffy after they've been cooked, which makes it an ideal choice to use as a side dish.

Hawaiian Chicken

Take a mental vacation to The Big Island as you enjoy this grilled chicken marinated in a mixture of pineapple juice, ketchup, soy sauce, and ginger.

- ¼ **cup pineapple juice**
- 2 **tablespoons ketchup**
- 2 **tablespoons lower-sodium soy sauce**
- 1½ **teaspoons minced peeled fresh ginger**
- 2 **garlic cloves, minced**
- 4 **(6-ounce) skinless, boneless chicken breast halves**
- **Cooking spray**
- ¾ **teaspoon salt, divided**
- ¼ **teaspoon freshly ground black pepper**
- 2 **cups hot cooked long-grain white rice**
- ¼ **cup chopped fresh cilantro**

1. Combine first 5 ingredients. Reserve ¼ cup marinade; place remaining marinade in a zip-top plastic bag. Add chicken to bag; seal. Marinate in refrigerator 4 hours.

2. Heat a grill pan over medium-high heat. Coat pan with cooking spray. Remove chicken from bag; discard marinade in bag. Sprinkle chicken with ½ teaspoon salt and pepper. Add chicken to pan; baste with 2 tablespoons reserved marinade. Cook 6 minutes. Turn chicken over; baste with 2 tablespoons reserved marinade. Cook 6 minutes.

3. Combine rice, remaining ¼ teaspoon salt, and cilantro; toss to combine. **Yield: 4 servings (serving size: 1 breast half and ½ cup rice).**

CALORIES 247; FAT 1.8g (sat 0.5g, mono 0.4g, poly 0.4g); PROTEIN 29.9g; CARB 25.2g; FIBER 0.5g; CHOL 68mg; IRON 1.9mg; SODIUM 674mg; CALC 26mg

Mediterranean-Stuffed Chicken Breasts

1 large red bell pepper + **¼ cup (1 ounce) crumbled feta cheese** + **2 tablespoons finely chopped pitted kalamata olives**

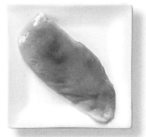

1 tablespoon minced fresh basil + **8 (6-ounce) skinless, boneless chicken breast halves**

Preheat broiler. Cut bell pepper in half lengthwise; discard seeds and membranes. Place pepper halves, skin sides up, on a foil-lined baking sheet; flatten with hand. Broil 15 minutes or until blackened. Place in a zip-top plastic bag; seal. Let stand 15 minutes. Peel and finely chop. Prepare grill to medium-high heat. Combine bell pepper, cheese, olives, and basil. Cut a horizontal slit through thickest portion of each chicken breast half to form a pocket. Stuff 2 tablespoons bell pepper mixture into each pocket; close opening with a wooden pick. Sprinkle chicken with ¼ teaspoon salt and ¼ teaspoon black pepper. Place chicken on grill rack coated with cooking spray. Grill 6 minutes on each side or until done. Remove from grill; cover loosely with foil, and let stand 10 minutes. **Yield: 8 servings (serving size: 1 stuffed chicken breast half).**

CALORIES 210; FAT 5.9g (sat 1.9g, mono 2.3g, poly 1g); PROTEIN 35.2g; CARB 1.8g; FIBER 0.5g; CHOL 98mg; IRON 1.3mg; SODIUM 266mg; CALC 43mg

Grilled Chicken with Mango-Pineapple Salsa

Salsa:
⅔ cup diced peeled ripe mango (1 medium)
⅔ cup diced fresh pineapple
2 tablespoons minced red onion
1 tablespoon minced seeded jalapeño pepper
1½ teaspoons chopped fresh cilantro
1½ teaspoons fresh lime juice
⅛ teaspoon salt
⅛ teaspoon freshly ground black pepper

Chicken:
4 (6-ounce) skinless, boneless chicken breast halves
¼ cup pineapple juice
3 tablespoons chopped fresh cilantro
3 tablespoons lower-sodium soy sauce
2 tablespoons honey
1 teaspoon fresh lime juice
Dash of crushed red pepper
Cooking spray

1. To prepare salsa, combine first 8 ingredients. Cover; refrigerate 30 minutes.
2. To prepare chicken, place each chicken breast half between 2 sheets of heavy-duty plastic wrap; pound to ½-inch thickness using a meat mallet or small heavy skillet. Combine pineapple juice and next 5 ingredients in a large zip-top plastic bag. Add chicken to bag; seal. Marinate in refrigerator 30 minutes.
3. Preheat grill to medium-high heat.
4. Remove chicken from bag, reserving marinade. Place chicken on grill rack coated with cooking spray; grill 3 minutes on each side or until done.
5. Place reserved marinade in a small saucepan; bring to a boil. Reduce heat, and cook until reduced to ¼ cup (about 5 minutes). Drizzle over chicken. Serve salsa with chicken. **Yield: 4 servings (serving size: 1 chicken breast half, 1 tablespoon sauce, and ¼ cup salsa).**

CALORIES 222; FAT 3.4g (sat 0.9g, mono 1.1g, poly 0.7g); PROTEIN 26.9g; CARB 21.1g; FIBER 1.3g; CHOL 70mg; IRON 1.4mg; SODIUM 537mg; CALC 27mg

Mango
What it adds: The mango—likened to a cross between a pineapple and a peach—adds sublime sweetness to this salsa.

Pineapple
What it adds: In addition to tropical flavor, pineapple is also a wonderful source of vitamin C.

Grilled Chicken with Bourbon Peach Butter

1½　pounds coarsely chopped peeled peaches
　　(about 5 medium)
　¼　cup fresh lemon juice
　3　tablespoons water
　½　cup bourbon
　⅓　cup packed dark brown sugar
　¾　teaspoon salt, divided
　½　teaspoon freshly ground black pepper
　6　(6-ounce) skinless, boneless chicken
　　breast halves
　　Cooking spray

1. Preheat oven to 250°.
2. Combine first 3 ingredients in a saucepan. Bring to a boil; cover, reduce heat, and simmer 30 minutes. Place peach mixture, bourbon, brown sugar, and ¼ teaspoon salt in a food processor or blender, and process 1 minute or until smooth. Transfer peach mixture to a 13 x 9–inch glass or ceramic baking dish. Bake at 250° for 2 hours and 15 minutes or until thickened.
3. Preheat grill to medium-high heat.
4. Sprinkle remaining ½ teaspoon salt and pepper evenly over chicken. Place chicken on grill rack coated with cooking spray; grill 6 minutes on each side or until done. Serve with sauce. **Yield: 6 servings (serving size: 1 breast half and ¼ cup sauce).**

CALORIES 304; FAT 2.5g (sat 0.6g, mono 0.6g, poly 0.6g); PROTEIN 40.4g; CARB 23.8g; FIBER 1.7g; CHOL 99mg; IRON 1.6mg; SODIUM 409mg; CALC 37mg

kitchen how-to:
make bourbon peach butter

The hands-free oven method helps prevent the sugary fruit butter from scorching.

1. Combine coarsely chopped peaches, lemon juice, and 3 tablespoons water. Bring to a boil; cover, reduce heat, and simmer 30 minutes.
2. Use a food processor or blender to process the bourbon-peach mixture until it's smooth.
3. Transfer the mixture to a 13 x 9–inch glass or ceramic baking dish, and bake until thickened. Reducing the sweet mixture in the oven offers gentle, controlled heat, which is one way to avoid scorching that could occur on the stovetop.

Curry Chicken Wraps with Nectarine Chutney

1 cup plain fat-free yogurt
3 tablespoons curry powder
3 tablespoons lime juice, divided
4 (6-ounce) skinless, boneless chicken breast halves
10 cilantro sprigs
6 garlic cloves, crushed
2 cups chopped nectarines
¾ cup finely sliced green onions
⅓ cup mango chutney
2 tablespoons chopped fresh cilantro
2 tablespoons chopped fresh mint
1 tablespoon grated peeled fresh ginger
¼ teaspoon ground red pepper
½ teaspoon salt
Cooking spray
6 (1.9-ounce) light whole-wheat flatbreads
24 (⅛-inch-thick) slices cucumber
1½ cups loosely packed baby arugula
1 cup vertically sliced red onion

1. Combine yogurt, curry, and 1 tablespoon lime juice in a large heavy-duty zip-top plastic bag; squeeze bag to mix. Cut 3 shallow slits in each chicken breast. Add chicken, cilantro sprigs, and garlic to bag, squeezing to coat chicken. Seal and marinate in the refrigerator 2 hours, turning occasionally.
2. Combine remaining 2 tablespoons lime juice, nectarines, and next 6 ingredients in a bowl; toss gently. Cover and set aside.
3. Preheat grill to medium-high heat.
4. Remove chicken from bag; discard marinade. Sprinkle chicken with salt; place chicken on grill rack coated with cooking spray. Cover and grill 4 minutes on each side or until chicken is done. Let stand 5 minutes. Cut chicken across grain into thin slices.
5. Place ⅓ cup nectarine chutney in center of each flatbread. Divide chicken evenly among flatbreads. Top each with 4 cucumber slices, ¼ cup arugula, and about 2½ tablespoons red onion; roll up. Cut each wrap in half diagonally. **Yield: 6 servings (serving size: 1 wrap).**

CALORIES 283; FAT 3.9g (sat 0.3g, mono 0.4g, poly 0.4g); PROTEIN 30.8g; CARB 38.4g; FIBER 11g; CHOL 49mg; IRON 2.8mg; SODIUM 732mg; CALC 89mg

kitchen how-to: use yogurt-based marinades

Buttermilk, milk, and yogurt are only mildly acidic and don't toughen meats the way highly acidic marinades can. For more information about acidic marinades, see page 108.

1. Combine yogurt marinade ingredients in a zip-top plastic bag; squeeze to mix.

2. Cut 3 shallow slits in each chicken breast. Cutting the surface of the chicken (or any meat) helps the marinade penetrate as quickly and deeply as possible.
3. Add the chicken to the bag, squeezing to coat chicken. Seal bag, and marinate in refrigerator, turning occasionally.

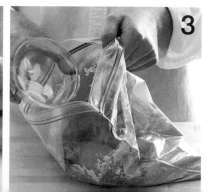

Chicken Kebabs and Nectarine Salsa

1	tablespoon brown sugar
1	tablespoon olive oil
1	tablespoon fresh lime juice
2	teaspoons chili powder
1	teaspoon bottled minced garlic
½	teaspoon kosher salt
½	teaspoon ground cumin
¼	teaspoon freshly ground black pepper
1½	pounds skinless, boneless chicken breast halves, cut into 24 (2-inch) pieces
1	large red onion, cut into 32 (2-inch) pieces
	Cooking spray
2	cups diced nectarine (about 3)
½	cup diced red bell pepper
¼	cup thinly sliced red onion
2	tablespoons fresh cilantro leaves
1½	tablespoons fresh lime juice
2	teaspoons minced seeded jalapeño pepper
¼	teaspoon kosher salt
½	cup diced peeled avocado

1. Preheat grill to medium-high heat.

2. Combine first 9 ingredients in a shallow dish; let stand 15 minutes.

3. Thread 4 onion pieces and 3 chicken pieces alternately onto each of 8 (12-inch) skewers. Place kebabs on grill rack coated with cooking spray. Grill 8 to 10 minutes or until chicken is done, turning occasionally.

4. Combine nectarine and next 6 ingredients in a bowl. Gently stir in avocado. **Yield: 4 servings (serving size: 2 kebabs and ¾ cup salsa).**

CALORIES 324; FAT 8.9g (sat 1.5g, mono 4.9g, poly 1.3g); PROTEIN 41.2g; CARB 18.5g; FIBER 3.8g; CHOL 99mg; IRON 1.9mg; SODIUM 547mg; CALC 44mg

Red Onion
What it adds: The relatively mild flavor of red onions doesn't overwhelm this dish. Their purple hue also adds a nice color contrast.

Nectarine Salsa

What it adds: The salsa offers the perfect sweet balance to the hint of spice in the chicken. Use peaches or plums instead of nectarines, if you like.

Chicken Fajitas

¾ cup dark Mexican beer
2 tablespoons lower-sodium soy sauce
2 tablespoons fresh lime juice
1 tablespoon canola oil
1 tablespoon Worcestershire sauce
3 garlic cloves, crushed
1 pound skinless, boneless chicken breast halves,
    cut across grain into ½-inch-thick strips
1 cup sliced onion
1 orange bell pepper, seeded and sliced
1 yellow bell pepper, seeded and sliced
Cooking spray
¼ teaspoon salt
¼ teaspoon freshly ground black pepper
8 (6-inch) flour tortillas
1 jalapeño pepper, thinly sliced
Salsa (optional)
Reduced-fat sour cream (optional)
Fresh cilantro leaves (optional)

1. Combine first 6 ingredients, stirring well. Place
chicken in a zip-top plastic bag. Add ¾ cup beer mixture
to bag; seal. Reserve remaining beer mixture. Marinate
in refrigerator 1 hour, turning occasionally. Combine
onion, bell peppers, and remaining mixture in a zip-top
plastic bag; seal. Marinate 1 hour at room temperature.
2. Heat a grill pan over medium-high heat. Coat pan
with cooking spray. Remove chicken from bag; discard
marinade. Sprinkle chicken evenly with salt and black
pepper. Add chicken to pan; cook 2 minutes on each
side or until done. Remove chicken from pan; keep
warm. Remove onion and bell peppers from bag,
and discard marinade. Add onion mixture to pan; cook
6 minutes or until tender, turning after 3 minutes. Toast
tortillas in pan, if desired. Place 2 tortillas on each of
4 plates, and divide chicken mixture evenly among
tortillas. Top evenly with onion mixture. Garnish with
jalapeño slices. Serve with salsa, sour cream, and
cilantro, if desired. **Yield: 4 servings.**

CALORIES 377; FAT 9.4g (sat 1.5g, mono 4.7g, poly 2.3g); PROTEIN 31.6g; CARB 39.8g;
FIBER 4.3g; CHOL 66mg; IRON 1.9mg; SODIUM 668mg; CALC 67mg

kitchen how-to:
get the most from salt when marinating

Added salt is something to keep in mind when
marinating. There are ways to make that salty flavor
go farther.

1. Marinades are one way to add flavor to meats
and poultry, but the salt can sometimes get lost if
it's added to the marinade, and even more so if the
marinade is discarded afterward.
2. To help ensure the salt goes as far as it can, sprinkle
it on the meat or poultry after it's been removed from
the marinade so the small amount of salt used has a
bigger impact on the overall taste.

Chicken Shawarma

Chicken:
- 2 tablespoons fresh lemon juice
- 1 teaspoon curry powder
- 2 teaspoons extra-virgin olive oil
- ½ teaspoon salt
- ½ teaspoon ground cumin
- 3 garlic cloves, minced
- 1 pound skinless, boneless chicken breast halves, cut into 16 (3-inch) strips

Sauce:
- ½ cup plain 2% reduced-fat Greek yogurt
- 2 tablespoons tahini
- 2 teaspoons fresh lemon juice
- 1 garlic clove, minced

Remaining ingredients:
- Cooking spray
- 4 (6-inch) pitas
- 1 cup chopped romaine lettuce
- 8 (¼-inch-thick) slices tomato

1. Preheat grill to medium-high heat.

2. To prepare chicken, combine first 6 ingredients in a medium bowl. Add chicken to bowl; toss well to coat. Let stand at room temperature 20 minutes.

3. To prepare sauce, combine yogurt and next 3 ingredients, stirring with a whisk.

4. Thread 2 chicken strips onto each of 8 (12-inch) skewers. Place kebabs on grill rack coated with cooking spray; grill 4 minutes on each side or until done.

5. Place pitas on grill rack; grill 1 minute on each side or until lightly toasted. Place 1 pita on each of 4 plates; top each serving with ¼ cup lettuce and 2 tomato slices. Top each serving with 4 chicken pieces; drizzle each serving with 2 tablespoons sauce. **Yield: 4 servings.**

CALORIES 384; FAT 9.8g (sat 2.1g, mono 4.1g, poly 2.7g); PROTEIN 34.4g; CARB 40g; FIBER 2.5g; CHOL 64mg; IRON 4.3mg; SODIUM 614mg; CALC 106mg

Greek Yogurt
What it adds: Greek yogurt provides a thick, creamy base for the cool savory sauce, which complements the hot grilled chicken.

Garlic Cloves
What they add: Garlic is a key ingredient in this Middle Eastern dish of garlicky meat or poultry served on pitas.

Grapes
What they add: Halved grapes add brightness to this chicken salad. Substitute red grapes, if you like.

Canola Mayonnaise
What it adds: Canola mayonnaise has far less saturated fat than conventional store-bought mayo.

Grilled Chicken Salad

1½ cups plain 2% reduced-fat Greek yogurt
1 tablespoon canola oil
1 tablespoon grated peeled fresh ginger
3 garlic cloves, minced
¾ teaspoon salt, divided
½ teaspoon ground red pepper
4 (8-ounce) bone-in chicken breast
  halves, skinned
Cooking spray
1 cup seedless green grapes, halved
½ cup chopped red onion
½ cup mango chutney
⅓ cup finely chopped celery
⅓ cup canola mayonnaise
3 tablespoons fresh lemon juice

1. Combine first 4 ingredients, stirring to combine. Stir in ¼ teaspoon salt and pepper. Place yogurt mixture in a heavy-duty zip-top plastic bag. Add chicken to bag; seal. Marinate in refrigerator 2 hours, turning occasionally.
2. Preheat grill to medium-high heat.
3. Remove chicken from bag; discard marinade. Place chicken, breast sides down, on grill rack coated with cooking spray; grill 10 minutes or until browned. Turn chicken over; grill 20 minutes or until done. Remove chicken from grill; let stand 10 minutes. Remove meat from bones; discard bones. Coarsely chop chicken and place in a medium bowl. Sprinkle chicken with remaining ½ teaspoon salt.
4. Add grapes and remaining ingredients to chicken mixture; toss gently to combine. Chill 30 minutes.
Yield: 5 servings (serving size: about 1 cup).

CALORIES 430; FAT 18.6g (sat 2.7g, mono 6.2g, poly 8.8g); PROTEIN 28.9g; CARB 35.1g; FIBER 1g; CHOL 68mg; IRON 1mg; SODIUM 718mg; CALC 100mg

Maple-Mustard Chicken Thighs

Speed up prep by marinating only 30 minutes. Serve with cabbage-carrot slaw.

- ⅓ **cup spicy brown mustard**
- 2 **tablespoons brown sugar**
- 3 **tablespoons maple syrup**
- 2 **tablespoons yellow mustard**
- 1 **tablespoon grated onion**
- 1 **tablespoon cider vinegar**
- 2 **teaspoons lower-sodium soy sauce**
- ½ **teaspoon freshly ground black pepper**
- 1 **garlic clove, minced**
- 8 **bone-in chicken thighs, skinned**
- ¼ **teaspoon kosher salt**
- **Cooking spray**

1. Combine first 9 ingredients. Place half of mixture in a zip-top plastic bag; reserve remaining mixture. Add chicken to bag; seal. Marinate in refrigerator 2 hours.
2. Preheat grill to medium-high heat.
3. Remove chicken from bag; discard marinade. Sprinkle chicken with salt. Place chicken on grill rack coated with cooking spray; grill 8 minutes on each side or until done. Serve with reserved mustard mixture. **Yield: 4 servings (serving size: 2 thighs and 2 tablespoons sauce).**

CALORIES 314; FAT 11.7g (sat 3.2g, mono 4.5g, poly 2.7g); PROTEIN 27.6g; CARB 18.2g; FIBER 0.4g; CHOL 99mg; IRON 1.8mg; SODIUM 565mg; CALC 36mg

all about chicken thighs

Rich thigh meat is higher in fat than lean white meat, so the thighs stay moist even when they're grilled without skin. They also have more flavor and are less expensive than skinless, boneless chicken breasts.

Tequila-Glazed Grilled Chicken Thighs

If you would rather not use tequila, you can substitute ⅓ cup pineapple juice. Start the grilling over direct heat to get good grill marks and charred bits, and then move to indirect heat to gently finish the cooking. Serve with lime wedges.

- 1½ teaspoons ground cumin
- 1 teaspoon chili powder
- ¾ teaspoon kosher salt
- ¼ teaspoon chipotle chile powder
- 6 bone-in chicken thighs (about 2 pounds), skinned
- ¾ cup pineapple juice
- ⅓ cup tequila
- ¼ cup honey
- 2 teaspoons cornstarch
- 2 teaspoons water
- 2 teaspoons grated lime rind
- 3 tablespoons fresh lime juice
- ¼ teaspoon crushed red pepper
- Cooking spray

1. Preheat grill to medium-high heat using both burners. After preheating, turn the left burner off (leave the right burner on).

2. Combine first 4 ingredients in a small bowl; rub evenly over chicken.

3. Combine pineapple juice, tequila, and honey in a small saucepan; bring to a boil. Cook until reduced to ¾ cup (about 10 minutes). Combine cornstarch and 2 teaspoons water in a small bowl, and stir well. Add cornstarch mixture to juice mixture, stirring constantly with a whisk. Bring to a boil, and cook 1 minute, stirring constantly. Remove from heat, and stir in lime rind, 3 tablespoons lime juice, and red pepper.

4. Place chicken on grill rack coated with cooking spray over right burner (direct heat). Cover and grill 5 minutes on each side, basting occasionally with juice mixture. Move chicken to grill rack over left burner (indirect heat). Cover and grill an additional 5 minutes on each side or until done, basting occasionally. **Yield: 6 servings (serving size: 1 thigh).**

CALORIES 241; FAT 7.6g (sat 2.1g, mono 2.8g, poly 1.7g); PROTEIN 18g; CARB 17.2g; FIBER 0.4g; CHOL 64mg; IRON 1.2mg; SODIUM 374mg; CALC 19mg

all about dry rubs

These spice blends have no added moisture, so they cook to a light crust—not chunky or thick, just a thin coating that enhances a food's basic flavors. Dry rubs are easy to prepare, made only with dried spices and herbs, so you may want to consider doubling or tripling the recipe to have extra on hand the next time you grill. When using a dry rub, sprinkle it evenly over the food on one side, gently pat in place, and then turn the food over and repeat. Store extra in an airtight container in a cool, dark place; use spicy rubs within two weeks because chiles can overpower more delicate herbs and spices during extended storage.

Yogurt-Marinated Chicken with Beet Salad

Tamarind lends the marinade a pleasant sweet-sour note. However, you can substitute 2 tablespoons lemon juice if tamarind paste isn't available.

- ¾ cup plain low-fat yogurt
- 1 tablespoon garam masala
- 3 tablespoons finely chopped garlic
- 2 tablespoons canola oil
- 1 tablespoon tamarind paste
- 1¼ teaspoons ground red pepper
- 1 teaspoon ground cumin
- 1 teaspoon minced peeled fresh ginger
- 12 skinless, boneless chicken thighs (about 2½ pounds)
- 1½ cups diced seeded tomato
- 1 cup thinly sliced peeled beet
- ¾ cup thinly sliced peeled daikon radish (about 4 ounces)
- ½ cup vertically sliced red onion
- ½ cup finely chopped fresh cilantro
- 3 tablespoons fresh lemon juice
- 1 tablespoon extra-virgin olive oil
- 1 teaspoon salt, divided
- Cooking spray

1. Combine first 8 ingredients in a bowl. Add chicken; toss to coat. Cover and marinate in refrigerator at least 4 hours.
2. Combine tomato and next 4 ingredients in a medium bowl. Combine juice, olive oil, and ½ teaspoon salt. Pour juice mixture over beet mixture, and toss to coat. Cover and chill at least 2 hours.
3. Heat a grill pan over high heat. Coat pan with cooking spray. Remove chicken from marinade, and discard marinade. Sprinkle chicken evenly with remaining ½ teaspoon salt. Add half of chicken to pan; cook chicken 4 minutes on each side or until done. Repeat procedure with remaining chicken. Serve with salad. **Yield: 6 servings (serving size: 2 chicken thighs and ½ cup salad).**

CALORIES 385; FAT 20.9g (sat 5g, mono 9.4g, poly 4.7g); PROTEIN 37.6g; CARB 11.2g; FIBER 2.6g; CHOL 125mg; IRON 2.6mg; SODIUM 550mg; CALC 69mg

all about tamarind paste

Tamarind sweetens as it ripens, but even mature fruit still has a sour bite. The paste is made by blending ripe tamarind fruit with water, sugar, and spices until it's a smooth consistency.

Grilled Chicken Thighs with Roasted Grape Tomatoes

1   tablespoon grated lemon rind
2   tablespoons fresh lemon juice
1   teaspoon olive oil
2   garlic cloves, minced
8   skinless, boneless chicken thighs (about
     1½ pounds)
½   teaspoon salt
¼   teaspoon freshly ground black pepper
Cooking spray
2   cups grape tomatoes
2   teaspoons olive oil
2   tablespoons chopped fresh parsley
1   teaspoon grated lemon rind
1   tablespoon fresh lemon juice
1   tablespoon capers
⅛   teaspoon salt
⅛   teaspoon freshly ground black pepper
Fresh parsley (optional)

1. Preheat grill to medium-high heat.
2. Combine first 4 ingredients in a large zip-top plastic bag. Add chicken to bag; seal. Marinate in refrigerator 15 minutes, turning bag occasionally.
3. Remove chicken from bag; discard marinade. Sprinkle chicken evenly with ½ teaspoon salt and ¼ teaspoon pepper. Place chicken on grill rack coated with cooking spray; grill 5 minutes on each side or until done.
4. Preheat oven to 425°.
5. Combine tomatoes and 2 teaspoons oil in an 8-inch square baking dish; toss gently. Bake at 425° for 18 minutes or until tomatoes are tender. Combine tomato mixture, parsley, and remaining ingredients, stirring gently. Serve with chicken. Garnish with parsley, if desired. **Yield: 4 servings (serving size: 2 chicken thighs and ¼ cup tomato mixture).**

CALORIES 194; FAT 7.8g (sat 1.7g, mono 3.4g, poly 1.6g); PROTEIN: 25.9g; CARB 4.5g; FIBER 1.1g; CHOL 106mg; IRON 1.9mg; SODIUM 329mg; CALC 23mg

Capers
What they add: These small, pickled buds of the caper plant can pack a wallop of briny taste. A little goes a long way.

Lemon Rind
What it adds: Fresh grated lemon rind intensifies the lemon flavor in the tangy marinade.

Grilled Chicken Sliders and Apricot Chutney Spread

⅜ teaspoon ground red pepper
½ teaspoon freshly ground black pepper
⅛ teaspoon salt
1½ pounds skinless, boneless chicken thighs
Cooking spray
3 apricots, halved and pitted
1 tablespoon water
1 tablespoon cider vinegar
1 tablespoon Dijon mustard
2 garlic cloves, chopped
8 (1.3-ounce) mini sandwich buns

1. Combine first 3 ingredients in a small bowl. Sprinkle chicken with pepper mixture. Place a large grill pan over medium-high heat; coat pan with cooking spray. Add chicken to pan; cook 5 minutes on each side or until done. Cool slightly; shred meat.
2. Recoat pan with cooking spray. Place apricots, cut sides down, on pan; cook 6 minutes on medium-high heat or until tender and lightly browned, turning after 4 minutes. Place apricots and next 4 ingredients in a food processor; process until smooth.
3. Spread about ½ teaspoon apricot chutney over cut side of each sandwich bun half. Place about ⅓ cup chicken on bottom bun; cover with top half of bun.
Yield: 4 servings (serving size: 2 sliders).

CALORIES 430; FAT 11g (sat 3.7g, mono 4.1g, poly 1.7g); PROTEIN 42.3g; CARB 41.9g;
FIBER 2.7g; CHOL 141mg; IRON 2mg; SODIUM 644mg; CALC 24mg

Dijon Mustard
What it adds: The mustard gives the apricot chutney the perfect amount of peppery tang to complement the grilled chicken.

Apricots
What they add: Apricots—one of the first fruits of summer—have a delicate sweet flavor and velvety texture.

Grilled Chicken with Sriracha Glaze

Customize the glaze according to what you have on hand; try pineapple preserves or apple jelly in place of mango jam, for example, or hot pepper sauce instead of Sriracha. Serve with rice and grilled bell peppers.

⅔ cup mango jam
2 tablespoons finely chopped fresh chives
2 tablespoons rice vinegar
2 tablespoons Sriracha (hot chile sauce)
1 tablespoon olive oil
4 (12-ounce) bone-in chicken leg-thigh quarters, skinned
½ teaspoon kosher salt
¼ teaspoon freshly ground black pepper

1. Preheat grill for indirect grilling. If using a gas grill, heat one side to medium-high, and leave one side with no heat. If using a charcoal grill, arrange hot coals on either side of charcoal grate, leaving an empty space in the middle.
2. Combine mango jam, chives, vinegar, and Sriracha, stirring until smooth. Reserve ¼ cup mango mixture; set aside.
3. Brush oil evenly over chicken. Sprinkle chicken with salt and pepper.
4. Carefully remove grill rack. Place a disposable aluminum foil pan on unheated part of grill. Carefully return grill rack to grill. Place chicken on grill rack over unheated part. Brush chicken with about 2 tablespoons remaining mango mixture. Close lid; grill 1 hour and 30 minutes or until a thermometer inserted into meaty part of thigh registers 165°, turning chicken and brushing with about 2 tablespoons mango mixture every 20 minutes. Transfer chicken to a platter. Drizzle chicken with reserved ¼ cup mango mixture. **Yield: 4 servings (serving size: 1 leg-thigh quarter and 1 tablespoon mango mixture).**

CALORIES 326; FAT 10.4g (sat 2.3g, mono 4.7g, poly 2.1g); PROTEIN: 38.7g; CARB 18.2g; FIBER 2.7g; CHOL 154mg; IRON 4.5mg; SODIUM 515mg; CALC 102mg

kitchen how-to:
avoid burning sweet glazes

Glazes and basting sauces that contain sugar can be susceptible to burning. The best advice when grilling with these sweet sauces is to add them at the end of cooking to shorten their time over the high heat of the grill, or use them when you're cooking over indirect heat.

Kansas City Barbecued Chicken

  4 **cups hickory wood chips**
  8 **(10-ounce) bone-in chicken leg-thigh quarters**
  ¼ **cup Kansas City Dry Rub**
  2 **cups water**
  Cooking spray
1½ **cups Kansas City Barbecue Sauce**

1. Soak wood chips in water 1 hour; drain well.
2. Loosen skin from thighs and drumsticks by inserting fingers, gently pushing between skin and meat. Rub Kansas City Dry Rub evenly under loosened skin; let stand at room temperature 30 minutes.
3. Remove grill rack; set aside. Prepare grill for indirect grilling, heating one side to medium-high and leaving one side with no heat.
4. Pierce bottom of a disposable aluminum foil pan several times with the tip of a knife. Place pan on heated side of grill; add half of wood chips to pan. Place another disposable aluminum foil pan (do not pierce pan) on unheated side of grill. Pour 2 cups water in pan. Coat grill rack with cooking spray; place grill rack on grill.
5. Place chicken on grill rack over foil pan on unheated side. Close lid; cook 1½ hours. Add additional wood chips halfway during cooking time. Turn chicken over; cover and cook 30 minutes or until a thermometer registers 165°. Remove chicken from grill; let stand 10 minutes. Remove and discard skin.
6. Bring sauce to a simmer in a small saucepan. Brush chicken with ½ cup sauce. Serve chicken with remaining sauce. **Yield: 8 servings (serving size: 1 chicken leg-thigh quarter and 2 tablespoons sauce).**

CALORIES 294; FAT 10.9g (sat 2.9g, mono 3.9g, poly 2.5g); PROTEIN 35g; CARB 12.7g; FIBER 0.4g; CHOL 119mg; IRON 2.1mg; SODIUM 591mg; CALC 36mg

Kansas City Dry Rub

Use this sweet, smoky blend on steaks, pork tenderloin, pork chops, or chicken. Store in an airtight container for up to a month. Combine ¼ cup paprika, 2 tablespoons Spanish smoked paprika, 2 tablespoons freshly ground black pepper, 1 tablespoon brown sugar, 2 teaspoons kosher salt, 2 teaspoons garlic powder, 1½ teaspoons chili powder, and ½ teaspoon celery salt. **Yield: ¾ cup (serving size: 1½ teaspoons).**

CALORIES 5; FAT 0g (sat 0g, mono 0g, poly 0g); PROTEIN 0.1g; CARB 1.1g; FIBER 0.2g; CHOL 0mg; IRON 0.1mg; SODIUM 178mg; CALC 3mg

Kansas City Barbecue Sauce

Thick, tomato-rich Kansas City sauces are sweeter than those from other barbecue regions. While commercial renditions can overdo the sugar, this version balances sweet with spice. Combine 1 cup plus 2 tablespoons ketchup, 1 cup water, ⅓ cup cider vinegar, ¼ cup packed brown sugar, 1 tablespoon onion powder, 1 tablespoon chili powder, 1 tablespoon freshly ground black pepper, 1½ tablespoons molasses, ¾ teaspoon ground celery seed, and ½ teaspoon smoked salt in a large saucepan; bring to a boil over medium heat. Reduce heat; simmer 25 minutes or until slightly thickened. **Yield: 2½ cups (serving size: about 2 tablespoons).**

CALORIES 31; FAT 0.1g (sat 0g, mono 0g, poly 0g); PROTEIN 0.3g; CARB 7.8g; FIBER 0.2g; CHOL 0mg; IRON 0.3mg; SODIUM 198mg; CALC 12mg

all about
Kansas City barbecue

Kansas City offers a variety of barbecue meat options, but what doesn't vary is the style of the sweet, sticky, tomato-based sauce. It adds color and zest to pulled pork and pork ribs, beef brisket, chicken, and sausage alike.

Chicken Satay

Serve skewers with rice noodles tossed with cilantro, sesame seeds, and dark sesame oil; top with thinly sliced cucumber. If using a gas grill, preheat it during the last 20 minutes of marinating time. By the time chicken is threaded onto skewers, the grill should be heated.

⅓ cup unsalted dry-roasted peanuts
1 tablespoon toasted cumin seeds
2 tablespoons fresh lime juice
1 tablespoon dark sesame oil
1 teaspoon toasted coriander seeds
2 garlic cloves
1 shallot, peeled
⅓ cup light coconut milk
3 tablespoons brown sugar
1 tablespoon grated peeled fresh ginger
¼ teaspoon ground turmeric
1 serrano chile, stem removed
6 skinless, boneless chicken thighs, cut into 36 pieces
½ teaspoon salt

1. Place first 7 ingredients in a food processor, and process until smooth. Add coconut milk and next 4 ingredients; process until smooth. Spoon peanut mixture into a large zip-top plastic bag. Add chicken to bag, and seal. Marinate in refrigerator 1 hour, turning after 30 minutes.
2. Preheat grill to medium-high heat.
3. Remove chicken from bag, and discard marinade. Thread chicken evenly onto 12 (6-inch) skewers; sprinkle evenly with salt. Grill 6 minutes on each side or until chicken is done. **Yield: 4 servings (serving size: 3 skewers).**

CALORIES 300; FAT 15.2g (sat 2.7g, mono 6.1g, poly 4.7g); PROTEIN 24.6g; CARB 17.5g; FIBER 2.1g; CHOL 86mg; IRON 2.2mg; SODIUM 508mg; CALC 51mg

Serrano Chile
What it adds: The unseeded serrano chile pepper gives this dish some heat. Feel free to use more if you'd like to amp up the fire.

Peanut Marinade
What it adds: There are many variations of satay, but this peanutty marinade imbues this dish with the most popular rendition: satay with peanut sauce. Using unsalted peanuts allows you to better control the sodium.

Apricot Grilled Duck Breasts

Serve this savory-sweet entrée over couscous, brown or white rice, or pasta.

½ **cup apricot preserves**   2½ **tablespoons sherry vinegar**   ¼ **teaspoon ground cumin**

⅛ **teaspoon ground red pepper**   4 **(6-ounce) boneless duck breast halves, skinned**

Combine apricot preserves, sherry vinegar, ¼ teaspoon salt, ground cumin, and ground red pepper in a bowl, stirring with a whisk. Add duck; cover and marinate in refrigerator 20 minutes. Preheat grill to medium heat. Remove duck from marinade, reserving marinade. Bring marinade to a boil in a small saucepan over medium-high heat, and boil 1 minute. Remove from heat. Place duck on grill rack coated with cooking spray. Grill 5 to 6 minutes on each side or until a thermometer inserted into thickest portion registers 165°, basting occasionally with reserved marinade. **Yield: 4 servings (serving size: 1 duck breast half).**

CALORIES 299; FAT 3.7g (sat 0.8g, mono 1.3g, poly 0.5g); PROTEIN 39.4g; CARB 26.8g; FIBER 0.2g; CHOL 203mg; IRON 6.7mg; SODIUM 311mg; CALC 23mg

Grilled Duck with Warm Mushroom Salad and Truffle Vinaigrette

2 tablespoons chopped fresh rosemary

2 tablespoons chopped fresh parsley

1 tablespoon olive oil

4 (6-ounce) boneless duck breast halves, skinned

3 garlic cloves, minced

½ teaspoon salt, divided

¼ teaspoon freshly ground black pepper, divided

Cooking spray

3 cups thinly sliced shiitake mushroom caps (about 5 ounces)

2 cups thinly sliced cremini mushroom caps (about 5 ounces)

¾ cup (¼-inch) diagonally cut asparagus

1½ tablespoons Champagne vinegar

1½ teaspoons truffle oil

1. Combine first 5 ingredients in a large zip-top plastic bag; seal and marinate in refrigerator overnight or up to 2 days.

2. Preheat grill to medium-high heat.
3. Remove duck from bag; sprinkle evenly with ¼ teaspoon salt and ⅛ teaspoon pepper. Place duck on grill rack coated with cooking spray, and grill 4 minutes on each side or until desired degree of doneness. Remove duck from grill; cover and let stand 10 minutes. Cut duck across grain into thin slices.
4. While duck stands, heat a large nonstick skillet over medium-high heat. Coat pan with cooking spray. Add mushrooms, ⅛ teaspoon salt, and remaining ⅛ teaspoon pepper; sauté 10 minutes or until tender. Add asparagus; sauté 2 minutes. Combine remaining ⅛ teaspoon salt, vinegar, and truffle oil, stirring with a whisk. Arrange about ½ cup mushroom mixture in center of each of 4 plates. Top each serving with slices of 1 duck breast half. Drizzle about 1½ teaspoons vinaigrette over each serving. **Yield: 4 servings.**

CALORIES 250; FAT 8.4g (sat 1.5g; mono 4.9g, poly 1g); PROTEIN 37.7g; CARB 5.3g; FIBER 0.9g; CHOL 182mg; IRON 7.2mg; SODIUM 434mg; CALC 35mg

Mix of Mushrooms

What they add: Using two varieties offers contrast in taste and texture. Cremini mushrooms (also called baby portabellos) have a firmer texture and deeper flavor than white mushrooms, while shiitakes provide a rich smokiness.

Duck

What it adds: For a sophisticated meal, it's hard to surpass the richness of duck. Duck skin is thick and fatty, but duck meat has little marbling and is only about 2 percent fat.

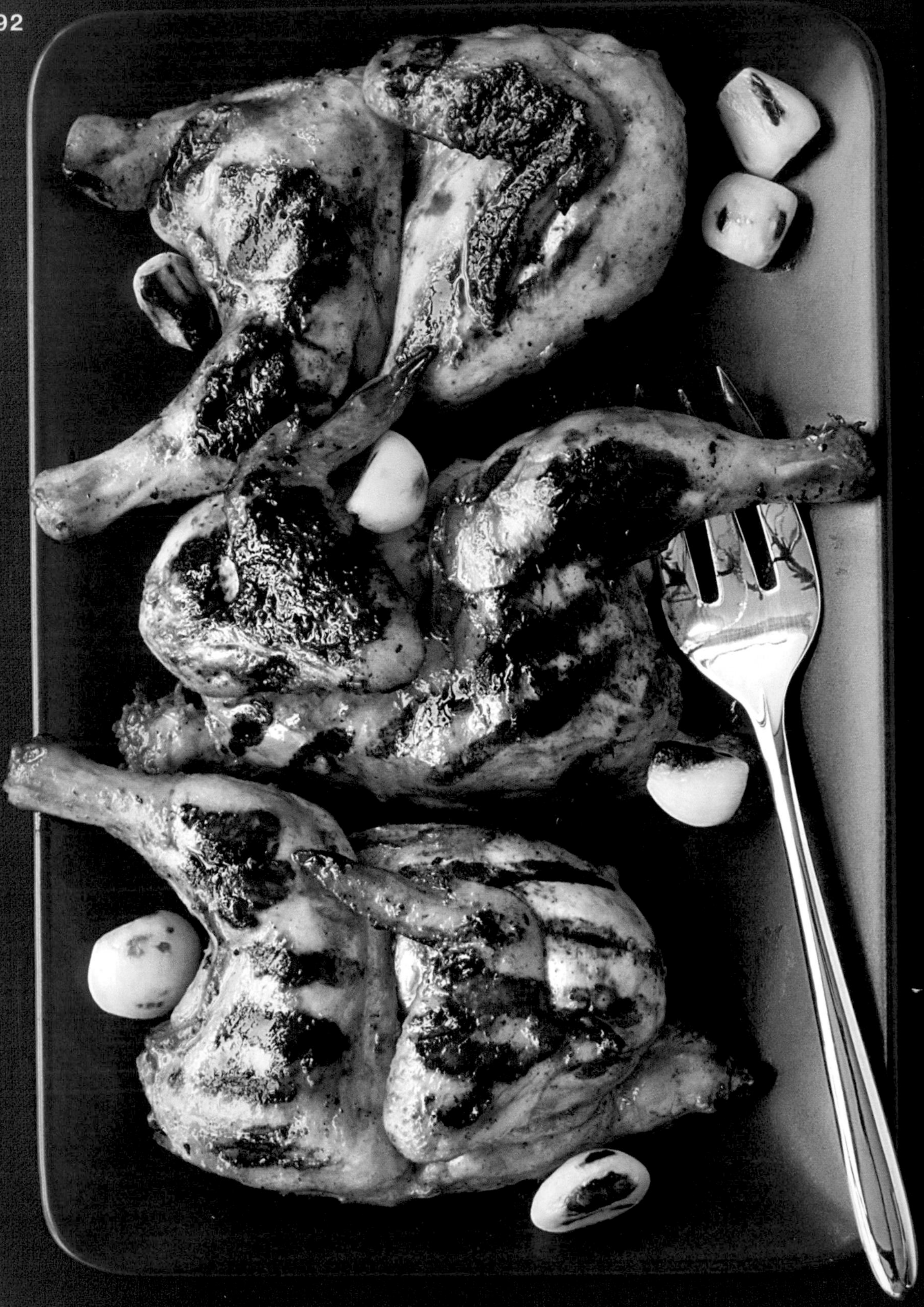

Asian-Style Grilled Cornish Hens

Raspberry vinegar provides a fruity, lightly tart note in the marinade for this dish.

- 3 tablespoons raspberry vinegar
- 2 tablespoons hoisin sauce
- 1 tablespoon dark sesame oil
- 1 tablespoon lower-sodium soy sauce
- 1 teaspoon Sriracha (hot chile sauce)
- 4 garlic cloves, minced
- 4 (1½-pound) Cornish hens, skinned and split in half lengthwise
- Cooking spray

1. Combine first 6 ingredients in a large zip-top plastic bag. Add hens to bag; seal and marinate in refrigerator overnight, turning occasionally. Remove hens from bag; discard marinade.

2. Preheat grill to medium-high heat.

3. Place hens on grill rack coated with cooking spray, and grill 7 to 8 minutes on each side or until a thermometer registers 165°. **Yield: 8 servings (serving size: ½ cornish hen).**

CALORIES 213; FAT 7.2g (sat 1.7g; mono 2.5g, poly 2.1g); PROTEIN 32.4g; CARB 2.5g; FIBER 0.2g; CHOL 146mg; IRON 1.2mg; SODIUM 235mg; CALC 23mg

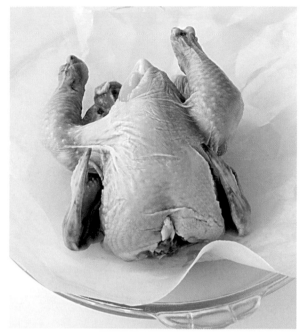

all about cornish hens

Cornish hens are a special breed of small chickens with short legs and broad breasts. Look for the smallest ones you can find—they'll be the most tender and have the best flavor. Remove the skin before grilling. The glaze will protect the meat and help keep it moist.

fish & shellfish

fish & shellfish

Grilling is an excellent way to add variety to fish and shellfish dishes. The key to grilling seafood successfully is knowing the best types to use and cooking them over the correct heat.

Grilling Seafood

The texture of seafood is an important element to consider before you grill. You want fish and shellfish that have a thick, firm texture so that they won't fall apart while cooking. Grouper, sea bass, mahimahi, salmon, swordfish, tuna, shrimp, and scallops are all excellent options. Halibut can handle the heat, but it's a bit more delicate than these others, so be careful when you're turning it on the grill.

To avoid overcooking seafood, check it several minutes before you think it's done. To check doneness, you can make a small slit in the flesh. Cooked seafood will be firm to the touch and opaque; undercooked seafood will be shiny and semi-translucent. For fish, you can also cut into a bit of the flesh with a fork to see if it flakes.

Prevent Sticking

Before you build your fire, make sure the grate is very clean. Any residue on the rack could interfere with the seafood's delicate flavors. Plus, a clean rack helps prevent sticking. Lightly coat the grill rack with cooking spray or brush it with oil before placing it on the grill. This one step will ensure that your seafood won't stick and that cleanup is a breeze.

For Your Health

There's a lot of buzz about the health benefits of seafood, but what makes it healthy? It's a lean protein option with very little saturated fat, and the fat it does contain is mostly good-for-you omega-3 fatty acids, polyunsaturated fats that have been shown to protect against heart disease and some forms of cancer. It's also been shown to help reduce blood pressure and control inflammation.

Sustainable Choices

Making sense of sustainable choices can be tricky. A primary reason for the confusion is that sustainable choices are often influenced by regional and seasonal conditions. Black-and-white choices are rare, leaving behind many shades of gray. The best bet is to check what species are considered sustainable for your area. The Monterey Bay Aquarium and the Blue Ocean Institute keep updated lists of sustainable choices on their websites at **montereybayaquarium.org** and **blueocean.org**, respectively.

kitchen how-to: fillet a fish

1

2

3

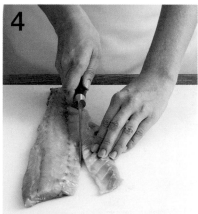
4

You may be wondering why you should fillet your own fish? Two reasons: better quality and lower price. Buying whole fish is the best way to determine freshness and get the most from your purchase (the bones and scraps make great fish stock). Buy a fish with firm flesh that springs back when pressed; eyes that are shiny and clear; and a smell like the ocean, not fish. Ask the fishmonger to scale and gut the fish, and then use these techniques to fillet any kind of round fish, such as striped bass (shown here). You may want to wear latex gloves to keep your hands from smelling fishy.

1. First, remove the head. Place a chef's knife behind the pectoral fin; make a diagonal downward cut through the bone. Repeat on the opposite side, and discard the head.
2. Next, remove the tail. Place a chef's knife where the tail fin joins the body, and make a straight cut down through the flesh and bone; discard tail fin.
3. Starting at the head end, run a fillet knife along the backbone in

a smooth motion. (This may take more than one cut.) Cut around the rib cage to separate the fillet.
4. Cut away the thin belly portion of the fillet. While fine to eat, it will cook quicker than the rest of the fillet and is higher in fat. It can be reserved for making stock.
5. With the fillet skin side down, place the chef's knife at the tail end between the skin and the flesh. Run the knife slowly along the fillet with the knife blade angled ever so slightly downward, firmly gripping the skin as you cut.

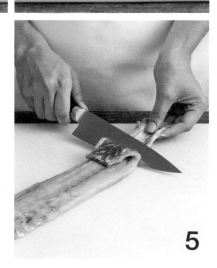
5

fish

Grilling fish can be a delicate business, but you can enjoy great grilled fish at home. We'll show you how.

Grilled Trout

2 cups water
1 tablespoon fine sea salt
2 teaspoons sugar
4 (7-ounce) dressed rainbow trout
Cooking spray
¼ teaspoon table salt
¼ teaspoon freshly ground black pepper
2 (1-ounce) bunches dill sprigs
2 medium limes, each thinly sliced

1. Combine 2 cups water, sea salt, and sugar in a shallow dish, stirring until salt and sugar dissolve; add fish. Let stand 20 minutes. Drain; pat fish dry.

2. Prepare charcoal fire in a chimney starter; let coals burn until flames die down. Pour hot coals out of starter; pile on one side of grill. Coat grill rack with cooking spray; put rack in place over coals.
3. Sprinkle ¼ teaspoon salt and pepper over fish. Divide dill and lime slices evenly among fish cavities. Coat outside of fish with cooking spray. Place fish over direct heat; grill 4 minutes. Turn over; move to indirect heat. Grill 12 minutes or until done. **Yield: 4 servings (serving size: 1 fish).**

CALORIES 230; FAT 8.9g (sat 2.5g, mono 2.7g, poly 2.8g); PROTEIN 35g; CARB 0.3g; FIBER: 0g; CHOL 105mg; IRON 0.6mg; SODIUM 405mg; CALC 132mg

kitchen how-to: grill fish

Let's face it: Grilling fish makes a lot of people nervous. Delicate fillets can stick to the grill and fall apart or, worse, they can overcook, leaving you with a dry, tough dinner. Follow these pointers to grill fish perfectly every time.

1. Indirect grilling is ideal for larger fish fillets because it cooks them more slowly and delicately, while individual fillets can often handle direct heat, and sometimes a combination of direct and indirect heat produces something delectable. Each recipe specifies the type of heat you'll need, so prepare the grill accordingly.
2. Season the fish to add interest and flavor. Stick to basic seasonings like salt, pepper, oil, and herbs when you really want the flavor of the fish to shine.
3. Make sure the grate is clean, and then oil it and the fish (or spray with cooking spray) to help prevent sticking. The fish should release easily when it's time to turn it over or remove it from the grill.

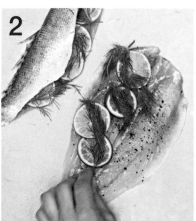

Striped Bass with Peach Salsa

2	**cups water**
1	**tablespoon fine sea salt**
2	**teaspoons sugar**
4	**(6-ounce) striped bass fillets**

Cooking spray

1½	**cups finely chopped peaches (about 2 medium)**
2	**tablespoons thinly sliced shallots**
1½	**tablespoons fresh lemon juice**
1	**tablespoon extra-virgin olive oil**
⅜	**teaspoon table salt, divided**
¼	**teaspoon freshly ground black pepper**
1½	**tablespoons torn small fresh mint leaves**

1. Combine first 3 ingredients in a shallow dish, stirring until sea salt and sugar dissolve; add fish. Let stand 20 minutes. Drain; pat fish dry.

2. Prepare charcoal fire in a chimney starter; let coals burn 15 to 20 minutes or until flames die down. Carefully pour hot coals out of starter, and pile them onto one side of grill. Coat grill rack with cooking spray; put in place over coals.

3. Combine peaches, shallots, juice, and oil in a medium bowl; stir in ⅛ teaspoon table salt. Sprinkle remaining ¼ teaspoon table salt and pepper evenly over fish. Lightly coat fish with cooking spray. Place fish fillets, skin sides down, over direct heat on grill rack coated with cooking spray; grill 2 minutes. Turn fish over, and move over indirect heat; grill 12 minutes or until desired degree of doneness. Stir mint into peach salsa. Serve with fish. **Yield: 4 servings (serving size: 1 fillet and about ⅓ cup salsa).**

CALORIES 231; FAT 7.7g (sat 1.4g, mono 3.7g, poly 1.9g); PROTEIN 31.9g; CARB 8.1g; FIBER 0.8g; CHOL 140mg; IRON 1.8mg; SODIUM 514mg; CALC 31mg

all about peaches

Look for fruit that is firm with taut, unblemished skin and no signs of bruising or wrinkling. If you smell peaches when you walk up to the stand, they're ripe and ready to go. If not, keep them at room temperature to let them ripen more fully. If ripe, put them in the refrigerator; they'll keep for a few days.

Grilled Char with Yukon Golds and Tomato–Red Onion Relish

1 small red onion, vertically sliced
4 (6-ounce) center-cut arctic char or salmon
   fillets
1 pound small Yukon gold or red potatoes
1 tablespoon chopped fresh thyme
2 tablespoons extra-virgin olive oil, divided
¾ teaspoon kosher salt, divided
½ teaspoon freshly ground black pepper,
   divided
1 pint heirloom cherry or grape tomatoes,
   quartered
2 tablespoons finely chopped fresh mint
1 tablespoon capers, chopped
2 teaspoons sherry vinegar
2 teaspoons Dijon mustard
Cooking spray

1. Place onion in a small bowl; add cool water
to cover. Let stand 30 minutes. Drain. Set aside.
2. Arrange fish fillets in a single layer on a large
plate lined with paper towels. Let stand, uncovered,
in refrigerator 1 hour (to allow surface to dry).
3. Preheat grill to medium-high heat.
4. Place potatoes in a large saucepan. Cover with
water to 2 inches above potatoes; bring to a boil.
Reduce heat; simmer 15 minutes or until tender.
Drain; cool slightly. Cut potatoes in half. Combine
potatoes, thyme, 1 tablespoon olive oil, ¼ teaspoon
salt, and ⅛ teaspoon pepper in a bowl, tossing to
coat. Thread potatoes onto 4 (6-inch) skewers, cut
sides facing out.
5. Combine onion, remaining 1 tablespoon oil, ⅛
teaspoon salt, ⅛ teaspoon pepper, tomatoes, mint,
capers, vinegar, and mustard in a bowl; toss gently.
Set aside.
6. Sprinkle remaining ⅜ teaspoon salt and ¼ teaspoon
pepper evenly over fish. Place fish and potatoes, cut
sides down, on grill rack coated with cooking spray.
Cover and grill potatoes 6 minutes without turning.

Grill fish 3 to 4 minutes on each side or until fish flakes
easily when tested with a fork or until desired degree
of doneness. Serve fish with potatoes; top with
tomato-onion relish. **Yield: 4 servings (serving size:
1 fillet, about 5 potato halves, and ½ cup relish).**

CALORIES 357; FAT 13.4g (sat 2.8g, mono 6.5g, poly 2.3g); PROTEIN 32.1g; CARB 25.6g;
FIBER 2.8g; CHOL 141mg; IRON 1.9mg; SODIUM 584mg; CALC 47mg

kitchen how-to:
remove the harsh bite of onions

Onions can sometimes have an overpowering
flavor. To cool their harsh bite a bit, soak the onions
in cool water, let them stand for 30 minutes, and
then drain.

Green Olives
What they add: Green olives are picked while still unripe, which gives them a denser texture and a slightly more bitter flavor than darker olives that stay on the tree to ripen. They add a bit of brininess to this dish, too.

Beefsteak Tomato
What it adds: This heirloom tomato is the crowning glory of this meal. It has a sweet and slightly acidic flavor.

Halibut with Grilled Tomato and Olive Relish

Mild halibut pairs nicely with this tangy relish, starring tasty late-summer tomatoes. Any other firm fish, such as wild salmon or striped bass, will also work.

2½ tablespoons extra-virgin olive oil, divided
1 (12-ounce) beefsteak tomato, halved crosswise and seeded
⅜ teaspoon salt, divided
½ teaspoon freshly ground black pepper, divided
Cooking spray
2 tablespoons thinly sliced fresh basil
1 tablespoon chopped fresh oregano
1½ tablespoons finely chopped shallots
½ teaspoon grated lemon rind
1½ teaspoons fresh lemon juice
2 ounces pitted green olives, coarsely chopped
1 garlic clove, minced
4 (6-ounce) halibut fillets
Lemon wedges (optional)

1. Preheat grill to medium-high heat.
2. Brush 1½ teaspoons oil over cut sides of tomato; sprinkle evenly with ⅛ teaspoon salt and ⅛ teaspoon pepper. Place tomato, cut sides down, on grill rack coated with cooking spray. Cover and grill 8 minutes. Cool slightly; peel and chop tomato. Combine tomato, ⅛ teaspoon salt, ⅛ teaspoon pepper, 1 tablespoon oil, basil, and next 6 ingredients, toss gently.
3. Brush fillets evenly with 1 tablespoon oil; sprinkle evenly with remaining ¼ teaspoon salt and remaining ¼ teaspoon pepper. Place fillets, flesh sides down, on grill rack coated with cooking spray. Grill 5 minutes; turn and grill 3 minutes or until desired degree of doneness. Serve with tomato relish. Serve with lemon wedges, if desired. **Yield: 4 servings (serving size: 1 fillet and about ⅓ cup tomato relish).**

CALORIES 318; FAT 16.3g (sat 2.2g, mono 10.3g, poly 2.6g); PROTEIN 35.3g; CARB 6.7g; FIBER 1.2g; CHOL 52mg; IRON 2mg; SODIUM 548mg; CALC 97mg

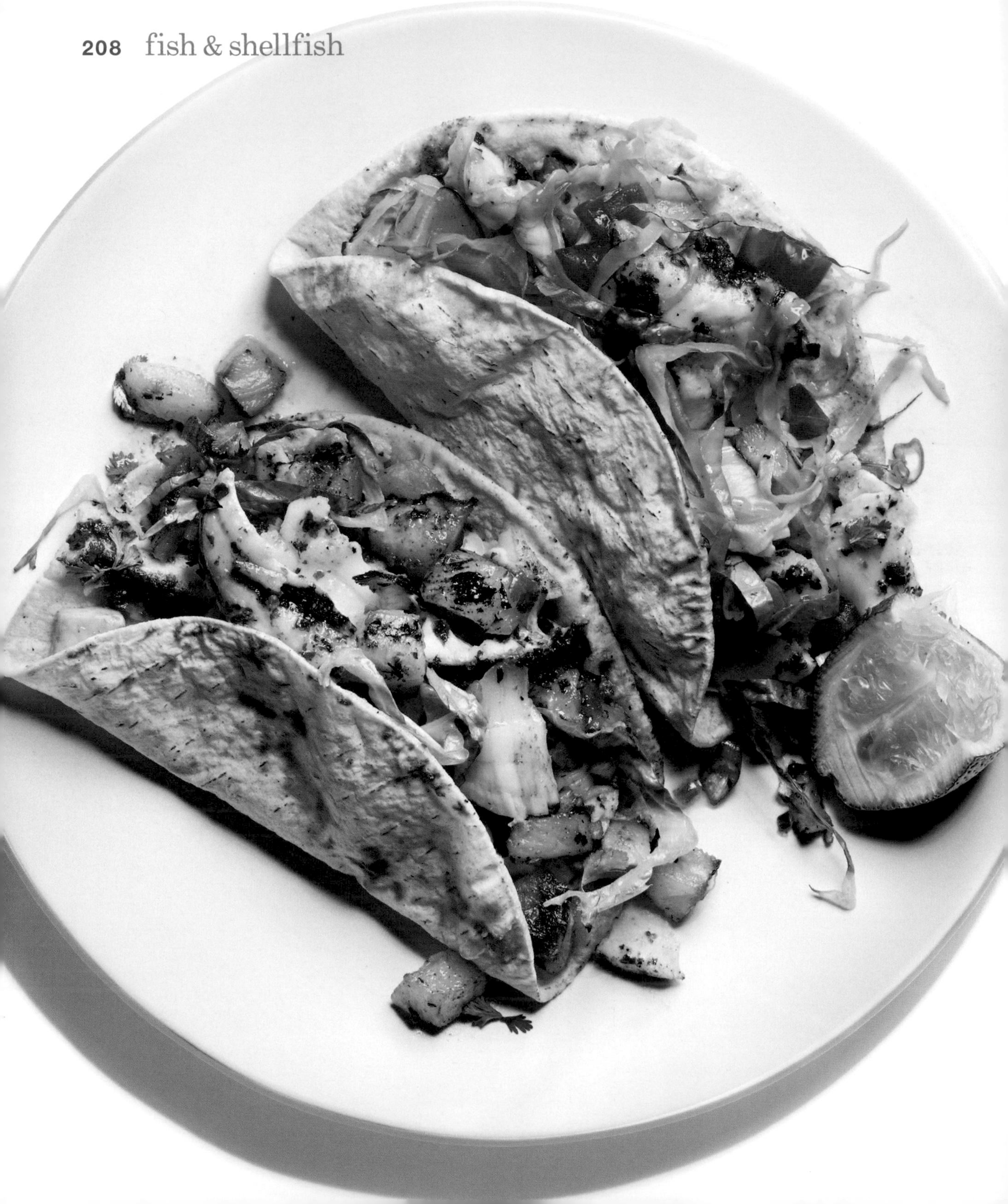

Chimichurri Halibut Tacos

You can also use striped bass or cod in this recipe. Serve with Grilled Pineapple-Avocado Salsa on page 302.

- 2 cups fresh flat-leaf parsley leaves
- 2 tablespoons chopped fresh oregano
- ¾ teaspoon ground cumin
- ¼ teaspoon ground red pepper
- 5 garlic cloves, crushed
- ⅓ cup extra-virgin olive oil
- 5 (6-ounce) halibut fillets
- 1 teaspoon kosher salt
- ½ teaspoon freshly ground black pepper
- Cooking spray
- 12 (6-inch) corn tortillas
- Shredded romaine lettuce (optional)
- Chopped fresh tomatoes (optional)
- Lime wedges (optional)

1. Place first 5 ingredients in a food processor; process until finely chopped. Slowly pour oil through food chute; process until smooth. Place fish in a shallow dish; rub mixture over fish. Cover and marinate in refrigerator 2 hours.
2. Preheat grill to high heat.
3. Sprinkle fish with salt and black pepper. Place fish on grill rack coated with cooking spray, and grill 4 minutes on each side or until desired degree of doneness. Remove from grill. Break fish into chunks. Heat tortillas according to package directions. Divide fish evenly among tortillas. Top with romaine and tomatoes, if desired. Serve with lime wedges, if desired. **Yield: 6 servings (serving size: 2 tacos).**

CALORIES 266; FAT 10.4g (sat 1.3g, mono 5.8g, poly 2g); PROTEIN 24.6g; CARB 19.8g; FIBER 2.6g; CHOL 34mg; IRON 1.6mg; SODIUM 394mg; CALC 93mg

all about corn tortillas

Corn tortillas have a coarser texture and more assertive flavor than wheat flour–based white or whole-wheat versions. Variations in color (white or yellow) are due to variations in the color of the kernels, and each variety offers its own mix of health-promoting antioxidants. Pick the version you like best or mix it up from time to time.

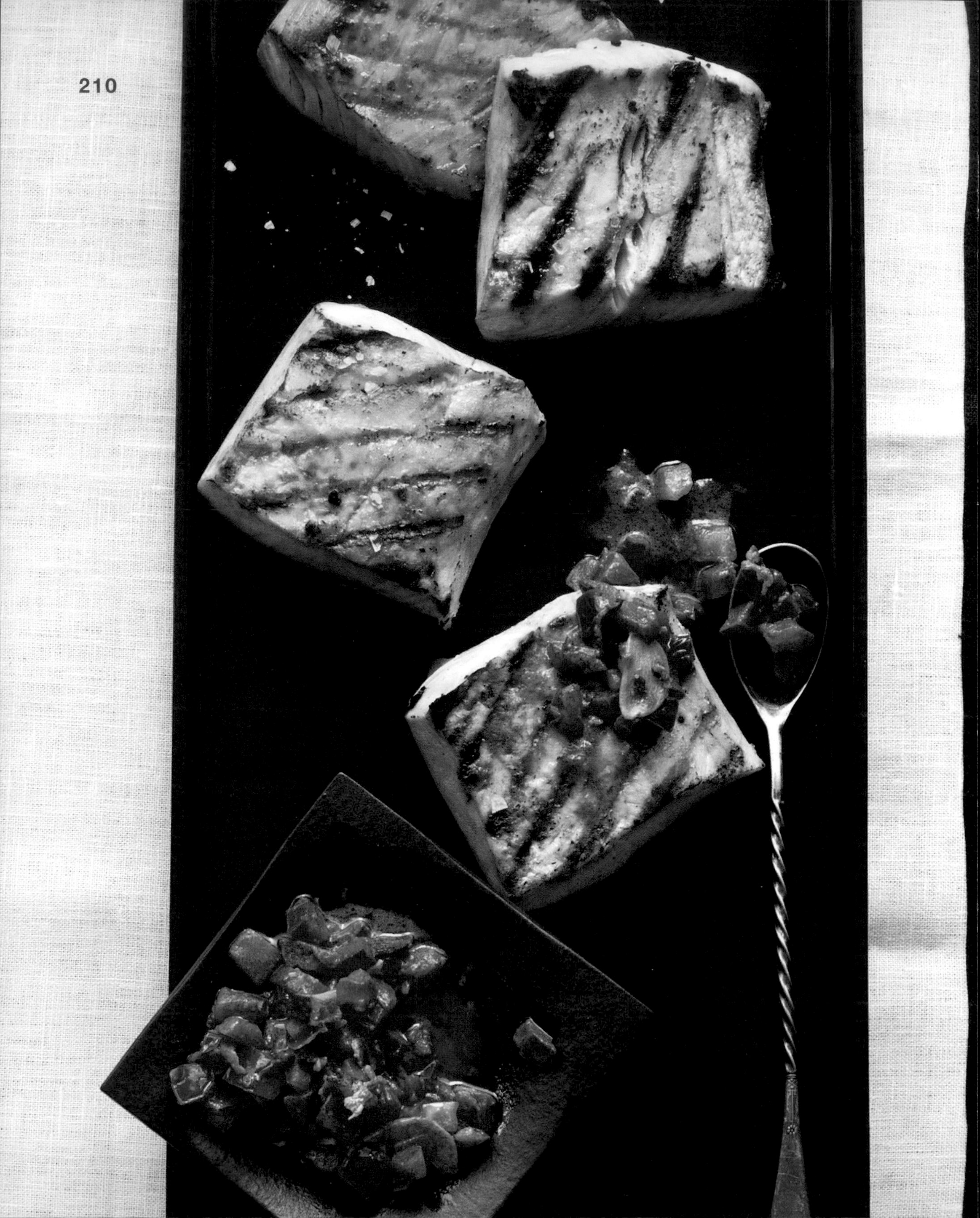

Mahimahi with Bacon-Tomato Butter

2 cups water
1 tablespoon fine sea salt
2 teaspoons sugar
4 (6-ounce) mahimahi or other firm white
   fish fillets
Cooking spray
⅛ teaspoon table salt
1 center-cut bacon slice, finely chopped
1 garlic clove, thinly sliced
¼ teaspoon hot smoked paprika
2 plum tomatoes, seeded and diced
2 tablespoons butter

1. Combine first 3 ingredients in a shallow dish, stirring until sea salt and sugar dissolve; add fish. Let stand 20 minutes. Drain; pat dry.
2. Prepare charcoal fire in a chimney starter; let coals burn 15 to 20 minutes or until flames die down. Carefully pour hot coals out of starter, and pile them onto one side of grill. Coat grill rack with cooking spray; put in place over coals.
3. Sprinkle ⅛ teaspoon table salt evenly over fish. Lightly coat fish with cooking spray. Place fish fillets, skin sides down, over direct heat on grill rack coated with cooking spray; grill 2 minutes or until well marked. Turn fish over, and move to indirect heat; grill 12 minutes or until desired degree of doneness.
4. Heat a small skillet over medium heat; add bacon to pan. Cook 5 minutes or until bacon is almost crisp, stirring occasionally. Add garlic; cook 2 minutes, stirring frequently. Add paprika, and cook 20 seconds, stirring constantly. Add tomatoes, and cook 3 minutes. Stir in butter. Remove from heat. Place 1 fillet on each of 4 plates; top each serving with about 2 tablespoons tomato mixture. **Yield: 4 servings.**

CALORIES 211; FAT 8g (sat 4.4g, mono 1.7g, poly 0.5g); PROTEIN 31.5g; CARB 1.9g; FIBER 0.4g; CHOL 137mg; IRON 2mg; SODIUM 487mg; CALC 31mg

kitchen how-to: make bacon-tomato butter

The bacon-tomato butter is rich and salty-sweet. Try it as a salad topping or paired with other fish.

1. Cook bacon in a small skillet over medium heat about 5 minutes or until it's almost crisp. It will finish cooking once the other ingredients are added.

2. Add garlic, and cook 2 minutes, stirring frequently. Add paprika, and cook 20 seconds, stirring constantly. Add tomatoes, and cook for 3 minutes. It's important to seed the tomatoes to prevent the mixture from being watery.
3. Stir in butter until it's melted. A bit of butter—2 tablespoons—adds a lot of richness and flavor.

Grilled Mahimahi with Mango Salsa

¼ cup light coconut milk, divided
6 tablespoons fresh lime juice (about 4 limes), divided
4 (6-ounce) mahimahi or other firm white fish fillets
1½ cups diced peeled ripe mango (about ½ pound)
¾ cup diced English cucumber (about ½ medium)
⅓ cup finely diced red bell pepper
2 tablespoons minced red onion
1 tablespoon chopped fresh cilantro
1 teaspoon minced peeled fresh ginger
1 serrano chile, minced
¾ teaspoon kosher salt, divided
¼ teaspoon freshly ground black pepper
Cooking spray
Lime slices (optional)

1. Combine 3 tablespoons milk and 3 tablespoons juice in a shallow dish; add fish, turning to coat. Cover and marinate at room temperature 15 minutes.
2. Combine remaining 1 tablespoon milk, remaining 3 tablespoons juice, mango, and next 6 ingredients in a bowl. Add ¼ teaspoon salt; toss well.
3. Remove fish from dish; discard marinade. Sprinkle fish with remaining ½ teaspoon salt and pepper. Heat a grill pan over medium-high heat. Coat pan with cooking spray. Cook fish 4 minutes on each side or until desired degree of doneness. Serve with mango salsa. Garnish with lime slices, if desired. **Yield: 4 servings (serving size: 1 fillet and ½ cup salsa).**

CALORIES 198; FAT 1.7g (sat 0.6g, mono 0.3g, poly 0.3g); PROTEIN 32.2g; CARB 12g; FIBER 1.6g; CHOL 124mg; IRON 2.2mg; SODIUM 507mg; CALC 39mg

English Cucumber
What it adds: The thin skins of the English cucumber mean you don't need to peel it. It adds a cool, refreshing crispness.

Fresh Cilantro
What it adds: Cilantro has a distinctive pungent, peppery taste. Because this herb loses much of its flavor when dehydrated, you should always try to use fresh leaves.

Brown Sugar and Mustard Salmon

2 tablespoons dark brown sugar
2 tablespoons whole-grain Dijon mustard
1 teaspoon freshly ground black pepper
¼ teaspoon kosher salt
¼ teaspoon ground ginger
¼ teaspoon ground coriander
1 garlic clove, minced
1 (1½-pound) center-cut salmon fillet

1. Preheat grill for indirect grilling. If using a gas grill, heat one side to medium-high and leave one side with no heat. If using a charcoal grill, arrange hot coals on either side of charcoal grate, leaving an empty space in the middle.
2. Combine first 7 ingredients, stirring until well blended. Spread mustard mixture evenly over fish; let stand 15 minutes.
3. Carefully remove grill rack. Place a disposable aluminum foil pan on unheated part of grill. Carefully return grill rack to grill. Place fish, skin side down, on grill rack over unheated side. Close lid; grill 30 minutes or until fish flakes easily when tested with a fork or until desired degree of doneness. Remove fish from grill by inserting a spatula between skin and fish. Discard skin. **Yield: 4 servings (serving size: about 5 ounces).**

CALORIES 267; FAT 11.1g (sat 2.5g, mono 4.6g, poly 2.5g); PROTEIN 31.6g; CARB 8.7g; FIBER 0.5g; CHOL 80mg; IRON 0.9mg; SODIUM 340mg; CALC 31mg

kitchen how-to:
easily remove fish skin

When grilling fish, use those that are an even thickness for best results; they will cook more evenly. When grilling, leave the skin on. Once the fish is cooked, insert a spatula between the skin and the fish. The fish and skin should easily separate when you lift off the fish. Scrape off the skin remaining on the grill once it has cooled.

Grilled Salmon with Smoky Tomato Salsa

If you prefer a milder relish, remove the seeds from the jalapeño before grilling.

4 (6-ounce) skinless   4 large plum
salmon fillets   tomatoes, halved

1 small red onion, cut   1 jalapeño pepper,   1 lime, divided
into ½-inch slices   halved

Preheat grill to medium-high heat. Sprinkle fillets with ¼ teaspoon salt and ¼ teaspoon black pepper. Place on grill rack coated with cooking spray, and grill 4 minutes on each side or until desired degree of doneness. Place tomatoes, onion, and jalapeño on grill rack coated with cooking spray; grill tomatoes, cut sides down, 6 minutes. Turn; grill 1 minute. Grill onion and jalapeño 6 minutes on each side or until lightly browned. Remove vegetables from grill, and cool slightly. Coarsely chop tomatoes and onion; finely chop jalapeño. Combine tomatoes, onion, jalapeño, ¼ teaspoon salt, ¼ teaspoon black pepper, and juice from ½ lime. Serve salsa over fish. Serve with lime wedges, if desired. **Yield: 4 servings (serving size: 1 fillet and about ½ cup salsa).**

CALORIES 336; FAT 18.6g (sat 3.7g, mono 6.6g, poly 6.8g); PROTEIN 34.7g; CARB 6.2g; FIBER 1.7g; CHOL 100mg; IRON 0.9mg; SODIUM 399mg; CALC 32mg

Plank-Grilled Salmon with Grape Relish

Substitute picholine or other green olives, if necessary.

- 1 (15 x 6½ x ⅜–inch) alder wood grilling plank
- 4 (6-ounce) salmon fillets
- ½ teaspoon freshly ground black pepper
- ¼ teaspoon kosher salt
- 1 tablespoon butter
- ⅓ cup chopped leek
- 3 tablespoons chopped shallots
- 1 cup seedless red grapes, quartered
- 12 Castelvetrano olives, pitted and chopped
- 4 teaspoons red wine vinegar

1. Immerse and soak plank in water 1 hour; drain.

2. Preheat grill to medium-high heat.

3. Place plank on grill rack; grill 3 minutes or until lightly charred. Sprinkle fillets with pepper and salt. Carefully turn plank over using sturdy long-handled tongs. Place fillets, skin sides down, on charred side of plank. Cover and grill 12 minutes or until desired degree of doneness.

4. Melt butter in a small skillet over medium-high heat. Add leek and shallots; sauté 2 minutes. Stir in grapes and olives; remove from heat. Stir in vinegar. Serve relish with salmon. **Yield: 4 servings (serving size: 1 fillet and about ⅓ cup relish).**

CALORIES 386; FAT 17.9g (sat 6.1g, mono 8.7g, poly 1.9g); PROTEIN 32.4g; CARB 22.1g; FIBER 1.2g; CHOL 64mg; IRON 4mg; SODIUM 496mg; CALC 181mg

kitchen how-to: plank-grill fish

You can cook everything from tuna to tenderloin on a wood plank for extra smoky flavor.

1. You'll need to soak the plank before using it to help keep the fish moist. A soaked plank also produces maximum smoke and is less likely to burn. Submerge it in water for at least 1 hour. Use the soaked plank right away since the wood will start to dry out.

2. Preheat the grill, and place the plank on the grill rack. Grill the plank for 3 minutes or until lightly charred.

3. Carefully turn the plank over using long-handled tongs. Food that touches the wood takes on more flavor, so arrange the fish on the plank in a single layer on the charred side.

4. After placing the food on the plank, immediately close the grill so that the smoke surrounds the food, and grill until the fish are done.

Maple Grilled Salmon

The sweet-sour marinade is cooked down to a syrupy glaze that's brushed on the fish as it cooks. These flavors would also be tasty with pork. Garnish the fillets with lemon or orange slices, if desired.

¼ cup rice wine vinegar **+** 3 tablespoons maple syrup **+** 2 tablespoons fresh orange juice

4 (6-ounce) skinless salmon fillets **+** ¼ teaspoon salt and ¼ teaspoon freshly ground black pepper

Combine vinegar, syrup, and juice in a large zip-top plastic bag; add fish. Seal and marinate in refrigerator 3 hours. Preheat grill or grill pan to medium-high heat. Remove fish from bag, reserving marinade. Pour marinade into a small saucepan; bring to a boil. Cook until reduced to 2 tablespoons (about 5 minutes). Place fish on grill rack or pan coated with cooking spray; grill 4 minutes on each side or until desired degree of doneness, basting occasionally with marinade. Remove fish from grill; sprinkle with salt and pepper. **Yield: 4 servings (serving size: 1 fillet).**

CALORIES 270; FAT 10.6g (sat 2.5g, mono 4.6g, poly 2.5g); PROTEIN 31.1g; CARB 11g; FIBER 0.1g; CHOL 80mg; IRON 0.7mg; SODIUM 216mg; CALC 27mg

Grilled Fresh Sardines

1 teaspoon fennel seeds
1 teaspoon ground coriander
1 shallot, peeled and chopped
1 tablespoon olive oil
¼ teaspoon kosher salt
12 (3-ounce) whole dressed sardines
Cooking spray

1. Place first 3 ingredients in a mini food processor; process until pureed. Add olive oil and kosher salt to shallot mixture; pulse to combine. Place sardines in a shallow dish; rub inside and outside of fish evenly with shallot mixture. Cover and chill 3 hours.
2. Prepare charcoal fire in a chimney starter; let coals burn until flames die down. Pour hot coals out of starter; pile on one side of grill. Coat grill rack with cooking spray; put in place over coals.
3. Place sardines on grill rack coated with cooking spray over direct heat; grill 2 minutes on each side. Move fish over indirect heat, and grill 5 minutes or until desired degree of doneness. **Yield: 4 servings (serving size: 3 fish).**

CALORIES 143; FAT 7.6g (sat 1g, mono 3.9g, poly 2.3g); PROTEIN 12.7g; CARB 2.8g; FIBER 0.2g; CHOL 69mg; IRON 0.3mg; SODIUM 368mg; CALC 6mg

all about sardines

The average weight of a fresh sardine is 3 to 6 ounces, but they can grow up to about a pound. The number of servings and serving size will vary depending on the size of the fish you find. Sardines are also a good source of heart-healthy omega-3 fatty acids.

Grilled Whole Red Snapper with Citrus-Ginger Hot Sauce

To make the sauce fiery, leave the seeds in the serrano chile and hot red chile.

Sauce:
- ⅓ cup fresh orange juice
- 2 tablespoons water
- 1½ tablespoons fresh lime juice
- 1 tablespoon fish sauce
- 1 teaspoon grated peeled fresh ginger
- 1 teaspoon grated garlic
- ½ teaspoon minced seeded serrano chile
- ½ teaspoon Sriracha (hot chile sauce)
- 1½ teaspoons honey
- 1 dried hot red chile, seeded and crushed

Fish:
- 2 (2-pound) cleaned whole red snapper
- 1 tablespoon olive oil
- ½ teaspoon freshly ground black pepper
- ¼ teaspoon kosher salt
- 2 lemons, thinly sliced
- 2 garlic cloves, thinly sliced
- Cooking spray

1. Preheat grill to medium heat.

2. To prepare sauce, combine first 10 ingredients in a bowl; set aside.

3. To prepare fish, score each fish with 3 diagonal cuts on both sides. Brush outside of fish evenly with olive oil. Sprinkle with black pepper and kosher salt. Stuff lemon and garlic slices into cuts. Place any remaining lemon slices into each fish cavity. Coat outside of fish with cooking spray.

4. Place fish on grill rack; grill 40 minutes or until fish flakes easily when tested with a fork. (Fish does not need to be turned.) Serve fish with sauce. **Yield: 4 servings (serving size: about 5 ounces fish and about 2½ tablespoons sauce).**

CALORIES 313; FAT 5.5g (sat 1.3g, mono 2.4g, poly 1g); CARB 25.3g; PROTEIN 40.9g; FIBER 3.3g; CHOL 50mg; IRON 3.1mg; SODIUM 578mg; CALC 93mg

kitchen how-to: grill a whole fish

Although fish is often grilled over indirect heat, cooking whole fish over moderate direct heat is another option. Anything hotter will burn the exterior before the inside is cooked.

1. Start with a whole fish that has already been cleaned (you can buy them like this from the grocery store), and then score each fish with 3 diagonal cuts on each side. This helps the fish cook evenly by allowing the heat of the grill to penetrate the interior of the fish more easily. If you skip this step, the thick middle will still be raw when the tail is overcooked.

2. Brush fish evenly with oil, season the fish, and then coat the fish with cooking spray. This helps prevent the fish from sticking to the grill and also helps the seasonings adhere. Add lemon, garlic, and other herbs into the diagonal cuts or cavity to add moisture and flavor the fish throughout.

3. Place the fish on the grill, and grill until done. Depending on the fish, you may not need to turn it, but in general, fish will need to cook 10 to 14 minutes per side. Just flip once, and when flipping, you'll need to use two spatulas to carefully turn the whole fish.

Grilled Snapper with Orange-Tarragon Butter

½ teaspoon canola oil
4 (6-ounce) red snapper fillets or other firm white fish fillets
½ teaspoon salt
⅛ teaspoon paprika
⅛ teaspoon freshly ground black pepper
Cooking spray
2 tablespoons Orange-Tarragon Butter

1. Preheat grill to medium-high heat.
2. Brush oil evenly over fish. Sprinkle fish with salt, paprika, and pepper. Place fish on grill rack coated with cooking spray; grill 3 minutes on each side or until fish flakes easily when tested with a fork or until desired degree of doneness. Cut butter into 4 equal portions; place one portion on top of each fillet. **Yield: 4 servings (serving size: 1 fillet and 1½ teaspoons Orange-Tarragon Butter).**

CALORIES 227; FAT 8.6g (sat 4.1g, mono 2.2g, poly 1.2g); PROTEIN 35g; CARB 0.3g; FIBER 0.1g; CHOL 78mg; IRON 0.3mg; SODIUM 444mg; CALC 58mg

Orange-Tarragon Butter

Use thyme, chives, or rosemary instead of tarragon, if you prefer.

¼ cup butter, softened
1 tablespoon finely chopped fresh tarragon
¼ teaspoon grated orange rind
2 teaspoons fresh orange juice

1. Combine all ingredients in a small bowl. Place butter mixture on a long sheet of plastic wrap, and roll into a 3-inch log, covering completely. Freeze 10 minutes or until firm. **Yield: 8 servings (serving size: 1½ teaspoons butter mixture).**

CALORIES 51; FAT 5.7g (sat 3.6g, mono 1.5g, poly 0.2g); PROTEIN 0.1g; CARB 0.2g; FIBER 0g; CHOL 15mg; IRON 0.0mg; SODIUM 40mg; CALC 3.2mg

kitchen how-to:
make compound butter

Compound butter—butter mixed with other ingredients, such as herbs and acids like wine or citrus juices—adds bright yet rich flavor to meat, poultry, fish, shrimp, or vegetables.

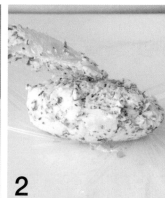

1. Place softened butter and chosen herbs, spices, or other flavorings in a bowl. If you're using salty seasonings, you may want to use unsalted butter to better control the flavor and the amount of sodium in the finished compound butter.
2. Transfer the butter mixture to a long sheet of plastic wrap or wax paper, and roll into a log.
3. Twist the ends of the plastic wrap or wax paper to seal, and freeze for 10 minutes or until firm.

Swordfish Kebabs with Orange-Basil Sauce

Leave a little space between the swordfish pieces on the kebabs so they cook evenly.

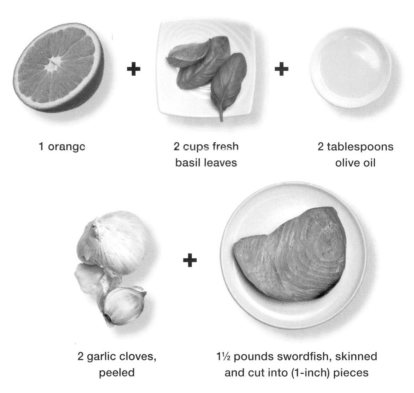

1 orange	**+**	2 cups fresh basil leaves	**+**	2 tablespoons olive oil

2 garlic cloves, peeled	**+**	1½ pounds swordfish, skinned and cut into (1-inch) pieces

Preheat grill to medium-high heat. Squeeze orange to extract ¼ cup juice. Place orange juice, basil leaves, olive oil, and garlic cloves in a mini chopper; add ¼ teaspoon salt. Process basil leaf mixture until finely chopped. Sprinkle ¼ teaspoon salt and ⅛ teaspoon freshly ground black pepper evenly over fish; thread fish onto 4 (12-inch) skewers. Place kebabs on grill rack coated with cooking spray. Grill fish 10 minutes or until fish flakes easily when tested with a fork or until desired degree of doneness, turning occasionally. Drizzle fish with sauce, or serve sauce separately. Garnish sauce with orange rind curls, if desired. **Yield: 4 servings (serving size: 1 kebab and 2 tablespoons sauce).**

CALORIES 280; FAT 14g (sat 2.9g, mono 7.7g, poly 2.6g); PROTEIN 34.3g; CARB 2.8g; FIBER 0.7g; CHOL 66mg; IRON 1.9mg; SODIUM 449mg; CALC 36mg

Skin-On Trout
What it adds: Skin-on fish holds together better on the grill—plus the skin gets deliciously crisp and lightly charred.

Canadian Bacon
What it adds: Also known as back bacon, this lean cut of bacon has a hamlike flavor and less fat compared to other cuts.

Ocean Trout with Coleslaw and Crisp Smoked Bacon

6   (¾-ounce) pieces Canadian bacon
6   (6-ounce) skin-on ocean trout, steelhead trout, or salmon fillets
¼   teaspoon kosher salt
½   teaspoon freshly ground black pepper, divided
Cooking spray
2¼   cups thinly sliced red cabbage
2   cups thinly sliced green cabbage
¾   cup fresh flat-leaf parsley leaves
½   cup thinly sliced red onion
1½   tablespoons white wine vinegar
1   tablespoon extra-virgin olive oil
1   teaspoon Dijon mustard
2   tablespoons canola mayonnaise
⅛   teaspoon kosher salt

1. Preheat grill to medium-high heat.
2. Place bacon on grill rack; grill 1½ minutes on each side or until browned. Remove from grill; set aside.
3. Sprinkle fish evenly with ¼ teaspoon salt and ¼ teaspoon pepper. Arrange fish on grill rack coated with cooking spray; grill 4 minutes on each side or until desired degree of doneness.
4. Combine cabbages, parsley, and onion in a large bowl. Combine vinegar, oil, and mustard in a small bowl, stirring with a whisk; stir in mayonnaise. Add vinegar mixture, ⅛ teaspoon salt, and remaining ¼ teaspoon pepper to cabbage mixture, tossing to coat. Top slaw with bacon just before serving with fish. **Yield: 6 servings (serving size: 1 fillet, ⅔ cup slaw, and 1 bacon piece).**

CALORIES 327; FAT 17.7g (sat 3.4g, mono 8g, poly 5.2g); PROTEIN 35.3g; CARB 5.1g; FIBER 1.6g; CHOL 90mg; IRON 1.5mg; SODIUM 457mg; CALC 51mg

Barbecue Squid

The spice rub and dipping sauce are hot, hot, hot (but quite good). Serve with slices of cucumber and fresh cilantro leaves for a cooling effect in the mouth. Thai chiles are very spicy, so you can use fewer (and increase the mild bell pepper) to tame the heat.

1½ **pounds whole cleaned skinless squid tubes**
 ⅓ **cup chopped red bell pepper**
13 **fresh red Thai chiles, stemmed**
 6 **large garlic cloves**
 3 **large peeled shallots, coarsely chopped**
 1 **(1-inch) piece peeled fresh ginger, coarsely chopped**
 6 **tablespoons sugar**
 2 **tablespoons lower-sodium soy sauce**
1½ **teaspoons freshly ground black pepper**
 ¼ **teaspoon kosher salt**
    Cooking spray

1. Score squid by making 4 (½-inch) crosswise cuts in each tube.
2. Place bell pepper and next 4 ingredients in a food processor; process until finely ground. Stir in sugar, soy sauce, black pepper, and salt. Combine squid and ⅔ cup chile mixture in a large zip-top plastic bag; seal. Marinate in refrigerator 3 hours, turning bag occasionally. Reserve remaining ⅔ cup chile mixture for dipping sauce.
3. Preheat grill to medium heat.
4. Remove squid from bag; discard marinade. Arrange squid in a single layer on grill rack coated with cooking spray. Grill 2 minutes on each side or until charred and squid begins to curl around edges. Serve with reserved sauce. **Yield: 4 servings (serving size: 4½ ounces squid and about 2½ tablespoons sauce).**

CALORIES 263; FAT 2.6g (sat 0.6g, mono 0.2g, poly 1g); PROTEIN 28.1g; CARB 30.9g; FIBER 1.1g; CHOL 396mg; IRON 1.8mg; SODIUM 466mg; CALC 75mg

kitchen how-to: grill squid

Squid, also called calamari, has a briny, slightly sweet flavor when grilled.

1. Score the squid by making 4 (½-inch) crosswise cuts in each tube, cutting into, but not through, to the other side.

2. Arrange the squid in a single layer on a grill rack coated with cooking spray.
3. When grilling squid, a short cook time is key. (If you go too long, it'll end up tough and rubbery.) The squid will begin to curl around the edges when it is nearly done.

shellfish

Shellfish take well to the grill. The sweet, smoky, and slightly charred results are divine.

Smoked Oysters with Olive Relish

If your experience with smoked oysters is limited to the oily, strong-flavored bivalves sold canned, you're in for a revelation. The brininess of the olive- and caper-laced relish echoes the fresh, oceany notes of the oysters. Keep as much of the oysters' juices as possible in the shells while shucking and grilling.

1½ cups hickory wood chips
½ cup chopped pitted kalamata olives
½ cup chopped seeded peeled plum tomato
2 tablespoons chopped fresh basil
2 tablespoons extra-virgin olive oil
1 tablespoon capers
1 tablespoon fresh lemon juice
½ teaspoon freshly ground black pepper
24 large shucked oysters (on the half shell)
12 lemon wedges

1. Soak wood chips in water 1 hour; drain.
2. Combine olives and next 6 ingredients in a small bowl.
3. Remove grill rack, and set aside. Prepare grill for indirect grilling, heating one side to medium-high and leaving one side with no heat. Maintain temperature at 300°. Pierce bottom of a disposable aluminum foil pan several times with the tip of a knife. Place pan on heat element on heated side of grill; add wood chips to pan. Place another disposable aluminum foil pan (do not pierce pan) on unheated side of grill. Pour 2 cups water in pan. Place grill rack on grill. Place oysters on grill rack over foil pan on unheated side, and close lid. Grill 9 minutes; remove oysters from grill. Top each oyster with 1½ teaspoons olive mixture; serve immediately with lemon wedges.
Yield: 6 servings (serving size: 4 topped oysters, 2 tablespoons relish, and 2 lemon wedges).

CALORIES 120; FAT 9.3g (sat 1.5g, mono 6.1g, poly 1.4g); PROTEIN 4.3g; CARB 5.1g; FIBER 0.7g; CHOL 30mg; IRON 3.9mg; SODIUM 373mg; CALC 37mg

kitchen how-to:
shuck oysters

Before shucking, scrub the shell with a stiff-bristled brush, and rinse under cold water to prevent any dirt from getting inside.

1. Hold 1 oyster, flat shell on top, inside a folded kitchen towel (to protect your hands) on a sturdy surface. Work the tip of an oyster knife with a round pointed tip into the hinge.
2. Twist the knife sharply until you hear or feel the hinge snap. Carefully slide the knife around the inside surface of the top shell to separate the oyster from the shell; discard the top shell.
3. Cautiously cut the muscle under the oyster to release it from the bottom shell (leave the oyster on the bottom shell for grilling). Try not to spill any of the tasty oyster juice.

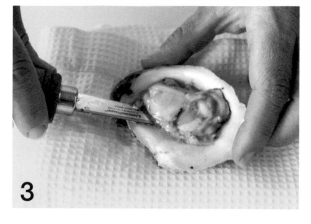

Grilled-Braised Clams and Chorizo in Tomato-Saffron Broth

3 cups hickory wood chips, divided
1½ cups fat-free, lower-sodium chicken broth
1 tablespoon chopped fresh thyme
½ teaspoon saffron threads
¼ teaspoon crushed red pepper
¼ teaspoon freshly ground black pepper
7 garlic cloves, thinly sliced
1 (14.5-ounce) can diced tomatoes, undrained
1 poblano chile
1 ear shucked corn
Cooking spray
4 green onions
1 (6-ounce) link dry-cured Spanish chorizo,
   cut in half lengthwise
24 littleneck clams (about 2½ pounds)
2 tablespoons chopped fresh flat-leaf parsley
1 tablespoon fresh lemon juice
4 (¾-inch-thick) slices Italian or French bread

1. Preheat grill to medium-high heat.
2. Pierce bottom of a disposable foil pan several times with the tip of a knife. Line pan with newspaper or paper towels; place 2 cups wood chips on top of paper in pan.
3. Combine broth and next 6 ingredients in a medium ovenproof saucepan. Place disposable pan on one side of grill rack; ignite newspaper with a long match. Place saucepan on other side of grill rack. Cover grill. Bring sauce to a simmer, and grill 15 minutes. Remove saucepan from grill, and keep warm.
4. Place poblano and corn on grill rack coated with cooking spray. Cover and grill 10 minutes, turning occasionally. Add green onions and chorizo, cut sides down, to grill rack; cover and grill 4 minutes or until poblano is blackened and charred, and corn is lightly charred, turning occasionally. Place poblano in a paper bag; fold to close tightly. Let stand 5 minutes. Peel and discard skins; cut poblano in half lengthwise. Discard stem, seeds, and membranes. Chop poblano, cut kernels from corn cob, slice green onions, and dice chorizo; add to broth mixture.
5. Add remaining 1 cup wood chips to disposable pan. Return saucepan to grill rack. Cover grill, and simmer. Place clams on grill rack. Cover and grill 2 minutes or until clams just begin to open. Discard unopened shells. Add clams to broth mixture; cover and grill 4 minutes or until shells open completely. Remove saucepan from grill; stir in parsley and juice. Cover and keep warm.
6. Place bread on grill rack, and grill 1 to 2 minutes on each side or until toasted. Ladle clam mixture into bowls. Serve with grilled bread. **Yield: 4 servings (serving size: about 6 clams, about 1 cup broth, and 1 bread slice).**

CALORIES 319; FAT 12.7g (sat 4.3g, mono 5.6g, poly 2.2g); PROTEIN 25.5g; CARB 27.6g; FIBER 2g; CHOL 28mg; IRON 13.5mg; SODIUM 500mg; CALC 142mg

kitchen how-to: grill-braise clams

This technique proves that the grill is multi-faceted. In this recipe, ingredients spend time over direct heat, absorb smoky flavor from the wood chips smoldering on one end of the grill, and also spend time braising in an ovenproof saucepan.

1. Preheat the grill to medium-high heat. Add the prepared disposable aluminum foil pan with wood chips on one end. The other end will be used for braising the broth mixture in an ovenproof saucepan, and the area in between the two will be used for direct grilling.
2. Place the clams on the grill rack.
3. Cover and grill the clams 2 minutes or until they just begin to open. Discard any unopened ones—that's a sign they died before they were cooked, and you don't want to consume those.
4. Add the clams to the broth mixture that's simmering in the saucepan.
5. Cover and grill until the clam shells open completely.

Smoky Mussels and Clams with White Wine Broth

Be sure to soak the wood chips in water before adding them to the grill so they'll smolder with flavorful smoke as the shellfish steam. We like the subtle, almost sweet flavor of applewood, though you can try hickory for a more assertive taste. If you're using a gas grill, place the wood chips inside a small disposable aluminum pan; cover with foil, and perforate the foil. Place the container on the cooking grate with the Dutch oven in Step 3.

  1 cup applewood wood chips
  2 tablespoons extra-virgin olive oil
  ⅓ cup chopped shallots
  6 garlic cloves, sliced
  2 cups chopped, seeded, peeled tomato
  ½ cup dry white wine
  3 thyme sprigs
  1 (8-ounce) bottle clam juice
  1½ pounds littleneck clams
  2 pounds mussels, scrubbed and debearded
  8 (½-ounce) slices French bread baguette
Cooking spray
  3 tablespoons butter
  3 tablespoons finely chopped fresh
     flat-leaf parsley
  1 tablespoon chopped fresh thyme

1. Soak wood chips in water 30 minutes; drain well.
2. Preheat grill to medium-high heat.
3. Place wood chips on hot coals. Place a large Dutch oven on grill rack. Close grill lid; heat 2 minutes. Add oil to pan; swirl to coat. Add shallots and garlic to pan; sauté 2 minutes, stirring frequently. Add tomato; close grill lid, and cook 3 minutes. Remove grill lid. Add wine; bring to a boil. Cook 5 minutes or until reduced to 2 tablespoons, stirring occasionally. Add thyme, juice, and clams; close grill lid, and cook 5 minutes. Remove grill lid. Stir in mussels; close grill lid, and cook 5 minutes. Coat bread slices with cooking spray; grill 1 minute on each side or until toasted.

4. Remove clams and mussels from pan using a slotted spoon, reserving cooking liquid in pan; discard any unopened shells. Cover clams and mussels; keep warm. Discard thyme sprigs. Bring reserved cooking liquid to a boil. Cook 15 minutes or until reduced to ¾ cup; remove from heat. Add butter, parsley, and chopped thyme, stirring until smooth. Return mussels and clams to pan; toss to coat. Serve with grilled bread. **Yield: 4 servings (serving size: about 2 cups clams and mussels, about ¼ cup broth, and 2 bread slices).**

CALORIES 402; FAT 19.5g (sat 7.1g, mono 8g, poly 2.3g); PROTEIN 26.6g; CARB 30.6g; FIBER 2g; CHOL 76mg; IRON 14.4mg; SODIUM 773mg; CALC 105mg

kitchen how-to:
scrub and debeard mussels

It takes just a few seconds to scrub and debeard a mussel. Here's how:

1. Using a stiff-bristled brush, scrub each mussel under running water to remove any sand or dirt on the shell.
2. The beards, also called byssal threads, hold the mussels to rocks or pilings when in the water. Grab the fibers with your fingers, and pull them out, tugging toward the hinged point of the shell.

Chile Crabs

Place each crab on its back, and snip off the small pointed flap at the lower part of the shell known as the apron; remove the fat beneath the apron. Rinse the entire crab well, and pat dry. Once cleaned, pop the crabs in the freezer for 30 minutes before marinating them.

- 10 fresh red Thai chiles, stemmed
- 9 large garlic cloves
- ½ medium-sized red bell pepper, chopped
- ⅓ cup ketchup
- 1½ tablespoons sugar
- 1 teaspoon salted bean paste or red miso
- 1 teaspoon fresh lime juice
- 8 (8-ounce) fresh blue crabs, rinsed and aprons removed
- 2 spring onions, trimmed and chopped

Fresh cilantro leaves (optional)

1. Place first 3 ingredients in a food processor; process until finely ground. Stir in ketchup, sugar, bean paste, and juice. Place crabs in a large bowl; top with ½ cup chile mixture. Toss to combine. Set remaining chile mixture aside. Marinate in refrigerator 1 hour.
2. Preheat grill to medium-high heat.
3. Remove crabs from marinade; discard marinade. Arrange crabs, shell sides up, on grill rack; grill 12 minutes or until shells turn red. Serve with remaining chile sauce and onions. Garnish with cilantro, if desired.
Yield: 4 servings (serving size: 2 crabs, ½ onion, and 1 tablespoon sauce).

CALORIES 158; FAT 2g (sat 0.3g, mono 0.3g, poly 0.8g); PROTEIN 20.9g; CARB 14.7g; FIBER 1.1g; CHOL 96mg; IRON 1.5mg; SODIUM 638mg; CALC 133mg

all about blue crabs

Two types of blue crabs are harvested: hard-shell and soft-shell. The meat in the hard-shelled body of the crab is thick and whitish in color, while the leg meat is smaller and flakier. Meat from the two large claws is firm, and there's more of it. The beautiful blue legs and gray body will turn red when grilled. Soft-shells are those that have recently molted, which happens when a crab has outgrown its shell, sheds it, and it is then replaced by a new, larger soft one that will eventually harden.

Grilled Maine Lobsters

8 (1⅛-pound) whole live lobsters
8 lemon wedges
Butter Sauce (optional)

1. Preheat grill to medium-high heat.
2. Plunge a heavy chef's knife through each lobster head just above the eyes, making sure the knife goes all the way through the head. Pull the knife in a downward motion between the eyes.
3. Place lobsters on grill rack; grill 6 minutes on each side or until done. Serve with lemon wedges and, if desired, Butter Sauce. **Yield: 8 servings (serving size: 1 lobster).**

CALORIES 122; FAT 0.7g (sat 0.1g, mono 0.2g, poly 0.1g); PROTEIN 25.2g; CARB 2.2g; FIBER 0.2g; CHOL 88mg; IRON 0.5mg; SODIUM 466mg; CALCIUM 77mg

Butter Sauce

This simple sauce is an emulsion—the end product should have a thick, creamy consistency and the light color of cold butter. It's an indulgent sauce but perfect for pairing with low-fat lobsters and steamed clams.

1 tablespoon fresh lemon juice
6 tablespoons chilled butter, cut into small pieces
Dash of ground red pepper

1. Heat lemon juice in a small saucepan over low heat. Gradually add pieces of butter, stirring constantly with a whisk until butter is melted and well blended. Stir in red pepper. **Yield: 8 servings (serving size: about 1 tablespoon).**

CALORIES 77; FAT 8.6g (sat 5.5g, mono 2.2g, poly 0.3g); PROTEIN 0.1g; CARB 0.2g; FIBER 0.0g; CHOL 23mg; IRON 0.0mg; SODIUM 61mg; CALC 3mg

kitchen how-to:
grill lobsters

If you don't have the grill capacity to cook all the lobsters at once, the relatively brief cooking time makes it easy to do them in batches.

1. Place the lobsters on a grill rack over medium-high heat.
2. Grill 6 minutes on each side or until done. The lobsters will be bright red with a few blackened spots when done cooking.
3. To check doneness, break a lobster open where the tail and body meet—the meat should be opaque and white.

Spicy Shrimp Tacos with Grilled Tomatillo Salsa

Salsa:
½ pound tomatillos
Cooking spray
⅔ cup chopped green onions (about 4 green onions)
¼ cup chopped fresh cilantro
3 tablespoons lime juice (about 1 lime)
¼ teaspoon salt
½ jalapeño pepper, seeds removed and chopped
1 garlic clove, minced

Tacos:
1 pound peeled and deveined medium shrimp
1 tablespoon hot pepper sauce
½ teaspoon ancho chili powder
½ teaspoon ground cumin
¼ teaspoon salt
8 (6-inch) corn tortillas
2 cups shredded cabbage
1 cup shredded carrot

1. Preheat grill to medium-high heat.
2. To prepare salsa, remove husks and stems from tomatillos. Place tomatillos on grill rack coated with cooking spray. Grill 10 minutes or until slightly blackened on each side, turning occasionally. Cool completely; chop. Place tomatillos, onions, and next 5 ingredients in a large bowl; toss to combine.
3. To prepare tacos, thread shrimp evenly on 6 (10-inch) skewers. Place skewers on grill rack coated with cooking spray. Grill 2 minutes or until shrimp are done, turning once. Remove shrimp from skewers, and place in a medium bowl. Add hot pepper sauce, chili powder, cumin, and ¼ teaspoon salt; toss to coat.
4. Heat tortillas on grill 1 minute on each side. Top each tortilla with ¼ cup cabbage and 2 tablespoons carrot. Divide shrimp mixture evenly among tortillas; top each with 2 tablespoons salsa. **Yield: 4 servings (serving size: 2 tacos).**

CALORIES 252; FAT 3.9g (sat 0.5g, mono 0.4g, poly 1.6g); PROTEIN 26.9g; CARB 30.2g; FIBER 5.5g; CHOL 172mg; IRON 3.8mg; SODIUM 507mg; CALC 125mg

kitchen how-to:
easily grill shrimp

If you have one, you can use a grill basket to cook the shrimp instead of threading them onto skewers. It'll save some time on prep, too.

Grilled Fiesta Shrimp

2 pounds peeled and deveined large shrimp
1 tablespoon olive oil
2 teaspoons Creole seasoning, divided
½ cup (2 ounces) preshredded Mexican-blend or cheddar cheese
½ cup drained canned whole-kernel corn with sweet peppers
3 tablespoons chopped fresh cilantro
1 (15-ounce) can black beans, rinsed and drained
4 cups hot cooked long-grain rice

1. Preheat grill to medium-high heat.
2. Arrange shrimp in center of a large piece of heavy-duty aluminum foil. Drizzle oil over shrimp; sprinkle with 1 teaspoon Creole seasoning, tossing to coat. Top shrimp with cheese, corn, cilantro, and beans; sprinkle with remaining 1 teaspoon Creole seasoning. Fold opposite ends of foil together; crimp to seal.
3. Place foil packet on grill rack; cover and cook 15 minutes or until shrimp are done. Serve over hot cooked rice. **Yield: 6 servings (serving size: about ¾ cup shrimp mixture and about ⅔ cup rice).**

CALORIES 391; FAT 8.3g (sat 2.9g, mono 2.6g, poly 1.3g); PROTEIN 37.6g; CARB 40.3g; FIBER 2.9g; CHOL 238mg; IRON 5.6mg; SODIUM 687mg; CALC 160mg

kitchen how-to: grill packets

1

2

The packets are easy to assemble, and they also make cleanup easy.

1. Arrange shrimp in the center of a large piece of heavy-duty aluminum foil. You can also use parchment paper.
2. Drizzle oil over shrimp, and add seasonings, tossing the shrimp to coat. Top with any additional ingredients—vegetables, beans, or fresh herbs.
3. Fold opposite ends of the foil together, and crimp edges to seal securely. You want to make sure all the liquid from the shrimp (and any added vegetables) stays inside the packet to create steam and help cook the ingredients. Place the packets on the grill, and cook until shrimp are done (about 15 minutes).

3

Mango Shrimp Kebabs

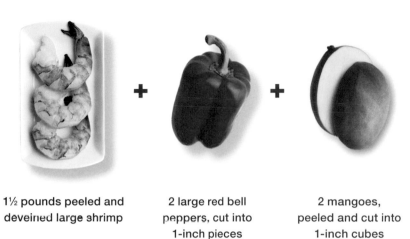

1½ pounds peeled and deveined large shrimp   +   **2 large red bell peppers, cut into 1-inch pieces**   +   **2 mangoes, peeled and cut into 1-inch cubes**

1 small red onion, cut into 1-inch pieces   +   **2 limes, cut into wedges**

Preheat grill to medium-high heat. Sprinkle shrimp evenly with ¼ teaspoon salt and ⅛ teaspoon freshly ground black pepper. Thread shrimp, bell pepper pieces, mango cubes, and onion pieces alternately onto each of 8 (12-inch) skewers. Place kebabs on grill rack coated with cooking spray; grill 2 minutes on each side or until shrimp are done. Squeeze juice from lime wedges over kebabs. **Yield: 4 servings (serving size: 2 kebabs).**

CALORIES 277; FAT 3.3g (sat 0.7g, mono 0.5g, poly 1.2g); PROTEIN 35.8g; CARB 27.1g; FIBER 4.2g; CHOL 259mg; IRON 4.5mg; SODIUM 403mg; CALC 109mg

Grilled Teriyaki Shrimp Kebabs

Tender and juicy, shrimp are a quick pick for a fresh meal.

¼	cup lower-sodium teriyaki sauce
1	tablespoon sesame seeds, toasted
48	large peeled and deveined shrimp (about 1½ pounds)
32	(1-inch) pieces cubed fresh pineapple (about ¾ pound)
1	medium red onion, cut into 8 wedges
	Cooking spray

1. Preheat grill to medium-high heat.

2. Combine teriyaki sauce and sesame seeds in a small bowl.

3. Thread 6 shrimp, 4 pineapple chunks, and 1 onion wedge alternately onto each of 8 (10-inch) skewers. Brush kebabs with teriyaki mixture. Place kebabs on grill rack coated with cooking spray; grill 8 minutes or until shrimp are done, turning once. **Yield: 4 servings (serving size: 2 kebabs).**

CALORIES 254; FAT 4g (sat 0.7g, mono 0.8g, poly 1.6g); PROTEIN 35.6g; CARB 17.6g; FIBER 1.9g; CHOL 259mg; IRON 4.6mg; SODIUM 514mg; CALC 110mg

all about shrimp size

Shrimp come in various sizes, and the terms used to describe them—small, medium, large, jumbo, and colossal—mean different things in different locations. A more universal technique for measuring size is the count or number. If the shrimp are 21–25, that means there are 21 to 25 shrimp per pound.

Cubed Pineapple
What it adds: Grilled pineapple cubes add sweet contrast to the savory flavors in this dish. Use precut pineapple from the produce section at your grocery to save time.

Sauce

What it adds: This simple, stir-together sauce adds salty flavor to the shrimp. You can also brush it over cubed chicken breasts or thighs or use it as a dipping sauce for spring rolls.

vegetables
& fruits

vegetables & fruits

When vegetables and fruits spend time on the grill, the fire caramelizes their natural sugars, and they're suffused by the smoke. The results are simply delicious.

What Works Best

The grill doesn't really discriminate when it comes to vegetables and fruits. A wide variety work, and all leave the fire quickly and easily with enhanced flavor and addicting aroma. Cut the vegetables and fruits in half or into slices to expose the maximum amount of flesh to the grill; this helps them cook quickly and evenly. For smaller pieces, use skewers or a grill basket or tray to keep them from falling in the fire. When grilling a variety of vegetables and fruits at once, you'll likely need to remove them from the grill at different times since they'll cook at different rates—thin asparagus spears will cook less than heartier corn on the cob.

On the Grill

Most vegetables and fruits can handle direct medium-high heat. Time on the grill is relatively short—just enough to get great grill marks and caramelize the sugars. Brushing the produce with oil and coating the grill rack with cooking spray prevents grill-stick and promotes even charring.

Keep it Seasonal

Cooking your vegetables or fruits to perfection without overcharring is an important factor in getting tasty results. Another important factor is using seasonal fruits and vegetables. You simply won't get the absolute peak of flavor outside the season. (For more information about seasonal produce, see the guide on page 308.) Luckily, since many vegetables and fruits take quite well to this technique, there's usually something in season to please your palate.

vegetables

You can grill a wide variety of vegetables, and the results are beautiful grill marks and bright, intense flavors.

kitchen how-to:
grill vegetables

Follow these guidelines for the best results on the grill.

1. Arrange the vegetables in a single layer on the grill rack. You don't want them to overlap or stack on top of each other. The allure of grilled vegetables comes from the flavor and marks created by contact with the grill.

2. Grill vegetables on each side so they're well marked. Smaller vegetables or those that have been sliced will cook more quickly than larger ones.

3. If you're grilling a variety of vegetables of different sizes, add the smaller ones after the larger ones have partially cooked so that they all come off the grill at the same time. Vegetables like corn on the cob and onions will need to cook a bit longer.

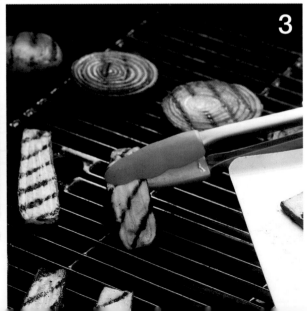

Italian Grilled Zucchini and Red Onion

This simple side dish is tastiest at room temperature, so it's an ideal make-ahead. Any leftovers would be good the next day for lunch with couscous.

1 tablespoon olive oil

4 (½-inch-thick) slices red onion (about 1 large)

2 pounds small zucchini, cut lengthwise into (¼-inch-thick) slices

½ teaspoon kosher salt, divided

½ teaspoon freshly ground black pepper, divided

2 tablespoons red wine vinegar

⅓ cup (about 1½ ounces) shaved fresh Parmigiano-Reggiano cheese

2 tablespoons thinly sliced fresh mint

1. Preheat grill to medium-high heat.

2. Combine first 3 ingredients in a large bowl. Sprinkle zucchini mixture with ¼ teaspoon salt and ¼ teaspoon pepper; toss gently to coat. Arrange vegetables in a single layer on grill rack; grill 4 minutes on each side or until zucchini is tender and vegetables are well marked. Remove zucchini from grill; reduce grill heat to medium-low. Grill onion an additional 5 minutes or until tender. Combine zucchini, onion, and vinegar in a large bowl, tossing to coat. Sprinkle with remaining ¼ teaspoon salt, remaining ¼ teaspoon pepper, cheese, and mint.

Yield: 8 servings (serving size: about ¾ cup).

CALORIES 63; FAT 3.3g (sat 1.2g, mono 1.7g, poly 0.3g); PROTEIN 3.5g; CARB 5.9g; FIBER 1.6g; CHOL 4mg; IRON 0.6mg; SODIUM 215mg; CALC 86mg

Grilled Vegetable Gazpacho

Make this soup up to 2 days ahead, cover, and chill until you're ready to serve. If you prepare it ahead, you may need to stir in a bit of water before serving, as it may thicken slightly as it sits.

- 3 ripe beefsteak tomatoes (about 3 pounds), cored and cut in half crosswise
- 1 onion, sliced crosswise into ¼-inch-thick slices
- ¼ cup extra-virgin olive oil, divided
- 1 (1-ounce) piece French bread baguette, cut into 2 slices
- Cooking spray
- 1 red bell pepper
- 1 jalapeño pepper
- ½ cup water
- 2½ tablespoons fresh lemon juice, divided
- ¾ teaspoon kosher salt, divided
- ¼ teaspoon freshly ground black pepper
- 2 garlic cloves, crushed
- 2 cups thinly sliced, quartered English cucumber
- ¼ cup minced green onions
- 3 tablespoons fresh cilantro leaves

1. Preheat grill to medium-high heat.
2. Brush cut sides of tomatoes and onion slices with 1 tablespoon oil. Lightly coat bread with cooking spray. Place bread on grill rack, and grill 1½ minutes on each side or until toasted. Remove from grill. Place peppers on grill rack coated with cooking spray. Grill 8 minutes or until blistered, turning peppers after 4 minutes. Remove peppers from grill. Place peppers in a small paper bag; fold tightly to seal. Let stand 20 minutes. Arrange onion on grill rack; grill 10 minutes. Turn onion over. Arrange tomatoes, cut sides down, on grill rack; grill onion and tomatoes 10 minutes. Peel and seed peppers.
3. Place 2 tablespoons oil, bread, grilled vegetables, ½ cup water, 2 tablespoons juice, ½ teaspoon salt, black pepper, and garlic in a blender; process until smooth. Combine remaining 1 tablespoon olive oil, remaining 1½ teaspoons lemon juice, remaining ¼ teaspoon salt, cucumber, and remaining ingredients; toss. Ladle about ⅔ cup soup in each of 6 bowls, and top each serving with about ⅓ cup cucumber mixture. **Yield: 6 servings.**

CALORIES 134; FAT 9.4g (sat 1.3g, mono 6.6g, poly 1.1g); PROTEIN 2.2g; CARB 11.5g; FIBER 2.5g; CHOL 0mg; IRON 0.8mg; SODIUM 280mg; CALC 29mg

Jalapeño
What it adds: For more heat, leave the seeds in the jalapeño, or remove them to tame the flames.

French Bread
What it adds: Pureeing the bread with the vegetables helps thicken the soup and adds body.

Grilled Stuffed Jalapeños

The rich and creamy combination of bacon, cream cheese, and cheddar is a nice foil for the muted spice of grilled jalapeño peppers. This recipe is a healthy, fresh alternative to the popular breaded and fried version. If you're making these poppers for a party, stuff the peppers ahead, cover, and chill. Then grill just before your guests arrive.

    2 center-cut bacon slices
    ½ cup (4 ounces) cream cheese, softened
    ½ cup (4 ounces) fat-free cream cheese,
        softened
    ¼ cup (1 ounce) shredded extrasharp
        cheddar cheese
    ¼ cup minced green onions
    1 teaspoon fresh lime juice
    ¼ teaspoon kosher salt
    1 small garlic clove, minced
   14 jalapeño peppers, halved lengthwise
        and seeded
       Cooking spray
    2 tablespoons chopped fresh cilantro
    2 tablespoons chopped seeded tomato

1. Preheat grill to medium-high heat.
2. Cook bacon in a skillet over medium heat until crisp. Remove bacon from pan, and drain on paper towels. Crumble bacon. Combine crumbled bacon, cheeses, and next 4 ingredients in a bowl, stirring to combine. Divide cheese mixture evenly among pepper halves. Place peppers, cheese sides up, on grill rack coated with cooking spray. Cover and grill peppers 8 minutes or until bottoms of peppers are charred and cheese mixture is lightly browned. Place peppers on a serving platter. Sprinkle with cilantro and tomato. **Yield: 14 servings (serving size: 2 pepper halves).**

CALORIES 56; FAT 4.1g (sat 2.2g, mono 1.1g, poly 0.2g); PROTEIN 2.9g; CARB 2.1g;
FIBER 0.5g; CHOL 13mg; IRON 0.2mg; SODIUM 157mg; CALC 55mg

kitchen how-to:
grill small or delicate vegetables

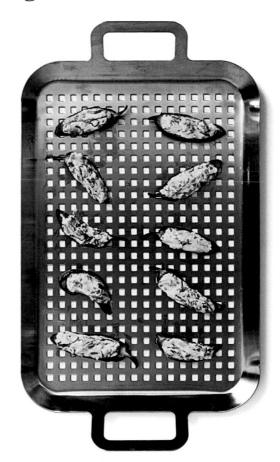

When vegetables are sliced or small, or generally run the risk of falling through the grate, then a grill basket or tray is a good option. It's also ideal for more delicate items (like these stuffed jalapeños) that you don't want to fall over or have to handle too much.

Grilled Farmers' Market Sandwiches

The stack of grilled eggplant, red onion, and zucchini is quite a mouthful but tasty to eat.

2 tablespoons olive oil, divided
8 (½-inch-thick) slices eggplant
2 (½-inch-thick) slices red onion
1 large zucchini, cut lengthwise into 4 pieces
2 teaspoons chopped fresh rosemary
¼ teaspoon freshly ground black pepper
⅛ teaspoon salt
1 tablespoon white balsamic vinegar
4 (2½-ounce) ciabatta bread portions, cut in half horizontally
Cooking spray
4 (1-ounce) slices provolone cheese, halved
8 (¼-inch-thick) slices tomato
8 fresh basil leaves

1. Preheat grill to medium-high heat.
2. Brush 1 tablespoon oil evenly over both sides of eggplant, onion, and zucchini. Sprinkle with rosemary, pepper, and salt.

3. Combine remaining 1 tablespoon oil and vinegar in a bowl. Brush vinegar mixture over cut sides of bread.
4. Place onion on grill rack coated with cooking spray, and grill 6 minutes on each side or until tender. Remove from grill, and separate into rings. Grill eggplant and zucchini 4 minutes on each side or until tender. Cut zucchini pieces in half crosswise.
5. Place bread, cut sides down, on grill rack; grill 2 minutes. Remove from grill. Place 1 piece of cheese on bottom halves of bread portions; top each serving with 1 eggplant slice, 1 tomato slice, 1 basil leaf, 2 pieces zucchini, one-fourth of onion rings, 1 eggplant slice, 1 tomato slice, 1 basil leaf, 1 piece of cheese, and top half of bread. Place sandwiches on grill rack; cover and grill 2 minutes or until cheese melts. **Yield: 4 servings (serving size: 1 sandwich).**

CALORIES 386; FAT 16.2g (sat 5.9g, mono 7.1g, poly 1.1g); PROTEIN 15.8g; CARB 45.5g; FIBER 6.4g; CHOL 20mg; IRON 3.2mg; SODIUM 670mg; CALC 249mg

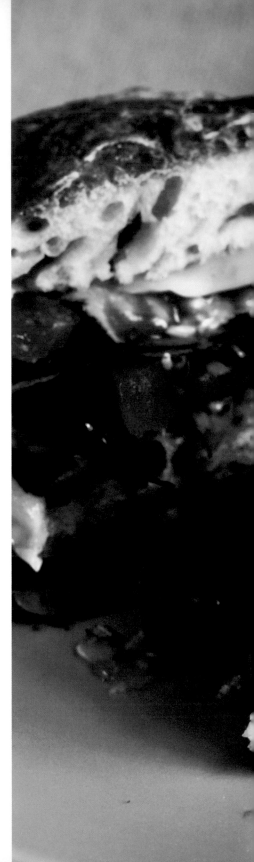

White Balsamic Vinegar

What it adds: White balsamic vinegar is slightly less sweet and a little less syrupy than the darker variety. It also doesn't discolor the bread in this recipe.

Provolone Cheese

What it adds: Provolone has a mild flavor and adds a creamy contrast to the grilled vegetables.

Grilled Asparagus with Caper Vinaigrette

1½	pounds asparagus spears, trimmed
3	tablespoons extra-virgin olive oil, divided
½	teaspoon kosher salt, divided

Cooking spray

1	tablespoon red wine vinegar
½	teaspoon Dijon mustard
¼	teaspoon freshly ground black pepper
1	garlic clove, minced
2	teaspoons capers, coarsely chopped
¼	cup small fresh basil leaves

1. Preheat grill to medium-high heat.

2. Place asparagus in a shallow dish. Add 1 tablespoon oil and ¼ teaspoon salt, tossing well to coat. Place asparagus on grill rack coated with cooking spray; grill 4 minutes or until crisp-tender, turning after 2 minutes.

3. Combine remaining ¼ teaspoon salt, vinegar, and next 3 ingredients; stir with a whisk. Slowly pour remaining 2 tablespoons oil into vinegar mixture, stirring constantly with a whisk. Stir in capers. Arrange asparagus on a serving platter; drizzle with vinaigrette, and sprinkle with basil. **Yield: 6 servings (serving size: about 4 asparagus spears and about 2 teaspoons vinaigrette).**

CALORIES 91; FAT 7.2g (sat 1.1g, mono 5g, poly 1.1g); PROTEIN 2.6g; CARB 4.8g; FIBER 2.5g; CHOL 0mg; IRON 2.5mg; SODIUM 198mg; CALC 32mg

kitchen how-to:
trim asparagus

To prepare asparagus, you'll need to remove the tough woody ends from each spear. A simple way to do this is to bend each spear near the base until it snaps. The asparagus will break where the fibrous part ends and the fresh green vegetable begins, so you won't break off too much or too little.

Grilled Baby Bok Choy

2 baby bok choy   **+**   1 tablespoon
lower-sodium soy sauce

2 teaspoons dark
sesame oil   **+**   ⅛ teaspoon salt

Cut baby bok choy in half lengthwise; place in a large bowl. Drizzle with lower-sodium soy sauce and sesame oil; toss to coat. Arrange bok choy on grill rack coated with cooking spray; grill 2 minutes on each side or until leaves begin to brown. Return bok choy to bowl; cover with plastic wrap. Let stand 3 minutes or until tender. Sprinkle evenly with salt. **Yield: 4 servings (serving size: 1 half).**

CALORIES 23; FAT 2.3g (sat 0.3g, mono 0.9g, poly 1g); PROTEIN 0.3g; CARB 0.4g; FIBER 0.1g; CHOL 0mg; IRON 0mg; SODIUM 227mg; CALC 6mg

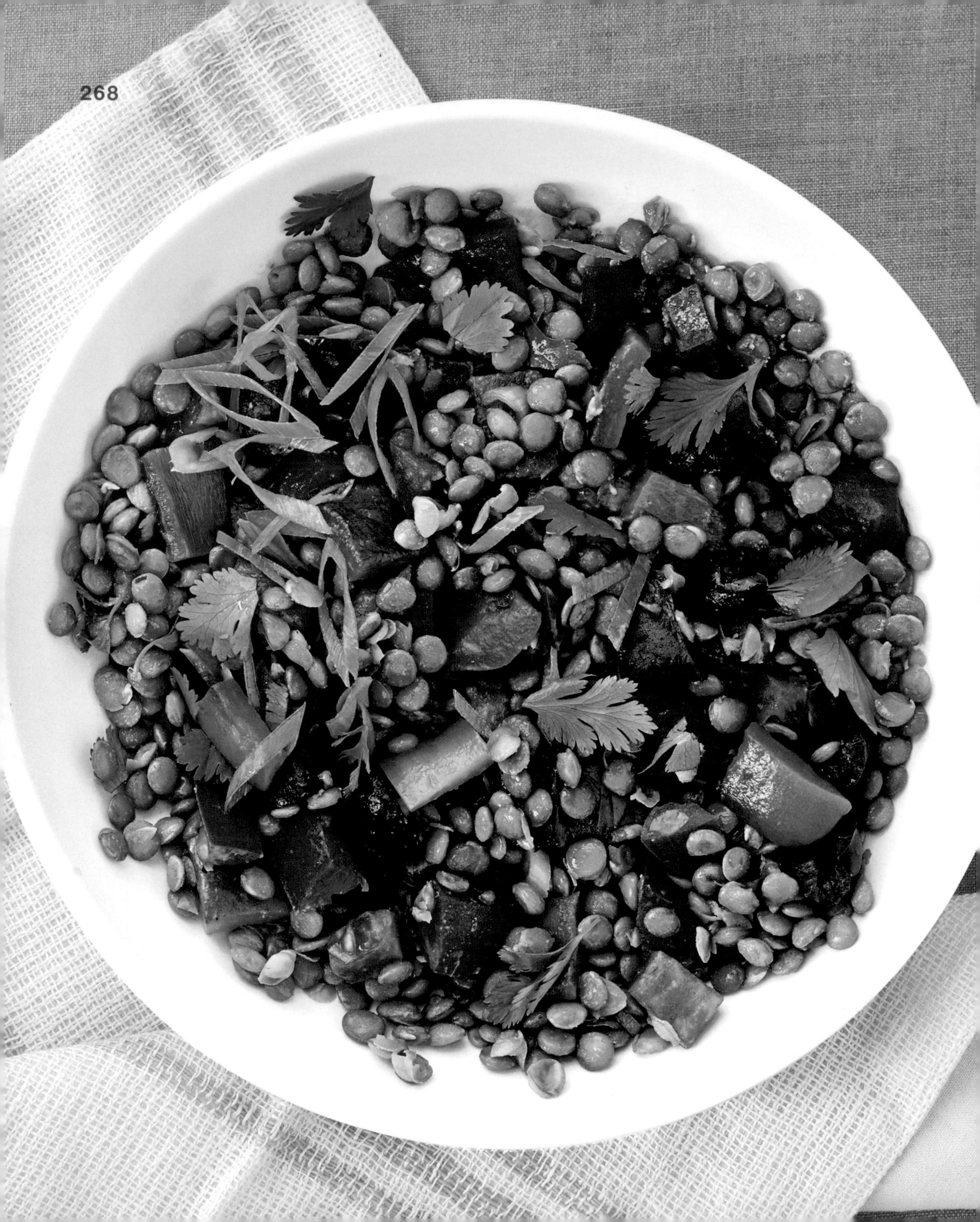

Grilled Peppers and Lentil Salad

        1   red bell pepper, quartered and seeded
        1   green bell pepper, quartered and seeded
        1   yellow bell pepper, quartered and seeded
        Cooking spray
    1⅛   teaspoons salt, divided
      ½   teaspoon freshly ground black pepper, divided
    1½   cups dried lentils (about ¾ pound)
        1   small onion, peeled and halved
        1   bay leaf
      ⅔   cup chopped plum tomato
      ½   cup chopped green onions
      ⅓   cup fresh cilantro leaves
      ⅓   cup fresh lime juice
      ¼   cup chopped pitted kalamata olives
        3   tablespoons extra-virgin olive oil
    1¼   teaspoons ground fennel seeds

1. Preheat grill to high heat.
2. Lightly coat bell pepper pieces with cooking spray. Place bell pepper pieces, skin sides down, on grill rack; grill 12 minutes or until skins are blackened. Place bell pepper pieces in a zip-top plastic bag; seal. Let stand 15 minutes; peel and chop bell peppers. Discard skins. Sprinkle with ½ teaspoon salt and ¼ teaspoon freshly ground black pepper. Place bell peppers in a large bowl.
3. Rinse and drain lentils; place in a large saucepan. Cover with water to 3 inches above lentils; add onion and bay leaf to pan. Bring to a boil. Cover, reduce heat, and simmer 20 minutes or until lentils are just tender. Drain lentils. Discard onion halves and bay leaf. Add lentils to bell peppers. Add remaining ⅝ teaspoon salt, remaining ¼ teaspoon black pepper, tomato, and remaining ingredients to lentil mixture; stir well. **Yield: 6 servings (serving size: 1⅓ cups).**

CALORIES 287; FAT 8.8g (sat 1.1g, mono 5g, poly 1.1g); PROTEIN 15.7g; CARB 41g; FIBER 8.4g; CHOL 0mg; IRON 5mg; SODIUM 596mg; CALC 22mg

kitchen how-to:
grill bell peppers

Grilled peppers are sweet, buttery-tender, and easy to make.

1. Cut the bell peppers in half; discard the seeds and membranes. Coat the peppers with cooking spray.
2. Grill the peppers for 12 minutes or until the skins are blackened.
3. Place the blackened peppers in a zip-top plastic bag, and let stand for 15 minutes. The steam created by the heat from the peppers will help the skins separate from the flesh.
4. The skins can easily be removed from the peppers and then cut.

Grilled Corn on the Cob with Roasted Jalapeño Butter

Charring the jalapeño eases the heat, yielding a versatile, not-too-spicy butter.

1   jalapeño pepper
Cooking spray
7   teaspoons unsalted butter, softened
1   teaspoon grated lime rind
2   teaspoons honey
¼   teaspoon salt
6   ears shucked corn

1. Preheat grill to medium-high heat.
2. Place jalapeño on grill rack coated with cooking spray; cover and grill 10 minutes or until blackened and charred, turning occasionally.
3. Place jalapeño in a small paper bag, and fold tightly to seal. Let stand 5 minutes. Peel and discard skins; cut jalapeño in half lengthwise. Discard stem, seeds, and membranes. Finely chop jalapeño. Combine jalapeño, butter, lime rind, honey, and salt in a small bowl; stir well.
4. Place corn on grill rack. Cover and grill 10 minutes or until lightly charred, turning occasionally. Place corn on serving plate; brush with jalapeño butter.
Yield: 6 servings (serving size: 1 ear corn).

CALORIES 124; FAT 5.5g (sat 3g, mono 1.5g, poly 0.7g); PROTEIN 3g; CARB 19.2g; FIBER 2.5g; CHOL 12mg; IRON 0.5mg; SODIUM 113mg; CALC 4mg

kitchen how-to: grill corn

Grilling is an ideal cooking method for corn on the cob, as it intensifies the vegetable's natural sweetness.

1. Place the corn on a grill rack coated with cooking spray.
2. Grill over medium-high heat for 10 minutes, turning it frequently to ensure one side doesn't get overly charred.

Grilled Corn and Potato Chowder

1 pound small red potatoes, quartered
1 tablespoon salt, divided
3 tablespoons softened butter, divided
4 ears shucked corn
Cooking spray
¾ cup finely chopped onion
⅛ teaspoon ground red pepper
3 cups 2% reduced-fat milk
½ cup half-and-half
2 thyme sprigs
3 tablespoons finely chopped fresh chives
1½ teaspoons chopped fresh thyme
½ teaspoon freshly ground black pepper

1. Preheat grill to medium-high heat.
2. Place a grill basket on grill.
3. Place potatoes and 2 teaspoons salt in a saucepan; cover with water. Bring to a boil; cook 2 minutes. Remove from heat. Let potatoes stand in hot water 5 minutes. Drain; cut into ¼-inch cubes.

4. Melt 1 tablespoon butter; brush evenly over corn. Place corn on grill rack coated with cooking spray. Place potatoes in grill basket coated with cooking spray. Grill corn and potatoes 15 minutes or until slightly charred, turning occasionally. Cool corn slightly; cut kernels from cobs. Place 1 cup corn kernels in a food processor; process until smooth.
5. Melt remaining 2 tablespoons butter in a medium saucepan over medium-high heat. Add onion; sauté 3 minutes, stirring occasionally. Add remaining 1 teaspoon salt and red pepper; cook 30 seconds, stirring frequently. Stir in potatoes, remaining corn kernels, pureed corn, milk, half-and-half, and thyme sprigs; bring to a simmer. Reduce heat; simmer 20 minutes, stirring occasionally. Discard thyme sprigs. Stir in chives and remaining ingredients. **Yield: 6 servings (serving size: 1 cup).**

CALORIES 268; FAT 12.3g (sat 6.6g, mono 2.2g, poly 0.4g); PROTEIN 9.9g; CARB 33.8g; FIBER 3.1g; CHOL 32mg; IRON 1mg; SODIUM 599mg; CALC 214mg

Half-and-half
What it adds: Using just a small amount of full-fat half-and-half with 2% reduced-fat milk as the base adds richness without going overboard on saturated fat.

Pureed Corn
What it adds: Pureeing
a portion of the corn in the
blender helps make this
soup creamy but also ensures
grilled corn flavor in every bite.

Grilled Eggplant Pita Sandwiches with Yogurt-Garlic Spread

You can also serve this sandwich cold the next day for lunch—to prevent the pita from getting soggy, don't assemble until you're ready to eat. We like thick, tangy Greek-style yogurt in this dish.

  2   **(1-pound) eggplants, cut crosswise into ½-inch-thick slices**
3½   **teaspoons kosher salt, divided**
  ½   **cup plain reduced-fat Greek-style yogurt**
  2   **tablespoons fresh lemon juice**
  2   **teaspoons chopped fresh oregano leaves**
  ⅛   **teaspoon black pepper**
  2   **small garlic cloves, minced**
  1   **small red onion, cut into ½-inch-thick slices**
  2   **tablespoons extra-virgin olive oil**
      Cooking spray
  4   **(6-inch) pitas, cut in half**
  2   **cups arugula**

1. Place eggplant slices in a colander; sprinkle with 1 tablespoon salt. Toss well. Drain 30 minutes. Rinse thoroughly; pat dry with paper towels.
2. Combine remaining ½ teaspoon salt, yogurt, and next 4 ingredients in a small bowl.
3. Preheat grill to medium-high heat.
4. Brush eggplant and onion slices with oil. Place eggplant and onion slices on grill rack coated with cooking spray; grill 5 minutes on each side or until vegetables are tender and lightly browned.
5. Fill each pita half with 1½ tablespoons yogurt mixture, one quarter of eggplant slices, one quarter of onion slices, and ¼ cup arugula. **Yield: 4 servings (serving size: 2 pita halves).**

CALORIES 311; FAT 8.2g (sat 1.6g, mono 5g, poly 1.2g); PROTEIN 12.7g; CARB 50.6g; FIBER 9.2g; CHOL 1.7mg; IRON 3.5mg; SODIUM 697mg; CALC 117mg

kitchen how-to:
grill eggplant

Eggplant can be fantastic on the grill, but it can also be overcooked and flavorless, or uncooked with a spongy texture.

1. By salting the eggplant first and allowing it to stand for 30 minutes, the salt will draw out moisture from the eggplant slices.
2. Pat the eggplant dry with paper towels before you put it on the grill. Less moisture will help it crisp up better.
3. Once it goes on the grill, it will emerge full of flavor with a crispy browned exterior and a creamy interior.

Grilled Romaine with Creamy Herb Dressing

1   large head romaine lettuce, trimmed
    and halved lengthwise
2   teaspoons olive oil
Cooking spray
½   teaspoon freshly ground black pepper,
    divided
⅜   teaspoon salt, divided
¼   cup canola mayonnaise
1½ teaspoons chopped fresh dill
1   tablespoon chopped fresh flat-leaf
    parsley
2   tablespoons fresh lemon juice
1   tablespoon water
2   garlic cloves, minced

1. Preheat grill to medium-high heat.
2. Brush cut sides of lettuce evenly with oil. Place lettuce, cut sides down, on grill rack coated with cooking spray, and grill 2 minutes. Remove from heat; cut each lettuce half lengthwise in half again to form 4 quarters. Sprinkle cut sides of lettuce with ¼ teaspoon black pepper and ⅛ teaspoon salt.
3. Combine remaining ¼ teaspoon pepper, remaining ¼ teaspoon salt, mayonnaise, and remaining ingredients in a small bowl, stirring well. Place 1 lettuce quarter on each of 4 salad plates; drizzle each serving with about 4 teaspoons dressing. Serve immediately. **Yield: 4 servings.**

CALORIES 132; FAT 13.4g (sat 1.3g, mono 7.7g, poly 3.3g); PROTEIN 0.7g; CARB 2.7g; FIBER 1g; CHOL 5mg; IRON 0.5mg; SODIUM 325mg; CALC 19mg

kitchen how-to: grill romaine

A brief turn over hot coals wilts hearty romaine lettuce ever so slightly and infuses it with smoky flavor, yielding a special salad that's simple to prepare. Serve with any type of grilled meat, fish, or burgers.

1. Halve each romaine lettuce head, and then brush cut sides evenly with oil.
2. Place the lettuce, cut sides down, on a grill rack coated with cooking spray.
3. It doesn't take long to grill lettuce—just 2 minutes should create a beautiful charring.

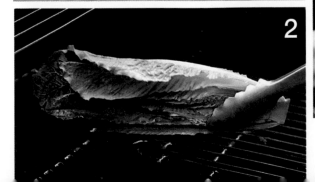

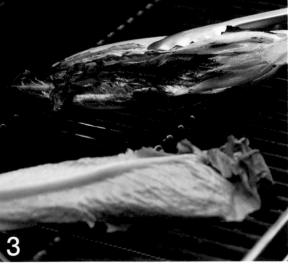

Smoked Chanterelles and Kale

- 2 **cups cedar wood chips**
- 6 **thyme sprigs**
- 3 **rosemary sprigs**
- 1 **pound chanterelle mushrooms, sliced lengthwise**
- 1 **center-cut bacon slice, thinly sliced**
- 1 **tablespoon butter**
- 2 **cups chopped kale**
- ¼ **cup fat-free, lower-sodium chicken broth**
- ¼ **teaspoon kosher salt**
- ⅛ **teaspoon freshly ground black pepper**

1. Prepare grill for indirect grilling, heating one side to high and leaving one side with no heat. Pierce bottom of a disposable aluminum foil pan several times. Place pan on heated side of grill; add wood chips, thyme sprigs, and rosemary sprigs to pan. When chips are smoking, place another foil pan (do not pierce) on unheated side of grill; add mushrooms. Cover and smoke 20 minutes.

2. Cook bacon in a large nonstick skillet over medium heat until crisp. Remove bacon from pan. Increase heat to medium-high. Heat butter in drippings in pan. Add mushrooms to pan; sauté 3 minutes or until tender. Add kale and next 3 ingredients; cook until kale is tender and liquid almost evaporates, stirring occasionally. Sprinkle with bacon. **Yield: 4 servings (serving size: ¾ cup).**

CALORIES 78; FAT 3.6g (sat 2g, mono 0.8g, poly 0.3g); PROTEIN 4.5g; CARB 8.1g; FIBER 1.4g; CHOL 9mg; IRON 1mg; SODIUM 211mg; CALC 67mg

kitchen how-to:
smoke vegetables

This technique generates a lot of smoke and imparts abundant flavor.

1. Indirect heat is a necessary part of the smoking process. Pierce the bottom of a disposable aluminum foil pan several times to allow the heat to easily circulate around the wood chips.

2. Add the wood chips to the pan. (See page 15 for more information about wood chips.) You can also add fresh herbs to the wood chips, if you like to add more depth to the smoked vegetables.

3. When the wood chips are smoking, place the vegetables in an aluminum foil pan (that has not been pierced) on the unheated side of the grill, and cover the grill.

4. The heat will circulate inside the closed grill and gently cook the vegetables while the smoke from the wood chips will infuse the vegetables with flavor.

Smoked Tomatoes

2 **cups wood chips, divided**
Cooking spray
3 **firm ripe tomatoes (about 1½ pounds),
cut in half crosswise and seeded**
2 **teaspoons extra-virgin olive oil**
3 **tablespoons finely chopped fresh parsley**
2 **tablespoons grated fresh Parmesan
cheese**
½ **teaspoon freshly ground black pepper**
¼ **teaspoon salt**
1 **garlic clove, minced**

1. Soak wood chips in water 30 minutes; drain well.
2. Prepare grill for indirect grilling, heating one side
to high and leaving one side with no heat. Place 1 cup
wood chips on hot coals. When chips begin to smoke,
coat grill rack with cooking spray, and place on grill.
Place tomato halves, cut sides down, on unheated
side of grill. Cover and cook 18 minutes or just until
tomatoes are tender. Add additional chips halfway
through cooking time, if necessary.
3. Place tomatoes, cut sides up, on a serving
platter, and drizzle with oil. Combine parsley and
remaining ingredients, and sprinkle over tomatoes.
Serve warm. **Yield: 6 servings (serving size:
1 tomato half).**

CALORIES 47; FAT 2.4g (sat 0.6g, mono 1.4g, poly 0.3g); PROTEIN 1.7g; CARB 5.7g;
FIBER 1.4g; CHOL 1mg; IRON 0.7mg, SODIUM 134mg; CALC 28mg

kitchen how-to:
select the right tomatoes for smoking

Perfectly ripe tomatoes can make all the difference. Very ripe tomatoes will overcook and become
mushy, and underripe ones won't have any flavor.
When buying tomatoes, select those that are still
slightly firm and that smell like a tomato, particularly
at the stem end.

Smoky Tomatillo Salsa

2   garlic cloves
2   jalapeño peppers
1   green bell pepper, halved and seeded
1   pound tomatillos, husks and stems removed
Cooking spray
1   cup coarsely chopped onion
⅓   cup chopped fresh cilantro
3   tablespoons chopped green onions
2   tablespoons fresh lime juice
½   teaspoon sugar
½   teaspoon salt

1. Preheat grill to medium-high heat.
2. Thread garlic cloves onto a 6-inch skewer. Arrange skewer, peppers, and tomatillos on grill rack coated with cooking spray; grill 8 minutes or until blackened, turning frequently. Remove seeds from jalapeño peppers. Place garlic, peppers, tomatillos, onion, and remaining ingredients in a food processor; process until finely chopped. **Yield: 7 servings (serving size: about ⅓ cup).**

CALORIES 41; FAT 0.7g (sat 0.1g, mono 0.1g, poly 0.3g); PROTEIN 1.2g; CARB 8.6g; FIBER 2.1g; CHOL 0mg; IRON 0.6mg; SODIUM 171mg; CALC 19mg

kitchen how-to: make smoky tomatillo salsa

For even smokier taste, add ¼ teaspoon Spanish smoked paprika to this mixture. Serve with tortilla chips, grilled chicken, or pork.

1. Grilling garlic produces amazing flavor, but you'll need to thread the cloves onto a skewer to prevent them from falling through the grate.
2. Grill the garlic, peppers, and tomatillos until they're blackened.
3. Process the grilled vegetables, raw vegetables, and seasonings until finely chopped.

Red Potatoes

What they add: These small, waxy potatoes are ideal for potato salad because of their firm texture. They hold their shape well and don't get mushy when mixed with the other ingredients.

Cornichons

What they add: A cornichon is the French version of a gherkin. You'll find these small, tart pickles in gourmet grocery stores; otherwise, gherkins will work just fine. Or, you can substitute 1 tablespoon drained capers for the pickles.

Potato Salad with Herbs and Grilled Summer Squash

Salad:

2 pounds small red potatoes
¾ pound yellow squash, cut lengthwise into ½-inch slices
Cooking spray
¼ teaspoon kosher salt
⅛ teaspoon freshly ground black pepper

Dressing:

⅓ cup chopped fresh chives
3 tablespoons chopped fresh parsley
2 tablespoons chopped fresh basil
1 tablespoon chopped fresh tarragon
¼ teaspoon grated lemon rind
3 tablespoons fresh lemon juice
2 tablespoons water
2 tablespoons extra-virgin olive oil
2 tablespoons finely chopped cornichons
¼ teaspoon kosher salt
⅛ teaspoon freshly ground black pepper

1. Preheat grill to medium-high heat.

2. To prepare salad, place potatoes in a large saucepan; cover with water. Bring to a boil. Reduce heat, and simmer 18 minutes or until tender. Drain; cut potatoes into quarters, and place in a large bowl. Set aside.

3. Lightly coat squash with cooking spray. Sprinkle evenly with ¼ teaspoon salt and ⅛ teaspoon pepper. Place squash on grill rack; grill 2 minutes on each side or until browned and tender. Remove squash from heat, and add to potatoes.

4. To prepare dressing, combine chives and remaining ingredients in a small bowl; stir with a whisk. Pour dressing over potato mixture, tossing gently to combine. Serve salad warm or chilled. **Yield: 6 servings (serving size: 1 cup).**

CALORIES 160; FAT 5g (sat 0.8g, mono 3.4g, poly 0.8g); PROTEIN 3.8g; CARB 27g; FIBER 3.4g; CHOL 0mg; IRON 1.5mg; SODIUM 206mg; CALC 33mg

Plank-Grilled Zucchini with Couscous, Spinach, and Feta Stuffing

2	(15 x 6½ x ⅜–inch) cedar grilling planks
2¼	cups organic vegetable broth
½	cup chopped shallots (about 1 large)
1	(10-ounce) package frozen chopped spinach, thawed and drained
¾	cup uncooked couscous
½	cup (2 ounces) diced feta cheese
¼	cup chopped fresh mint
2	teaspoons grated lemon rind
3	tablespoons fresh lemon juice
1	tablespoon extra-virgin olive oil
¼	teaspoon freshly ground black pepper
6	medium zucchini (about 2 pounds)
½	teaspoon kosher salt

1. Soak planks in water 1 hour; drain.

2. Preheat grill to medium-high heat.

3. Place broth in a large skillet over medium-high heat; bring to a boil. Add shallots and spinach; cook 5 minutes. Stir in couscous. Remove from heat; cover and let stand 5 minutes. Stir in cheese and next 5 ingredients.

4. Cut each zucchini in half lengthwise; scoop out pulp, leaving a ¼-inch-thick shell. Sprinkle salt evenly over zucchini. Spoon about ⅔ cup stuffing into each zucchini half.

5. Place planks on grill rack; grill 3 minutes or until lightly charred. Turn planks over; place zucchini on charred sides of planks. Cover; grill 12 minutes or until tender. **Yield: 6 servings (serving size: 2 stuffed zucchini halves).**

CALORIES 192; FAT 5.8g (sat 2.4g, mono 2.3g, poly 0.7g); PROTEIN 8.7g; CARB 28.7g; FIBER 4.5g; CHOL 11mg; IRON 2mg; SODIUM 564mg; CALC 172mg

Cedar Planks
What they add: Cedar planks lend this dish a pleasant smokiness. If you don't have planks, cook the zucchini halves directly on the grill. (See page 219 for more information about plank grilling.)

Zucchini

What it adds: Zucchini has a mild flavor, which pairs well with the seasoned stuffing. Use zucchini with some heft; if it's too thin, it may get too soft.

way to grill

fruits

The high sugar content of fruits produces delicious results on the grill. The fire caramelizes the sugars, intensifying the sweetness and creating a lovely caramelized exterior.

kitchen how-to: grill fruits

Grilled fruits are perfect as a side dish or served over ice cream for an easy dessert.

1. Depending on the fruit, you'll need to cut it in half or in slices to expose the skin to the grill. For smaller pieces, use skewers or a grill basket.

2. Brush the fruit with oil or coat with cooking spray to keep it from sticking to the grill. A sweet glaze made with honey or sugar is also a delicious addition and will create a thin crust when grilled.

3. Arrange the fruit, cut sides down, in a single layer on the grill rack, and grill.

Mixed Greens with Grilled Apricots and Prosciutto

1 tablespoon olive oil
1 teaspoon honey
6 apricots (about ¾ pound), halved and pitted
Cooking spray
⅛ teaspoon black pepper
1 ounce prosciutto
9 cups mixed greens
¼ cup blush wine vinaigrette
¼ cup sliced almonds, toasted
1 teaspoon chopped fresh thyme

1. Preheat grill to medium-high heat.
2. Combine olive oil and honey; brush over cut sides of apricots. Arrange apricots, cut sides down, on grill rack coated with cooking spray. Grill 2 minutes or until apricots are well marked. Remove from grill; sprinkle with black pepper.
3. Heat a medium nonstick skillet over medium heat. Add prosciutto, and cook 2 to 3 minutes or until crisp.
4. Place 1½ cups greens on each of 6 plates. Top evenly with apricot halves, prosciutto, and vinaigrette. Sprinkle with almonds and thyme. **Yield: 6 servings.**

CALORIES 128; FAT 7.3g (sat 0.8g, mono 3.3g, poly 1.1g); PROTEIN 3.7g; CARB 13.8g; FIBER 2.3g; CHOL 3mg; IRON 1.3mg; SODIUM 233mg; CALC 64mg

Marinated Grilled Apples with Mint

Serve these highly flavored apple rings as a
side with pork or chicken. This recipe is wonderful
with Granny Smiths. For a dessert version,
use Pink Lady apples, and serve with light ice
cream. Or use a combination of the two for
color and flavor variation.

 ⅔ **cup fresh orange juice**
 1 **tablespoon chopped fresh mint**
 2 **tablespoons honey**
 1 **teaspoon vanilla extract**
 ½ **teaspoon ground ginger**
 ¼ **teaspoon freshly ground black pepper**
 3 **Granny Smith or Pink Lady apples,**
  cored and each cut crosswise into
  4 (½-inch) slices
 Cooking spray

1. Combine first 6 ingredients in a large zip-top plastic
bag. Add apple slices; seal and marinate in refrigerator
1 to 2 hours, turning bag occasionally.
2. Preheat grill to medium-high heat.
3. Remove apple from bag, reserving marinade. Place
apple slices on grill rack coated with cooking spray;
grill 2 to 3 minutes on each side, turning and basting
frequently with reserved marinade. Arrange apple slices
on a platter; drizzle with remaining marinade. **Yield:
4 servings (serving size: 3 apple slices).**

CALORIES 116; FAT 0.5g (sat 0.1g, mono 0g, poly 0.1g); PROTEIN 0.6g; CARB 29.3g;
FIBER 3g; CHOL 0mg; IRON 0.4mg; SODIUM 1mg; CALC 14mg

kitchen how-to:
core apples

If you won't be using the apple slices right away,
sprinkle them with lemon juice to prevent browning.
Pierce the center of the fruit with an apple corer, and
rotate the apple to remove the core. Use a paring knife
to slice the apple.

Caramelized Fresh Figs with Sweet Cream

Honey-coated figs caramelize on the grill to star in this simple dessert.

  2 teaspoons honey
  8 large fresh figs, cut in half lengthwise
  Cooking spray
  ¼ cup crème fraîche
  ½ teaspoon sugar

1. Preheat grill to high heat.
2. Brush honey on cut sides of figs. Lightly spray cut sides of figs with cooking spray.
3. Place figs, cut sides down, on grill rack, and grill 3 minutes or until grill marks appear. Remove from grill. Combine crème fraîche and ½ teaspoon sugar; spoon over figs. **Yield: 4 servings (serving size: 4 fig halves and 1 tablespoon sauce).**

CALORIES 159; FAT 5.6g (sat 3.3g, mono 1.7g, poly 0.4g); PROTEIN 1.4g; CARB 28g; FIBER 3.7g; CHOL 14mg; IRON 0.5mg; SODIUM 6mg; CALC 45mg

Crème Fraîche
What it adds: This rich cream has a slightly sour taste and velvety smooth texture. Just a little can go a long way.

Honey
What it adds: The honey brushed on the figs caramelizes on the grill, adding a sweet crunch.

Grilled Mango and Avocado

This dish features a Vietnamese-style sauce known as *nuoc cham* [noo-ahk CHAHM] that traditionally includes fish sauce, lime juice, chiles, and sugar. Your avocados should be ripe but still slightly firm so they'll slice easily and not break apart as they grill. Leaving the skin on helps them maintain their shape—remove the skin before serving, if you like.

¼ cup water
1 teaspoon sugar
2 tablespoons fresh lime juice (about 1 lime)
1 tablespoon fish sauce
1 small garlic clove, minced
2 ripe unpeeled avocados, halved
2 peeled mangoes, each cut into 6 wedges
Cooking spray
12 lime wedges
6 large Bibb lettuce leaves
Chopped fresh cilantro (optional)

1. Combine first 5 ingredients in a small bowl.
2. Preheat grill to medium-high heat.
3. Cut avocado halves into thirds lengthwise. Brush marinade over mango and avocado wedges; coat with cooking spray. Arrange in a single layer on grill rack coated with cooking spray. Coat lime wedges with cooking spray; place on grill rack. Grill fruit 2 minutes on each side or until marked but not soft, basting frequently with marinade.
4. Place 1 lettuce leaf on each of 6 salad plates; top each leaf with 2 mango wedges, 2 lime wedges, and 2 avocado wedges. Sprinkle with cilantro, if desired.
Yield: 6 servings.

CALORIES 162; FAT 10.1g (sat 1.5g, mono 6.6g, poly 1.3g); PROTEIN 2.1g; CARB 19.8g; FIBER 6g; CHOL 0mg; IRON 0.7mg; SODIUM 239mg; CALC 24mg

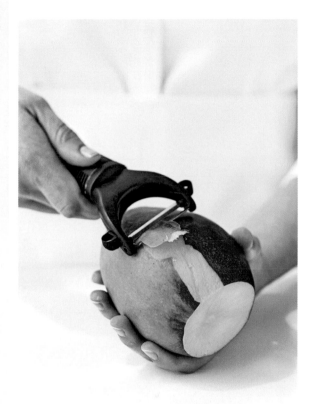

kitchen how-to:
peel & cut mangoes

Mangoes have a bright, fresh flavor. Their bright orange flesh is loaded with vitamins A and C and contains a healthy dose of fiber. To prepare them, use a vegetable peeler to easily remove the skin. They have a large, flat seed in the center that you'll need to cut around, and then cut them to the desired shape and size.

Grilled Peaches with Amaretto-Pecan Caramel Sauce

1 cup granulated sugar
⅓ cup water
½ cup apple cider
2 tablespoons amaretto (almond-flavored liqueur)
1 teaspoon chilled butter
⅓ cup chopped pecans, toasted
6 firm ripe peaches (about 3 pounds), halved
   and pitted
1 tablespoon brown sugar
¼ teaspoon salt
   Cooking spray

1. Preheat grill to medium-high heat.
2. Combine granulated sugar and ⅓ cup water in a medium, heavy saucepan over medium-high heat; cook until sugar dissolves, stirring gently as needed to dissolve sugar evenly. Continue cooking 8 minutes or until golden brown (do not stir); gently tilt pan and swirl mixture until evenly brown. Remove from heat. Slowly add cider, amaretto, and butter, stirring constantly with a long-handled wooden spoon (mixture will bubble vigorously). Cook over medium-low heat 5 minutes or until smooth. Stir in pecans. Remove from heat.
3. Sprinkle cut sides of peaches evenly with brown sugar and salt. Place peaches, cut sides up, on grill rack coated with cooking spray; grill 2 minutes on each side or until tender. Serve warm with sauce.
Yield: 6 servings (serving size: 2 peach halves and about 3 tablespoons sauce).

CALORIES 269; FAT 5.8g (sat 0.8g, mono 3g, poly 1.6g); PROTEIN 2g; CARB 55g; FIBER 3g; CHOL 2mg; IRON 0.6mg; SODIUM 106mg; CALC 17mg

kitchen how-to: make caramel sauce

Caramel is nothing more than melted, browned sugar; we add water to hasten the melting process and reduce the risk of burning the sugar.

1. Combine granulated sugar and ⅓ cup water in a medium, heavy saucepan over medium-high heat; cook until sugar dissolves, stirring gently as needed to dissolve sugar evenly.

2. Continue cooking without stirring until the sugar mixture is golden brown. Gently tilt the pan and swirl the mixture until it is evenly brown.
3. Remove from heat. Slowly add cider, amaretto, and butter, stirring constantly with a long-handled wooden spoon (mixture will bubble vigorously). Cook over medium-low heat 5 minutes or until smooth. Stir in pecans. Remove from heat.

Grilled Summer Stone Fruit with Cherry-Port Syrup

Syrup:
1¾ cups ruby port or other sweet red wine
⅔ cup sugar
¼ cup dried tart cherries
2 tablespoons red wine vinegar

Fruit:
2 apricots, halved and pitted
2 peaches, halved and pitted
2 nectarines, halved and pitted
2 plums, halved and pitted
1½ tablespoons canola oil
1 tablespoon sugar
¼ teaspoon ground cinnamon
Cooking spray

1. To prepare syrup, combine first 4 ingredients in a medium saucepan over medium-high heat; bring to a boil. Cook 10 minutes or until slightly syrupy. Cover and set aside.
2. Preheat grill to medium-high heat.
3. To prepare fruit, brush outsides of apricots, peaches, nectarines, and plums with oil, and sprinkle cut sides of fruit evenly with 1 tablespoon sugar and cinnamon. Place fruit on grill rack coated with cooking spray. Grill 4 minutes on each side or until tender. Place fruit on a cutting board; cool 5 minutes. Cut each fruit half into 2 wedges. Divide fruit evenly among 8 bowls. Drizzle with syrup. Serve immediately. **Yield: 8 servings (serving size: 4 fruit wedges and 3 tablespoons syrup).**

CALORIES 200; FAT 2.8g (sat 0.2g, mono 1.7g, poly 0.8g); PROTEIN 0.9g; CARB 36.2g; FIBER 2g; CHOL 0mg; IRON 0.4mg; SODIUM 4mg; CALC 10mg

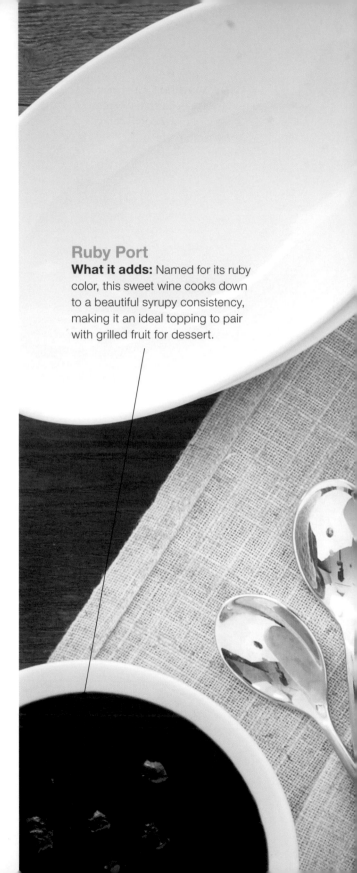

Ruby Port
What it adds: Named for its ruby color, this sweet wine cooks down to a beautiful syrupy consistency, making it an ideal topping to pair with grilled fruit for dessert.

Stone Fruit

What it adds: Firm stone fruit will maintain its shape when grilled. Use any combination of fruit you prefer.

Rum-Spiked Grilled Pineapple with Toasted Coconut

¼ cup packed brown sugar
¼ cup dark spiced rum
1 pineapple (about 1½ pounds), peeled, cored, halved lengthwise, and sliced lengthwise into 12 wedges
1 tablespoon butter
2 tablespoons sweetened flaked coconut, toasted
3 cups light vanilla ice cream

1. Combine sugar and rum in a microwave-safe bowl. Microwave at HIGH 1½ minutes or until sugar dissolves. Brush rum mixture evenly over pineapple wedges.
2. Melt butter in a grill pan over medium-high heat. Add pineapple to pan; grill 3 minutes on each side or until grill marks form and pineapple is thoroughly heated. Sprinkle with coconut. Serve with ice cream. **Yield: 6 servings (serving size: 2 pineapple wedges, 1 teaspoon coconut, and ½ cup ice cream).**

CALORIES 258; FAT 6.2g (sat 3.9g, mono 1.5g, poly 0.3g); PROTEIN 4.3g; CARB 44.4g; FIBER 2g; CHOL 26mg; IRON 0.6mg; SODIUM 79mg; CALC 146mg

kitchen how-to:
cut fresh pineapples

Fresh pineapples should be slightly soft to the touch, but avoid those with overly soft or dark areas on the skin, which is a sign of over-ripeness.

1. Cut off the leafy top—called the plume—and the base.
2. Stand the pineapple upright, and cut down the sides of the pineapple to remove the prickly rind. Try to remove as little flesh as possible.
3. While the pineapple is upright, cut it into thirds, carefully slicing downward around the fibrous core.

Grilled Pineapple-Avocado Salsa

1 tablespoon olive oil
1 tablespoon honey
1 pineapple, peeled, cored, and cut into ½-inch-thick slices
Cooking spray
⅓ cup finely chopped red onion
¼ cup minced fresh cilantro
1 tablespoon fresh lime juice
½ teaspoon salt
½ teaspoon ground red pepper
¼ teaspoon ground cumin
1 serrano chile, minced
1 avocado

1. Preheat grill to high heat.
2. Combine oil and honey, stirring well. Brush oil mixture over pineapple. Place pineapple on grill rack coated with cooking spray; grill 2 minutes on each side or until golden. Remove from grill; cool 5 minutes. Chop. Combine pineapple, onion, and next 6 ingredients; toss gently.
3. Peel, seed, and dice avocado. Add avocado to pineapple mixture, and toss gently. **Yield: 6 servings (serving size: ½ cup).**

CALORIES 166; FAT 7.5g (sat 1.1g, mono 5g, poly 0.9g); PROTEIN 1.7g; CARB 26.8g; FIBER 4.6g; CHOL 0mg; IRON 0.7mg; SODIUM 201mg; CALC 27mg

Ground Red Pepper
What it adds: A half teaspoon of this spice amps up the heat index of this salsa. Use less, if you like.

Avocado

What it adds: The creaminess of the avocado provides a nice contrast to the sweetness of the pineapple and the heat from the red pepper. It also provides healthy unsaturated fats.

Grilled Plantains

3   **soft black plantains (about 1½ pounds), unpeeled**
2   **tablespoons butter, melted**
1   **teaspoon brown sugar**
⅛   **teaspoon ground red pepper**
Cooking spray
6   **lime wedges**

1. Preheat grill to medium heat.
2. Cut plantains in half lengthwise. Cut plantain halves in half crosswise. Combine butter, sugar, and pepper; brush evenly over cut sides of plantain sections.
3. Place plantain sections, cut sides up, on grill rack coated with cooking spray; grill 7 minutes or until flesh is soft and skins begin to pull away from the flesh. Turn plantain sections over; grill 3 minutes. Serve warm with lime wedges. **Yield: 6 servings (serving size: 2 plantain sections and 1 lime wedge).**

CALORIES 174; FAT 4.3g (sat 2.6g, mono 1.2g, poly 0.2g); PROTEIN 1.5g; CARB 36.7g; FIBER 2.6g; CHOL 10mg; IRON 0.7mg; SODIUM 44mg; CALC 5mg

all about plantains

Plantains usually have less sugar and are firmer than common bananas. And while bananas can and often are eaten raw, plantains are generally cooked. You'll usually find them in your supermarket when they are just beginning to turn black. Let them sit at room temperature for a few days until they turn black and feel soft when lightly pressed, which are signs they're ripe. Black plantains are extremely ripe, and their deep yellow pulp is much sweeter than immature green-skinned ones.

Ingredient Substitution Guide

If you're right in the middle of cooking and realize you don't have
a particular ingredient, refer to the substitutions in this list.

Ingredient	Substitution
Fruits and Vegetables	
Lemon, 1 medium	2 to 3 tablespoons juice and 2 teaspoons grated rind
Juice, 1 teaspoon	½ teaspoon vinegar
Peel, dried	2 teaspoons freshly grated lemon rind
Orange, 1 medium	½ cup juice and 2 tablespoons grated rind
Tomatoes, fresh, chopped, 2 cups	1 (16-ounce) can (may need to drain)
Tomato juice, 1 cup	½ cup tomato sauce and ½ cup water
Tomato sauce, 2 cups	¾ cup tomato paste and 1 cup water
Miscellaneous	
Broth, beef or chicken, canned, 1 cup	1 bouillon cube dissolved in 1 cup boiling water
Chile paste, 1 teaspoon	¼ teaspoon hot red pepper flakes
Chili sauce, 1 cup	1 cup tomato sauce, ¼ cup brown sugar, 2 tablespoons vinegar, ¼ teaspoon ground cinnamon, dash of ground cloves, and dash of ground allspice
Tahini (sesame seed paste), 1 cup	¾ cup creamy peanut butter and ¼ cup sesame oil
Vinegar, cider, 1 teaspoon	2 teaspoons lemon juice mixed with a pinch of sugar
Seasonings	
Bay leaf, 1 whole	¼ teaspoon crushed bay leaf
Chives, chopped, 1 tablespoon	1 tablespoon chopped green onion tops
Garlic, 1 clove	1 teaspoon bottled minced garlic
Ginger	
Crystallized, 1 tablespoon	⅛ teaspoon ground ginger
Fresh, grated, 1 tablespoon	⅛ teaspoon ground ginger
Herbs, fresh, 1 tablespoon	1 teaspoon dried herbs or ¼ teaspoon ground herbs (except rosemary)
Lemongrass, 1 stalk, chopped	1 teaspoon grated lemon zest
Mint, fresh, chopped, 3 tablespoons	1 tablespoon dried spearmint or peppermint
Mustard, dried, 1 teaspoon	1 tablespoon prepared mustard
Parsley, fresh, chopped, 1 tablespoon	1 teaspoon dried parsley

Nutritional Analysis

How to Use It and Why

Glance at the end of any *Cooking Light* recipe, and you'll see how committed we are to helping you make the best of today's light cooking. With chefs, registered dietitians, home economists, and a computer system that analyzes every ingredient we use, *Cooking Light* gives you authoritative dietary detail like no other magazine. We go to such lengths so you can see how our recipes fit into your healthful eating plan. If you're trying to lose weight, the calorie and fat figures will probably help most. But if you're keeping a close eye on the sodium, cholesterol, and saturated fat in your diet, we provide those numbers, too. And because many women don't get enough iron or calcium, we can also help there, as well. Finally, there's a fiber analysis for those of us who don't get enough roughage.

Here's a helpful guide to put our nutritional analysis numbers into perspective. Remember, one size doesn't fit all, so take your lifestyle, age, and circumstances into consideration when determining your nutrition needs. For example, pregnant or breast-feeding women need more protein, calories, and calcium. And women older than 50 need 1,200mg of calcium daily, 200mg more than the amount recommended for younger women and men.

We Use These Abbreviations in Our Nutritional Analysis

sat saturated fat
mono monounsaturated fat
poly polyunsaturated fat
CARB carbohydrates

CHOL cholesterol
CALC calcium
g gram
mg milligram

Daily Nutrition Guide

	Women Ages 25 to 50	Women over 50	Men over 24
Calories	2,000	2,000 or less	2,700
Protein	50g	50g or less	63g
Fat	65g or less	65g or less	88g or less
Saturated Fat	20g or less	20g or less	27g or less
Carbohydrates	304g	304g	410g
Fiber	25g to 35g	25g to 35g	25g to 35g
Cholesterol	300mg or less	300mg or less	300mg or less
Iron	18mg	8mg	8mg
Sodium	2,300mg or less	1,500mg or less	2,300mg or less
Calcium	1,000mg	1,200mg	1,000mg

The nutritional values used in our calculations either come from The Food Processor, Version 8.9 (ESHA Research), or are provided by food manufacturers.

Seasonal Produce Guide

When you use fresh fruits, vegetables, and herbs, you don't have to do much to make them taste great. Although many fruits, vegetables, and herbs are available year-round, you'll get better flavor and prices when you buy what's in season. The Seasonal Produce Guide below helps you choose the best produce so you can create sensational meals all year long.

Spring

Fruits
Bananas
Blood oranges
Coconuts
Grapefruit
Kiwifruit
Lemons
Limes
Mangoes
Navel oranges
Papayas
Passionfruit
Pineapples
Strawberries
Tangerines
Valencia oranges

Vegetables
Artichokes
Arugula
Asparagus
Avocados
Baby leeks
Beets
Belgian endive
Broccoli
Cauliflower
Dandelion
  greens
Fava beans
Green onions
Green peas
Kale
Lettuce
Mushrooms
Radishes
Red potatoes
Rhubarb
Snap beans
Snow peas
Spinach
Sugar snap peas
Sweet onions
Swiss chard

Herbs
Chives
Dill
Garlic chives
Lemongrass
Mint
Parsley
Thyme

Summer

Fruits
Blackberries
Blueberries
Boysenberries
Cantaloupes
Casaba melons
Cherries
Crenshaw melons
Grapes
Guava
Honeydew melons
Mangoes
Nectarines
Papayas
Peaches
Plums
Raspberries
Strawberries
Watermelons

Vegetables
Avocados
Beets
Bell peppers
Cabbage
Carrots
Celery
Chile peppers
Collards
Corn
Cucumbers
Eggplant
Green beans
Jicama
Lima beans
Okra
Pattypan squash
Peas
Radicchio
Radishes
Summer squash
Tomatoes

Herbs
Basil
Bay leaves
Borage
Chives
Cilantro
Dill
Lavender
Lemon balm
Marjoram
Mint
Oregano
Rosemary
Sage
Summer savory
Tarragon
Thyme

Autumn

Fruits
Apples
Cranberries
Figs
Grapes
Pears
Persimmons
Pomegranates
Quinces

Vegetables
Belgian endive
Bell peppers
Broccoli
Brussels
  sprouts
Cabbage
Cauliflower
Eggplant
Escarole
Fennel
Frisée
Leeks
Mushrooms
Parsnips
Pumpkins
Red potatoes
Rutabagas
Shallots
Sweet potatoes
Winter squash
Yukon gold
  potatoes

Herbs
Basil
Bay leaves
Parsley
Rosemary
Sage
Tarragon
Thyme

Winter

Fruits
Apples
Blood oranges
Cranberries
Grapefruit
Kiwifruit
Kumquats
Lemons
Limes
Mandarin oranges
Navel oranges
Pears
Persimmons
Pomegranates
Pomelos
Tangelos
Tangerines
Quinces

Vegetables
Baby turnips
Beets
Belgian endive
Brussels sprouts
Celery root
Chile peppers
Dried beans
Escarole
Fennel
Frisée
Jerusalem
  artichokes
Kale
Leeks
Mushrooms
Parsnips
Potatoes
Rutabagas
Sweet potatoes
Turnips
Watercress
Winter squash

Herbs
Bay leaves
Chives
Parsley
Rosemary
Sage
Thyme

Metric Equivalents

The information in the following charts is provided to help cooks outside the United States successfully use the recipes in this book. All equivalents are approximate.

Cooking/Oven Temperatures

	Fahrenheit	Celsius	Gas Mark
Freeze Water	32° F	0° C	
Room Temp.	68° F	20° C	
Boil Water	212° F	100° C	
Bake	325° F	160° C	3
	350° F	180° C	4
	375° F	190° C	5
	400° F	200° C	6
	425° F	220° C	7
	450° F	230° C	8
Broil			Grill

Liquid Ingredients by Volume

¼ tsp	=	1 ml				
½ tsp	=	2 ml				
1 tsp	=	5 ml				
3 tsp	=	1 tbl	=	½ fl oz	=	15 ml
2 tbls	=	⅛ cup	=	1 fl oz	=	30 ml
4 tbls	=	¼ cup	=	2 fl oz	=	60 ml
5⅓ tbls	=	⅓ cup	=	3 fl oz	=	80 ml
8 tbls	=	½ cup	=	4 fl oz	=	120 ml
10⅔ tbls	=	⅔ cup	=	5 fl oz	=	160 ml
12 tbls	=	¾ cup	=	6 fl oz	=	180 ml
16 tbls	=	1 cup	=	8 fl oz	=	240 ml
1 pt	=	2 cups	=	16 fl oz	=	480 ml
1 qt	=	4 cups	=	32 fl oz	=	960 ml
				33 fl oz	=	1000 ml = 1 l

Dry Ingredients by Weight

(To convert ounces to grams, multiply the number of ounces by 30.)

1 oz	=	¹⁄₁₆ lb	=	30 g
4 oz	=	¼ lb	=	120 g
8 oz	=	½ lb	=	240 g
12 oz	=	¾ lb	=	360 g
16 oz	=	1 lb	=	480 g

Length

(To convert inches to centimeters, multiply the number of inches by 2.5.)

1 in	=			2.5 cm	
6 in	=	½ ft	=	15 cm	
12 in	=	1 ft	=	30 cm	
36 in	=	3 ft	= 1 yd =	90 cm	
40 in	=			100 cm	= 1 m

Equivalents for Different Types of Ingredients

Standard Cup	Fine Powder (ex. flour)	Grain (ex. rice)	Granular (ex. sugar)	Liquid Solids (ex. butter)	Liquid (ex. milk)
1	140 g	150 g	190 g	200 g	240 ml
¾	105 g	113 g	143 g	150 g	180 ml
⅔	93 g	100 g	125 g	133 g	160 ml
½	70 g	75 g	95 g	100 g	120 ml
⅓	47 g	50 g	63 g	67 g	80 ml
¼	35 g	38 g	48 g	50 g	60 ml
⅛	18 g	19 g	24 g	25 g	30 ml

subject index

A

all about
  blue crabs, 241
  chicken thighs, 173
  cornish hens, 193
  corn tortillas, 209
  dry rubs, 174
  ground beef, 29
  ground chicken vs. ground chicken
    breast, 64
  ground veal, 53
  Kansas City barbecue, 185
  peaches, 202
  plantains, 305
  sardines, 223
  shrimp size, 250
  tamarind paste, 177
aluminum foil pan, 11, 16, 17
amchur powder, 72
antioxidants, 24, 209
apples
  kitchen how-to: core apples, 290
apricots, 181
  dried, 59
asparagus
  kitchen how-to: trim asparagus, 265
avocado, 303

B

bacon, 116, 211
barbecue, 40
  all about Kansas City barbecue,
    185
  kitchen how-to:
    avoid burning sweet glazes, 182
    make Memphis-style sauce, 125
    make mustard sauce, 121
baste, 13, 81, 108. *See also*
    marinade, marinating.
  bourbon-butter baste, 143
beef, 82-99. *See also* ground beef,
    meats.
  doneness of, 81, 83
  flank steak, 90, 91
  New York Strip, 86
  rib-eye steak, 89

bison, 100-101
  kitchen how-to: make
    kebabs, 101
bourbon, 142, 161
brine, 115
  bourbon, 142
  kitchen how-to: brine
    meats, 115
bulgogi, 40
burgers, 18-77
  adding ingredients to
    patties, 21, 36
  all about ground chicken vs.
    ground chicken breast, 64
  all about ground beef, 29
  all about ground veal, 53
  buns for, 22, 59
    Burger-to-Bun Ratio, 22
    pita bread, 49
  condiments for, 21
  doneness of, 22, 54, 57
  grinding meat for, 22
  ground lamb for, 49
  How Do Burgers Stack Up?, 21
    different types of burgers, 21
  keeping moist, 27
  kitchen how-to:
    amp up burgers with homemade
      slaw, 39
    grill burgers indoors, 35
    grind meat for burgers, 45
    make delicious salmon
      burgers, 69
    make island-inspired
      burgers, 67
    make perfect poultry burgers, 57
    make stuffed burgers, 31
    make sweet potato–pecan
      burgers, 77
    make veggie burgers, 71
    shape burgers, 21
    shape mini burgers, 51
    use a panade to keep lean
      burgers juicy, 27
  let rest, 20
  mix of meats, 54

  seasoning, 21, 40
  shaping, 20, 21, 51
  stuffed, 31
  toppings for, 23
    easy tzatziki sauce, 48
    grilled Vidalia onions, 32
    radishes, 41
    roasted peppers, 46
    sautéed mushrooms, 36
    tahini, 62
    yogurt-mint sauce, 47
    vegetarian options for, 23
butter
  bourbon-butter baste, 143
  kitchen how-to
    make bacon-tomato butter, 211
    make bourbon peach butter, 161
    make compound butter, 227

C

calamari, 233
Canadian bacon, 230
capers, 178
caramel
  kitchen how-to: make caramel
    sauce, 297
caramelization, 13, 46, 255
cheese
  Cheese Glossary, 23
  provolone, 263
chicken, 21, 136-187
  all about chicken thighs, 173
  all about ground chicken vs.
    ground chicken breast, 64
  kitchen how-to:
    break down a whole
      chicken, 145
    grill chicken under a brick, 146
    grill a whole chicken, 141
    make root beer–can
      chicken, 149
chimichurri, 106
cilantro, fresh, 213
clams
  kitchen how-to: grill-braise
    clams, 237
cleanup, easy, 13, 108, 197, 247

condiments, 21, 23, 25
  Blue Cheese Mayo, 25, 32
  canola mayonnaise, 25
  Chipotle-Poblano Ketchup, 25
  Easy Tzatziki Sauce, 25
  Ginger-Honey Mustard, 25
  kitchen how-to:
    make mayonnaise, 23
    make tomato ketchup, 24
  Pesto Mayonnaise, 25
  vadouvan, 46
cooking spray, proper use of
    around grill, 13
cornichons, 285
Cornish hens, 192-193
  all about Cornish hens, 193
corn
  kitchen how-to: grill corn, 270
  pureed, 273
crab
  all about blue crabs, 241
crème fraîche, 292
cucumber, English, 213
cut "across the grain," 91

D

Dijon mustard, 181
direct grilling, 11, 12, 225
  best foods for, 11, 139
doneness of cooked foods, 12, 21,
    81, 97, 129, 139, 197. *See also*
    thermometer.
dry rubs, 174
duck, 188-191

E

eggplant
  kitchen how-to: grill eggplant, 275
equipment, 11-12. *See also* grill,
    thermometer.
  chimney starter, 11, 12
  drip pans, 11
  food processor, 45
  grill basket or tray, 11, 244, 261
  grill pan, 11, 20, 95
  grinder attachment for stand
    mixer, 22, 45
  meat grinder, 22, 45
  meat mallet, 119

spatula, 20
tongs, 12
wire brush, 12

F

fat, 21, 170, 173, 191, 230, 272, 303
  percentages of in
    ground beef, 29
    ground chicken, 64
    ground lamb, 49
    ground veal, 53
  polyunsaturated, 197
  unsaturated, in nuts, 77
fiber, 22, 23, 59, 71, 295
fish, 194-231
  check doneness of, 197
  kitchen how-to:
    easily remove fish
      skin, 215
    fillet a fish, 199
    grill fish, 201
    grill a whole fish, 225
    plank-grill fish, 219
  skin-on trout, 230
  Sustainable Choices, 198
flare-ups, preventing, 13
food safety, 13, 133
  storing food, 13
  using a thermometer, 13
  when marinating, 13, 81, 101,
    108, 139
French bread, pureeing to thicken
    soup, 259
fruits, 252-255, 288-305.
    See also specific types.
  kitchen how-to:
    core apples, 290
    cut fresh pineapples, 301
    grill fruits, 288
    peel & cut mangoes, 295
  stone fruit, 299
  using seasonal, 255, 308

G

garam masala, 46, 72
garlic, 169
glazes
  kitchen how-to: avoid burning
    sweet glazes, 182

grapes, 170
grate, 12, 13, 197, 201
grill, *See also* equipment.
  charcoal, 11, 12
    adjust the charcoal, 16
    kitchen how-to: get the fire
      going, 12
    kitchen how-to: smoke on
      a charcoal grill, 16
    maintaining even cooking
      temperature, 16
    and smoky flavor, 11
    vents, 16
  cleaning, 12, 13
  gas, 11, 12
    kitchen how-to: get the fire
      going, 12
    kitchen how-to: smoke on
      a gas grill, 17
    maintaining even cooking
      temperature, 16
grill marks, 11, 13, 35,
    85, 255
  kitchen how-to: ceate great
    grill marks, 85
grill pan, 11, 20, 35, 51, 95
  kitchen how-to: grill burgers
    indoors, 35
grinding meat for
    burgers, 22
  kitchen how-to: grind meat
    for burgers, 45
ground beef, 21, 27, 29
  all about ground beef, 29
ground chicken, 21,
  all about ground chicken, 64
ground lamb, 21, 49
ground red pepper,
    116, 302
ground veal, 21, 53

H

half-and-half, 272
herbs
  cilantro, fresh, 213
  fresh and dried, 88
  mint, fresh, 47
  substitutions, 306
honey, 293

I

indirect grilling, 11, 12, 139, 141, 225. *See also* smoke.
  best foods for, 11, 12, 141, 201
indoor grilling, 11, 35, 51
  kitchen how-to: grill steak indoors, 95

K

kebabs
  kitchen how-to: make kebabs, 101
ketchup
  Chipotle-Poblano Ketchup, 25
  kitchen how-to: make tomato ketchup, 24
kitchen how-to:
  amp up burgers with homemade slaw, 39
  avoid burning sweet glazes, 182
  break down a whole chicken, 145
  brine meats, 115
  cook dried lentils, 75
  core apples, 290
  create great grill marks, 85
  cut fresh pineapples, 301
  cut fresh watermelon, 133
  determine doneness, 83
  easily grill shrimp, 244
  easily remove fish skin, 215
  easily slice meat, 122
  fillet a fish, 199
  French a rack of lamb, 103
  get the fire going, 12
  get the most from salt when marinating, 167
  grill bell peppers, 269
  grill-braise clams, 237
  grill burgers indoors, 35
  grill chicken under a brick, 146
  grill corn, 270
  grill eggplant, 275
  grill fish, 201
  grill fruits, 288
  grill lobsters, 243
  grill packets, 247
  grill poblanos, 61
  grill poultry, 139

grill romaine, 277
grill small or delicate vegetables, 261
grill squid, 233
grill steak indoors, 95
grill tortillas, 135
grill vegetables, 256
grill a whole chicken, 141
grill a whole fish, 225
grind meat for burgers, 45
keep lean poultry moist on the grill, 153
make bacon-tomato butter, 211
make bourbon peach butter, 161
make caramel sauce, 297
make compound butter, 227
make delicious salmon burgers, 69
make island-inspired burgers, 67
make kebabs, 101
make mayonnaise, 23
make Memphis-style sauce, 125
make mustard sauce, 121
make perfect poultry burgers, 57
make root beer–can chicken, 149
make smoky tomatillo salsa, 283
make stuffed burgers, 31
make sweet potato–pecan burgers, 77
make Texas-style sauce, 99
make tomato ketchup, 24
make veggie burgers, 71
marinate meats, 108
peel & cut mangoes, 295
plank-grill fish, 219
pound pork, 119
quick-smoke meats, 97
remove the harsh bite of onions, 205
scrub and debeard mussels, 239
select the right tomatoes for smoking, 281
shape burgers, 21
shape mini burgers, 51
shuck oysters, 235
slice flank steak, 91
smoke on a charcoal grill, 16

smoke on a gas grill, 17
smoke vegetables, 279
stuff a pork tenderloin, 111
test for doneness, 129
trim asparagus, 265
use a panade to keep lean burgers juicy, 27
use yogurt-based marinades, 163

L

labels
  on ground beef, 29
  on ground poultry, 64
lamb, 102-107
  ground, 49
  kitchen how-to: French a rack of lamb, 103
  loin chops, 107
  marbling in, 102
lemon
  juice, 86
  rind, 179
lentils, 75
  kitchen how-to: cook dried lentils, 75
lobster
  kitchen how-to: grill lobsters, 243

M

mango, 159
  kitchen how-to: peel & cut mangoes, 295
marbling, 102
  in duck, 191
  in lamb, 102
  in pork, 108
marinade, 13, 40, 101, 154
  capers, 178
  chimichurri as a, 106
  kitchen how-to: use yogurt-based marinades, 163
  leftover, 13, 81, 108
  lemon rind, 179
  peanut, 186
marinating, 13, 81, 139
  kitchen how-to:
    get the most from salt when marinating, 167

marinate meats, 108
poultry, 139
mayonnaise,
blue cheese, 25, 32
canola, 25, 170
kitchen how-to: make
mayonnaise, 23
pesto, 25
meats, 78-135. *See also* specific
types.
handling safely, 13
kitchen how-to:
brine meats, 115
create great grill marks, 85
determine doneness, 83
easily slice meat, 122
grill steak indoors, 95
grind meat for burgers, 45
make kebabs, 101
marinate meats, 108
pound pork, 119
quick-smoke meats, 97
slice flank steak, 91
stuff a pork tenderloin, 111
test for doneness, 129
let it stand, 81
mix of, 49, 54
mushrooms, 36, 190
mussels
kitchen how-to: scrub and debeard
mussels, 239
mustard, ginger-honey, 25

N
nectarine salsa, 165
nuts, 77

O
oil the food, 13, 197, 201, 255
olives, green, 206
omega-3 fatty acids, 197, 223
onions
grilled Vidalia, 32
kitchen how-to: remove the harsh
bite of onions, 205
red, 164
oysters, kitchen how-to: shuck
oysters, 235

P
packets
kitchen how-to: grill packets, 247
panade
kitchen how-to: use a panade to
keep lean burgers juicy, 27
peaches, all about, 202
peanuts, 54, 186
butter, 161
marinade, 186
pecans
kitchen how-to: make sweet
potato–pecan burgers, 77
peppers
chipotle chile powder, 90
jalapeño, 259
kitchen how-to:
grill bell peppers, 269
grill poblanos, 61
roasted, 46
serrano chile, 186
pineapple, 159
cubed pineapple, 250
kitchen how-to: cut fresh
pineapples, 301
plank grilling
cedar planks, 286
kitchen how-to: plank-grill
fish, 219
plantains
all about plantains, 305
kitchen how-to: make island-
inspired burgers, 67
pork, 108-135
bone-in pork chops, 126
ground, 21, 54
kitchen how-to:
marinate meats, 108
pound pork, 119
stuff a pork tenderloin, 111
marbling in, 108
potatoes
red, 284
sweet, 77
poultry, 21, 136-193. *See also*
chicken, Cornish hens, turkey.
kitchen how-to:
grill poultry, 139

keep lean poultry moist on
the grill, 153
make perfect poultry
burgers, 57
marinating, 139
testing for doneness, 54, 139
protein, 71, 77, 197

R
radishes, 41
rest, let meat, 81
rice, long-grain white, 154
romaine
kitchen how-to: grill romaine, 277
ruby port, 298

S
sake, 127
salmon
kitchen how-to: make delicious
salmon burgers, 69
salsas, 159
for burger toppings, 23
kitchen how-to: make smoky
tomatillo salsa, 283
nectarine, 165
salt, 167
sardines, all about, 223
satay, 186
sauces, 47, 48, 81, 251
all about Kansas City
barbecue, 185
chimichurri, 106
kitchen how-to:
make caramel sauce, 297
make Memphis-style
sauce, 125
make mustard sauce, 121
make Texas-style sauce, 99
seafood, 194-251. *See also* specific
types and Fish, Shellfish.
handling safely, 13
health benefits of, 197
Sustainable Choices, 198
seasonings, 21, 141, 153, 167, 201
all about dry rubs, 174
all about tamarind paste, 177
amchur powder, 72

(continued)

for burgers, 21, 31, 40, 46
chipotle chile powder, 90
fresh & dried herbs, 88
garam masala, 46, 72
ground red pepper, 116
Marmite, 57
sake, 127
saté flavors, 54
tahini, 62
tzatziki sauce, easy, 25
shellfish, 196-198, 234-251. *See also* specific types and Fish, Seafood.
all about blue crabs, 241
doneness of, 197
kitchen how-to:
easily grill shrimp, 244
grill-braise clams, 237
grill lobsters, 243
scrub and debeard mussels, 239
shuck oysters, 235
Sustainable Choices, 198
shrimp
all about shrimp size, 250
kitchen how-to:
easily grill shrimp, 244
grill packets, 247
slicing
kitchen how-to:
easily slice meat, 122
slice flank steak, 91
pineapples, 301
watermelon, 133
smoke, 11, 14-17
best foods for, 15
Chips vs. Chunks, 15
equipment for, 11, 15
kitchen how-to:
quick-smoke meats, 97
select the right tomatoes for smoking, 281
smoke on a charcoal grill, 16
smoke on a gas grill, 17
smoke vegetables, 279
maintaining even cooking temperature, 16

sodium, 24, 186
soy crumbles, 21
squid
kitchen how-to: grill squid, 233
storing food, 13, 174
Sustainable Choices, 198
sweet potatoes
kitchen how-to: make sweet potato–pecan burgers, 77

T

tahini, 62
tamarind paste, all about, 177
tenderizing meat, 119. *See also* marinating.
kitchen how-to: pound pork, 119
thermometer, 12, 13, 22, 81, 129
chicken, 149
instant-read, 12, 83
kitchen how-to: determine doneness, 83
meat, 22, 97, 129, 149
placement of in meat, 13, 81, 129
tomatillos
kitchen how-to: make smoky tomatillo salsa, 283
tomatoes
Beefsteak, 206
kitchen how-to:
make bacon-tomato butter, 211
make tomato ketchup, 24
select the right tomatoes for smoking, 281
tortillas, 135
all about corn tortillas, 209
kitchen how-to: grill tortillas, 135
truffle oil, 36
turkey
ground, 21, 49, 54
kitchen how-to: make perfect poultry burgers, 57

U

U.S. Department of Agriculture (USDA)

recommendation for doneness temperature of cooked food, 22, 54, 57, 81, 83, 129

V

vadouvan, 46
veal, ground, 21, 53
all about ground veal, 53
vegetables, 12, 23, 252-287. *See also* specific types.
for burger toppings, 23, 32, 36, 39
kitchen how-to:
grill bell peppers, 269
grill corn, 270
grill eggplant, 275
grill romaine, 277
grill small or delicate vegetables, 261
grill vegetables, 256
smoke vegetables, 279
trim asparagus, 265
using seasonal, 255, 308
vegetarian burger options, 21, 71, 75, 77
kitchen how-to: make veggie burgers, 71

W

watermelon
kitchen how-to: cut fresh watermelon, 133
white balsamic vinegar, 263
wood chips or chunks, 11, 15, 16, 17, 97
types to use for smoking, 15

Y

yogurt, 47, 48
Greek-style, 63, 169
kitchen how-to: use yogurt-based marinades, 163

Z

zucchini, 287

recipe index

A

Apples with Mint, Marinated
Grilled, 290
Apricots
Burgers, Apricot Turkey, 58
Duck Breasts, Apricot Grilled, 189
Mixed Greens with Grilled Apricots
and Prosciutto, 289
Spread, Grilled Chicken Sliders and
Apricot Chutney, 180
Artichoke Salad, Tuscan-Style New
York Strip with Arugula-, 87
Asparagus with Caper Vinaigrette,
Grilled, 265
Avocados
Burger, Out-N-In California, 29
Flank Steak with Onions, Avocado,
and Tomatoes, Grilled, 93
Mango and Avocado, Grilled, 295
Salsa, Grilled Pineapple-
Avocado, 302

B

Bacon
Butter, Mahimahi with Bacon-
Tomato, 211
Crisp Smoked Bacon, Ocean Trout
with Coleslaw and, 231
Pancetta and Swiss Cheese–
Stuffed Burgers with Pesto
Mayonnaise, 30
Barbecue
Burgers, Korean Barbecue, 40
Burgers with Slaw, Chipotle
Barbecue, 39
Chicken, Kansas City
Barbecued, 184
Chicken, Quick Barbecue, 153
Pork Chops, Barbecued, 126
Sauces
Kansas City Barbecue
Sauce, 184
Mustard Barbecue Sauce,
Spice-Rubbed Pork
Tenderloin with, 117

Squid, Barbecue, 233
Barley Burgers with Fiery Fruit Salsa,
Lentil-, 74
Beans
Black
Burgers with Mango Salsa,
Black Bean, 71
Shrimp, Grilled Fiesta, 247
Burgers, Vegetable, 73
Beef. See also Beef, Ground; Veal.
Brisket
Burgers, Brisket, 44
Coffee-Rubbed Texas-Style
Brisket, 98
Steaks
Cucumber-Radish Salad,
Steak with, 95
Filet Mignon, Grilled Miso-
Marinated, 85
Flank Steak with Fresh Salsa,
Spice-Rubbed, 91
Flank Steak with Onions,
Avocado, and Tomatoes,
Grilled, 93
Herb Steak, Grilled, 89
New York Strip with Arugula-
Artichoke Salad, Tuscan-
Style, 87
Rosemary Grilled Steak with
Tomato Jam, 83
Tri-Tip, Santa Maria
Smoked, 96
Beef, Ground
Burgers
Barbecue Burgers,
Korean, 40
Blue Cheese Mayo and Sherry
Vidalia Onions, Burgers
with, 33
Chipotle Barbecue Burgers
with Slaw, 39
Mushroom Burgers with Fried
Eggs and Truffle Oil, 37
Out-N-In California
Burger, 29

Pancetta and Swiss Cheese–
Stuffed Burgers with Pesto
Mayonnaise, 30
Pesto Sliders, 43
Poblano Burgers with Pickled
Red Onions and Chipotle
Cream, Spicy, 26
Southwest Salsa
Burgers, 35
Beet Salad, Yogurt-Marinated
Chicken with, 177
Bison Rib-eye Kebabs, 101
Bok Choy, Grilled Baby, 267
Broth
Tomato-Saffron Broth, Grilled-
Braised Clams and Chorizo
in, 236
White Wine Broth, Smoky Mussels
and Clams with, 239
Butter
Bacon-Tomato Butter, Mahimahi
with, 211
Bourbon Peach Butter, Grilled
Chicken with, 161
Orange-Tarragon Butter, 227
Roasted Jalapeño Butter, Grilled
Corn on the Cob with, 270
Sauce, Butter, 243

C

Caramel Sauce, Grilled Peaches with
Amaretto-Pecan, 297
Cheese
Jalapeños, Grilled Stuffed, 261
Lamb Burgers with Blue Cheese,
Mini, 51
Cherries
Couscous, Pork Chops with
Cherry, 129
Syrup, Grilled Summer Stone Fruit
with Cherry-Port, 298
Chicken
Barbecue Chicken, Quick, 153
Barbecued Chicken, Kansas
City, 184

(continued)

Bourbon Peach Butter, Grilled Chicken with, 161
Burgers, Chicken Parmesan, 64
Burgers, Jamaican Chicken, 66
Fajitas, Chicken, 167
Hawaiian Chicken, 155
Kebabs and Nectarine Salsa, Chicken, 164
Mango-Pineapple Salsa, Grilled Chicken with, 158
Maple-Mustard Chicken Thighs, 173
Salad, Grilled Chicken, 171
Satay, Chicken, 186
Shawarma, Chicken, 168
Sliders and Apricot Chutney Spread, Grilled Chicken, 180
Sriracha Glaze, Grilled Chicken with, 182
Stuffed Chicken Breasts, Mediterranean-, 157
Tequila-Glazed Grilled Chicken Thighs, 174
Thighs with Roasted Grape Tomatoes, Grilled Chicken, 178
Tomatoes and Olives, Chicken Breasts with, 151
Whole
    Bourbon Smoked Chicken, Fantastic, 142
    Lemon and Sage Chicken, 144
    Marinated Chicken Cooked Under a Brick, 147
    Root Beer–Can Chicken, 148
    Spice-Rubbed Whole Chicken, Grilled, 140
Wraps with Nectarine Chutney, Curry Chicken, 163
Yogurt-Marinated Chicken with Beet Salad, 177
Chowder, Grilled Corn and Potato, 272
Chutney
    Apricot Chutney Spread, Grilled Chicken Sliders and, 180
    Nectarine Chutney, Curry Chicken Wraps with, 163

Clams
    Grilled-Braised Clams and Chorizo in Tomato-Saffron Broth, 236
    Smoky Mussels and Clams with White Wine Broth, 239
Coconut, Rum-Spiked Grilled Pineapple with Toasted, 301
Corn
    Chowder, Grilled Corn and Potato, 272
    Cob with Roasted Jalapeño Butter, Grilled Corn on the, 270
    Salsa, Grilled Pork Tacos with Summer Corn and Nectarine, 135
Cornish Hens, Asian-Style Grilled, 193
Couscous
    Cherry Couscous, Pork Chops with, 129
    Stuffing, Plank-Grilled Zucchini with Couscous, Spinach, and Feta, 286
Crabs, Chile, 241
Cucumber-Radish Salad, Steak with, 95

D
Desserts
    Apples with Mint, Marinated Grilled, 290
    Figs with Sweet Cream, Caramelized Fresh, 292
    Peaches with Amaretto-Pecan Caramel Sauce, Grilled, 297
    Pineapple with Toasted Coconut, Rum-Spiked Grilled, 301
    Summer Stone Fruit with Cherry-Port Syrup, Grilled, 298
Duck
    Apricot Grilled Duck Breasts, 189
    Mushroom Salad and Truffle Vinaigrette, Grilled Duck with Warm, 190

E
Eggplant
    Roasted Eggplant, Turkey Burgers with, 56

Sandwiches with Yogurt-Garlic Spread, Grilled Eggplant Pita, 275
Eggs and Truffle Oil, Mushroom Burgers with Fried, 37

F
Fajitas, Chicken, 167
Figs with Sweet Cream, Caramelized Fresh, 292
Fish. *See also* Salmon, Sardines, Seafood, Shellfish.
    Char with Yukon Golds and Tomato–Red Onion Relish, Grilled, 205
    Halibut Tacos, Chimichurri, 209
    Halibut with Grilled Tomato and Olive Relish, 207
    Mahimahi with Bacon-Tomato Butter, 211
    Mahimahi with Mango Salsa, Grilled, 212
    Ocean Trout with Coleslaw and Crisp Smoked Bacon, 231
    Red Snapper with Citrus-Ginger Hot Sauce, Grilled Whole, 224
    Snapper with Orange-Tarragon Butter, Grilled, 227
    Striped Bass with Peach Salsa, 202
    Swordfish Kebabs with Orange-Basil Sauce, 229
    Trout, Grilled, 201
Fruit. *See also* specific types.
    Salsa, Lentil-Barley Burgers with Fiery Fruit, 74
    Summer Stone Fruit with Cherry-Port Syrup, Grilled, 298

G
Garlic
    Burgers with Fried Eggs and Truffle Oil, Mushroom, 37
    Chicken Cooked Under a Brick, Marinated, 147
    Chicken Wraps with Nectarine Chutney, Curry, 163
    Crabs, Chile, 241

New York Strip with Arugula-Artichoke Salad, Tuscan-Style, 87
Squid, Barbecue, 233
Grape Relish, Plank-Grilled Salmon with, 218

J

Jicama Relish, Brined Pork Tenderloin with Plum and, 114

K

Kale, Smoked Chanterelles and, 278
Kebabs
Bison Rib-eye Kebabs, 101
Chicken Kebabs and Nectarine Salsa, 164
Chicken Satay, 186
Lamb Kebabs, Spiced, 105
Mango Shrimp Kebabs, 249
Shrimp Kebabs, Grilled Teriyaki, 250
Swordfish Kebabs with Orange-Basil Sauce, 229
Ketchup
Chipotle-Poblano Ketchup, 25
Tomato Ketchup, 24

L

Lamb
Burgers, Greek Lamb, 48
Burgers with Blue Cheese, Mini Lamb, 51
Burgers with Indian Spices and Yogurt-Mint Sauce, Lamb, 47
Chops with Roasted Summer Squash and Chimichurri, Grilled Lamb, 106
Kebabs, Spiced Lamb, 105
Rack of Lamb with Saffron Rice, Grilled, 103
Lemon and Sage Chicken, 144
Lentils
Burgers with Fiery Fruit Salsa, Lentil-Barley, 74
Salad, Grilled Peppers and Lentil, 269
Lobsters, Grilled Maine, 243

M

Mangoes
Avocado, Grilled Mango and, 295
Kebabs, Mango Shrimp, 249
Salsa, Black Bean Burgers with Mango, 71
Salsa, Grilled Chicken with Mango-Pineapple, 158
Salsa, Grilled Mahimahi with Mango, 212
Maple
Chicken Thighs, Maple-Mustard, 173
Salmon, Maple Grilled, 221
Marinated. See also Rubbed.
Apples with Mint, Marinated Grilled, 290
Chicken Cooked Under a Brick, Marinated, 147
Chicken Fajitas, 167
Chicken, Hawaiian, 155
Chicken, Lemon and Sage, 144
Chicken Salad, Grilled, 171
Chicken Satay, 186
Chicken Shawarma, 168
Chicken Thighs, Maple-Mustard, 173
Chicken Thighs with Roasted Grape Tomatoes, Grilled, 178
Chicken with Beet Salad, Yogurt-Marinated, 177
Chicken with Mango-Pineapple Salsa, Grilled, 158
Chicken Wraps with Nectarine Chutney, Curry, 163
Cornish Hens, Asian-Style Grilled, 193
Crabs, Chile, 241
Duck Breasts, Apricot Grilled, 189
Duck with Warm Mushroom Salad and Truffle Vinaigrette, Grilled, 190
Filet Mignon, Grilled Miso-Marinated, 85
Lamb Kebabs, Spiced, 105
Mahimahi with Mango Salsa, Grilled, 212

New York Strip with Arugula-Artichoke Salad, Tuscan-Style, 87
Pork, Cantonese-Style Grilled, 122
Pork Chops, Barbecued, 126
Pork Tacos with Summer Corn and Nectarine Salsa, Grilled, 135
Pork Tenderloin with Grilled Pepper Relish, Saffron-Marinated, 109
Salmon, Brown Sugar and Mustard, 215
Salmon, Maple Grilled, 221
Squid, Barbecue, 233
Steak, Grilled Herb, 89
Mayonnaise
Blue Cheese Mayo and Sherry Vidalia Onions, Burgers with, 33
Pesto Mayonnaise, Pancetta and Swiss Cheese–Stuffed Burgers with, 30
Meatball Burgers, Swedish, 53
Melon Salsa, Grilled Pork Chops with Two-, 133
Microwave
Pineapple with Toasted Coconut, Rum-Spiked Grilled, 301
Miso-Marinated Filet Mignon, Grilled, 85
Mushrooms
Burgers with Fried Eggs and Truffle Oil, Mushroom, 37
Chanterelles and Kale, Smoked, 278
Salad and Truffle Vinaigrette, Grilled Duck with Warm Mushroom, 190
Mussels and Clams with White Wine Broth, Smoky, 239
Mustard, Ginger-Honey, 25

N

Nectarines
Chutney, Curry Chicken Wraps with Nectarine, 163
Salsa, Chicken Kebabs and Nectarine, 164

(continued)

Salsa, Grilled Pork Tacos
with Summer Corn and
Nectarine, 135

O

Olives
Chicken Breasts with Tomatoes
and Olives, 151
Relish, Halibut with Grilled Tomato
and Olive, 207
Relish, Smoked Oysters with
Olive, 235
Onions
Caramelized Onions, Sweet
Potato–Pecan Burgers with, 76
Flank Steak with Onions, Avocado,
and Tomatoes, Grilled, 93
Red Onion, Italian Grilled Zucchini
and, 257
Red Onion Relish, Grilled Char with
Yukon Golds and Tomato–, 205
Red Onions, Pickled, 27
Vidalia Onions, Burgers with Blue
Cheese Mayo and Sherry, 33
Orange
Butter, Orange-Tarragon, 227
Sauce, Swordfish Kebabs with
Orange-Basil, 229
Oysters with Olive Relish,
Smoked, 235

P

Peaches
Amaretto-Pecan Caramel Sauce,
Grilled Peaches with, 297
Butter, Grilled Chicken with
Bourbon Peach, 161
Salsa, Striped Bass with
Peach, 202
Pecans
Burgers with Caramelized Onions,
Sweet Potato–Pecan, 76
Sauce, Grilled Peaches with
Amaretto-Pecan Caramel, 297
Peppers
Chile
Burgers, Southwest Salsa, 35
Burgers, Southwest Turkey, 61

Chipotle Barbecue Burgers
with Slaw, 39
Chipotle-Poblano Ketchup, 25
Crabs, Chile, 241
Poblano Burgers with Pickled
Red Onions and Chipotle
Cream, Spicy, 26
Squid, Barbecue, 233
Sriracha Glaze, Grilled Chicken
with, 182
Jalapeño
Roasted Jalapeño Butter,
Grilled Corn on the Cob
with, 270
Stuffed Jalapeños, Grilled, 261
Relish, Saffron-Marinated
Pork Tenderloin with Grilled
Pepper, 109
Salad, Grilled Peppers and
Lentil, 269
Pesto
Mayonnaise, Pancetta and Swiss
Cheese–Stuffed Burgers with
Pesto, 30
Sliders, Pesto, 43
Pineapple
Rum-Spiked Grilled Pineapple with
Toasted Coconut, 301
Salsa, Grilled Chicken with Mango-
Pineapple, 158
Salsa, Grilled Pineapple-
Avocado, 302
Salsa, Pan-Grilled Pork Chops with
Grilled Pineapple, 131
Plantains
Burgers, Jamaican Chicken, 66
Grilled Plantains, 305
Plum and Jicama Relish, Brined Pork
Tenderloin with, 114
Pork. *See also* Bacon, Sausage.
Burgers, Saté, 54
Cantonese-Style Grilled Pork, 122
Chops
Barbecued Pork Chops, 126
Cherry Couscous, Pork Chops
with, 129
Pan-Grilled Pork Chops with
Grilled Pineapple Salsa, 131

Tacos with Summer Corn
and Nectarine Salsa, Grilled
Pork, 135
Two-Melon Salsa, Grilled Pork
Chops with, 133
Sandwiches with Mustard Sauce,
Pulled Pork, 120
Sandwiches, Memphis Pork and
Coleslaw, 124
Tenderloin
Brined Pork Tenderloin
with Plum and Jicama
Relish, 114
Roulade, Grilled Pork
Tenderloin, 113
Saffron-Marinated Pork
Tenderloin with Grilled
Pepper Relish, 109
Salsa Verde, Grilled Pork
Tenderloin with, 118
Spice-Rubbed Pork Tenderloin
with Mustard Barbecue
Sauce, 117
Stuffed Cuban Pork
Tenderloin, 110
Potatoes. *See also* Sweet Potato.
Chowder, Grilled Corn and
Potato, 272
Salad with Herbs and Grilled
Summer Squash, Potato, 285
Yukon Golds and Tomato–Red
Onion Relish, Grilled Char
with, 205
Prosciutto, Mixed Greens with Grilled
Apricots and, 289

R

Radish Salad, Steak with
Cucumber-, 95
Relishes
Grape Relish, Plank-Grilled Salmon
with, 218
Olive Relish, Smoked Oysters
with, 235
Pepper Relish, Saffron-Marinated
Pork Tenderloin with Grilled, 109
Plum and Jicama Relish, Brined
Pork Tenderloin with, 114

Tomato and Olive Relish, Halibut with Grilled, 207

Tomato–Red Onion Relish, Grilled Char with Yukon Golds and, 205

Rice, Grilled Rack of Lamb with Saffron, 103

Roulade, Grilled Pork Tenderloin, 113

Rubbed. *See also* Marinated.

Brisket, Coffee-Rubbed Texas-Style, 98

Chicken, Grilled Spice-Rubbed Whole, 140

Chicken, Kansas City Barbecued, 184

Chicken, Quick Barbecue, 153

Chicken Thighs, Tequila-Glazed Grilled, 174

Flank Steak with Fresh Salsa, Spice-Rubbed, 91

Halibut Tacos, Chimichurri, 209

Lamb with Saffron Rice, Grilled Rack of, 103

Pork and Coleslaw Sandwiches, Memphis, 124

Pork Chops with Two-Melon Salsa, Grilled, 133

Pork Tenderloin with Mustard Barbecue Sauce, Spice-Rubbed, 117

Pulled Pork Sandwiches with Mustard Sauce, 120

Sardines, Grilled Fresh, 223

Steak with Cucumber-Radish Salad, 95

S

Salads and Salad Dressings

Arugula-Artichoke Salad, Tuscan-Style New York Strip with, 87

Beet Salad, Yogurt-Marinated Chicken with, 177

Chicken Salad, Grilled, 171

Cucumber-Radish Salad, Steak with, 95

Mixed Greens with Grilled Apricots and Prosciutto, 289

Mushroom Salad and Truffle Vinaigrette, Grilled Duck with Warm, 190

Peppers and Lentil Salad, Grilled, 269

Potato Salad with Herbs and Grilled Summer Squash, 285

Romaine with Creamy Herb Dressing, Grilled, 277

Slaws

Burgers with Slaw, Chipotle Barbecue, 39

Coleslaw and Crisp Smoked Bacon, Ocean Trout with, 231

Coleslaw Sandwiches, Memphis Pork and, 124

Salmon

Brown Sugar and Mustard Salmon, 215

Burgers, Salmon, 69

Maple Grilled Salmon, 221

Plank-Grilled Salmon with Grape Relish, 218

Smoky Tomato Salsa, Grilled Salmon with, 217

Salsa

Corn and Nectarine Salsa, Grilled Pork Tacos with Summer, 135

Fresh Salsa, Spice-Rubbed Flank Steak with, 91

Fruit Salsa, Lentil-Barley Burgers with Fiery, 74

Mango-Pineapple Salsa, Grilled Chicken with, 158

Mango Salsa, Black Bean Burgers with, 71

Mango Salsa, Grilled Mahimahi with, 212

Melon Salsa, Grilled Pork Chops with Two-, 133

Nectarine Salsa, Chicken Kebabs and, 164

Peach Salsa, Striped Bass with, 202

Pineapple-Avocado Salsa, Grilled, 302

Pineapple Salsa, Pan-Grilled Pork Chops with Grilled, 131

Santa Maria Salsa, 96

Tomatillo Salsa, Smoky, 283

Tomatillo Salsa, Spicy Shrimp Tacos with Grilled, 244

Tomato Salsa, Grilled Salmon with Smoky, 217

Verde, Grilled Pork Tenderloin with Salsa, 118

Sandwiches. *See also* Beef, Ground; Burgers.

Eggplant Pita Sandwiches with Yogurt-Garlic Spread, Grilled, 275

Farmers' Market Sandwiches, Grilled, 262

Pork and Coleslaw Sandwich, Memphis, 124

Pulled Pork Sandwiches with Mustard Sauce, 120

Sliders and Apricot Chutney Spread, Grilled Chicken, 180

Sardines, Grilled Fresh, 223

Sauces. *See also* Pesto, Relishes, Toppings.

Amaretto-Pecan Caramel Sauce, Grilled Peaches with, 297

Barbecue

Kansas City Barbecue Sauce, 184

Mustard Barbecue Sauce, Spice-Rubbed Pork Tenderloin with, 117

Butter Sauce, 243

Citrus-Ginger Hot Sauce, Grilled Whole Red Snapper with, 224

Memphis-style Sauce, 125

Mustard Sauce, Pulled Pork Sandwiches with, 120

Orange-Basil Sauce, Swordfish Kebabs with, 229

Tahini Sauce, Turkey Burger Pitas with, 62

Tzatziki Sauce, Easy, 25

Yogurt-Mint Sauce, Lamb Burgers with Indian Spices and, 47

Sausage
  Chorizo in Tomato-Saffron Broth,
    Grilled-Braised Clams and, 236
Seasoning
  Kansas City Dry Rub, 184
Shawarma, Chicken, 168
Shrimp
  Fiesta Shrimp, Grilled, 247
  Kebabs, Grilled Teriyaki
    Shrimp, 250
  Kebabs, Mango Shrimp, 249
  Tacos with Grilled Tomatillo Salsa,
    Spicy Shrimp, 244
Soups. *See also* Broth.
  Chowder, Grilled Corn and
    Potato, 272
  Gazpacho, Grilled Vegetable, 258
Spinach, and Feta Stuffing,
  Plank-Grilled Zucchini with
    Couscous, 286
Spreads. *See also* Butter,
  Mayonnaise.
  Apricot Chutney Spread, Grilled
    Chicken Sliders and, 180
  Yogurt-Garlic Spread, Grilled
    Eggplant Pita Sandwiches
    with, 275
Squash. *See also* Zucchini.
  Roasted Summer Squash and
    Chimichurri, Grilled Lamb Chops
    with, 106
  Summer Squash, Potato Salad
    with Herbs and Grilled, 285
Squid, Barbecue, 233
Sweet Potato–Pecan Burgers with
  Caramelized Onions, 76
Syrup, Grilled Summer Stone Fruit
  with Cherry-Port, 298

T
Tacos
  Halibut Tacos, Chimichurri, 209
  Pork Tacos with Summer Corn and
    Nectarine Salsa, Grilled, 135
  Shrimp Tacos with Grilled
    Tomatillo Salsa, Spicy, 244

Teriyaki Shrimp Kebabs,
  Grilled, 250
Tomatillos
  Salsa, Smoky Tomatillo, 283
  Salsa, Spicy Shrimp Tacos with
    Grilled Tomatillo, 244
Tomatoes
  Broth, Grilled-Braised Clams
    and Chorizo in Tomato-
    Saffron, 236
  Butter, Mahimahi with Bacon-
    Tomato, 211
  Chicken Breasts with Tomatoes
    and Olives, 151
  Flank Steak with Onions,
    Avocado, and Tomatoes,
    Grilled, 93
  Jam, Rosemary Grilled Steak with
    Tomato, 83
  Ketchup, Tomato, 24
  Relish, Grilled Char with Yukon
    Golds and Tomato–Red
    Onion, 205
  Relish, Halibut with Grilled Tomato
    and Olive, 207
  Roasted Grape Tomatoes,
    Grilled Chicken Thighs
    with, 178
  Salsas
    Fresh Salsa, Spice-Rubbed
      Flank Steak with, 91
    Santa Maria Salsa, 96
    Smoky Tomato Salsa, Grilled
      Salmon with, 217
  Smoked Tomatoes, 281
Toppings
  Caper Vinaigrette, Grilled
    Asparagus with, 265
  Pickled Red Onions, 27
  Sweet Cream, Caramelized Fresh
    Figs with, 292
  Tomato Jam, Rosemary Grilled
    Steak with, 83
Truffles
  Oil, Mushroom Burgers with Fried
    Eggs and, Truffle, 37

Vinaigrette, Grilled Duck
  with Warm Mushroom Salad
  and, Truffle, 190
Turkey
  Burger Pitas with Tahini Sauce,
    Turkey, 62
  Burgers, Apricot Turkey, 58
  Burgers, Greek Lamb, 48
  Burgers, Saté, 54
  Burgers, Southwest
    Turkey, 61
  Burgers with Roasted Eggplant,
    Turkey, 56

V
Veal
  Burgers, Swedish Meatball, 53
Vegetables. *See also* specific types.
  Burgers, Vegetable, 73
  Gazpacho, Grilled
    Vegetable, 258
  Sandwiches, Grilled Farmers'
    Market, 262

W
Wraps with Nectarine Chutney, Curry
  Chicken, 163

Y
Yogurt
  Chicken with Beet Salad, Yogurt-
    Marinated, 177
  Sauce, Lamb Burgers with Indian
    Spices and Yogurt-Mint, 47
  Spread, Grilled Eggplant Pita
    Sandwiches with Yogurt-
    Garlic, 275
  Tzatziki Sauce, Easy, 25

Z
Zucchini
  Italian Grilled Zucchini and Red
    Onion, 257
  Plank-Grilled Zucchini with
    Couscous, Spinach, and Feta
    Stuffing, 286